.NET Web Services For Dummies®

Built-In XML Datatypes

Datatype	Explanation
anyURI	Holds any valid Universal Resource Identifier
Base64Binary	Special type that defines Base64-encoded binary data
boolean	Holds binary data (either 1 or 0), but specified as true or false
date	Holds a specific date — namely the day, month, and year
dateTime	Holds a specific instance in time, including both date and time values
decimal	Holds a floating-point number with an unknown, arbitrary precision
double	Holds a 64-bit, double-precision, floating-point number with values in the range of negative 1.79769313486232e308 to positive 1.79769313486232e308
duration	Holds a specific duration of time
float	Holds a 32-bit, single-precision, floating-point number with values in the range of negative 3.402823e38 to positive 3.402823e38
gDay, gMonth, gMonthDay, gYear, gYearMonth	Using the Gregorian calendar, holds a specific day of the month, month number, day in a month, year, or month in a specific year, respectively
hexBinary	Special type that defines hexadecimal-encoded binary data
NOTATION	Holds a special attribute for some XML elements that indicates how to interpret data in a specific way
QName	Represents a fully-qualified name, including namespace information
string	Holds string data, including characters, numbers, and symbols
time	Holds a specific instance in time without a date value

Web Services Acronyms to Know and Love

Acronym	What It Stands For	Description
ADO	ActiveX Data Objects	A set of programmable objects that enables programmers to access relational databases in their own custom programs.
ASP	Active Server Pages	A server-side technology that enables developers to embed scripts and other code into Web pages to enable active Web content.
CLR	Common Language Runtime	A core component of the .NET Framework that makes sure that programs written in a variety of programming languages can manage server resources and proper code execution in a consistent way. The CLR also provides a common library, or *cache*, of operating system and utility routines.
CTS	Common Type System	A core component of the .NET Framework that ensures compatible datatypes among programming languages supported by the .NET CLR.

.NET Web Services
For Dummies®

Cheat Sheet

DISCO	Discovery	A file used in Web services technology that enables dynamic Web service discovery.
DLL	Dynamic Link Library	A small package of code that can be executed only as part of an executable file. A DLL can be shared between many programs to enable code reuse.
DOM	Document Object Model	A programmable set of objects for accessing parts of an HTML Web page.
DTD	Document Type Definition	A document (written in XML) that defines the *schema* (or format) that other XML documents should conform to. *See* XSD.
IIS	Internet Information Services	Microsoft's implementation of a Web server that runs on Windows 2000, Windows XP, or any of the Windows .NET servers. Some scaled-down versions of IIS, called Personal Web Servers (PWS) also run on Windows 98 and 95.
IL	Intermediate Language	Programming code that is compiled as far as possible without needing to include processor-specific instructions. Using an IL allows code written in any language to have a common starting point, from which another compiler can further compile code into processor-specific (or *machine-level)* instructions.
MSIL	Microsoft Intermediate Language	Microsoft's interpretation of IL. MSIL runs on the .NET platform, enabling all .NET languages (such as Visual Basic .NET and Visual C# .NET) to operate on the .NET Framework seamlessly.
SOAP	Simple Object Access Protocol	A protocol that packages Web services object instructions so that objects can be transferred over the Internet.
SSL	Secure Sockets Layer	A layer of network communication that digitally encrypts data for transmission over the Internet.
UDDI	Universal Description, Discovery, and Integration	A centralized repository of Web services offered by providers (also known as organizations).
WSDL	Web Services Description Language	A markup language that, used in conjunction with a DISCO file, enables dynamic discovery of the *interface* (or structure) of your Web services.
XML	Extensible Markup Language	A language that uses custom tags to describe data without any screen presentation instructions. XML is a core technology used in Web services.
XMLDOM	XML Document Object Model	A programmable set of objects for accessing parts of an XML document.
XSD	XML Schema Definition	A document (written in XML) that contains the definition of the schema that other XML documents should conform to.
XSL	XML Stylesheet Language	A markup language used to contain instructions on how an XML document should be formatted and presented on a computer screen or some other computer system.

Copyright © 2003 Wiley Publishing, Inc.
All rights reserved.

Item 1647-7.

For more information about Wiley Publishing, call 1-800-762-2974.

For Dummies: Bestselling Book Series for Beginners

.NET Web Services

FOR DUMMIES®

.NET Web Services FOR DUMMIES®

by Anthony T. Mann

Wiley Publishing, Inc.

.NET Web Services For Dummies®

Published by
Wiley Publishing, Inc.
909 Third Avenue
New York, NY 10022

www.wiley.com

Copyright © 2003 by Wiley Publishing, Inc., Indianapolis, Indiana

Published by Wiley Publishing, Inc., Indianapolis, Indiana

Published simultaneously in Canada

For general information on our other products and services or to obtain technical support, please contact our Customer Care Department within the U.S. at 800-762-2974, outside the U.S. at 317-572-3993, or fax 317-572-4002.

Wiley also publishes its books in a variety of electronic formats. Some content that appears in print may not be available in electronic books.

Library of Congress Control Number: 2002114823

ISBN: 0-7645-1644-7

Manufactured in the United States of America

10 9 8 7 6 5 4 3 2 1

1O/RZ/QT/QT/IN

About the Author

Anthony T. Mann is the President/CEO of Transport:80 Incorporated, based in New Hampshire. Transport:80 creates business-related .NET Web services that are available over the Internet for Customer Relationship Management (CRM) applications and other critical business functions. In addition, Transport:80 is a Microsoft Certified Partner and a Microsoft Great Plains Business Solutions Partner that also offers professional services, solutions, and training. For more information about Transport:80, visit the Web site at www.transport80.com.

Anthony has also been a software architect and developer for more than 12 years and holds the Microsoft Certified Database Administrator (MCDBA), Microsoft Certified Solution Developer (MCSD), and Microsoft Certified Trainer (MCT) certifications.

Anthony is a veteran author (or co-author) of many other technical books, including *SharePoint Portal Server: A Beginner's Guide* (Osborne/McGraw-Hill); *Microsoft SQL Server 2000 For Dummies* and *Microsoft SQL Server 7 For Dummies* (Wiley Publishing, Inc.); *Real-World Programming with Visual Basic, Visual Basic 4 Developer's Guide, Real-World Programming with Visual Basic 4, Visual Basic 5 Developer's Guide*, and *Visual Basic 5 Development Unleashed* (SAMS Publishing).

He lives in beautiful southeastern New Hampshire with his wife and shelties (Shetland Sheepdogs) and can be e-mailed at tmann@transport80.com.

Dedication

To my wife, Alison, who stands by my side and gives me the courage to tackle anything.

Author's Acknowledgments

I'd like to express my sincere appreciation to the many people who worked to help make this book come together. I cannot name them all, but I'd like to extend my special thanks to Steve Hayes for bringing me into this project and believing in me. I'd also like to thank Nicole Haims for doing such a great job in keeping me on my toes and not letting me get away with anything substandard. Nicole was also instrumental in working through the very complicated issues of organizing this book so that it makes sense! Thanks Nicole! David Williams also kept me on my toes by making sure everything in the book is technically accurate. Additionally, I appreciate the help of all the copy editors — Rebekah Mancilla, Rebecca Huehls, and Diana Conover. Thanks again everyone for working so hard on this book!

Publisher's Acknowledgments

We're proud of this book; please send us your comments through our online registration form located at `www.dummies.com/register/`.

Some of the people who helped bring this book to market include the following:

Acquisitions, Editorial, and Media Development

Senior Project Editor: Nicole Haims

Senior Acquisitions Editor: Steven Hayes

Copy Editors: Rebekah Mancilla, Diana Conover

Technical Editor: David M. Williams, MCSD

Editorial Manager: Leah Cameron

Senior Permissions Editor: Carmen Krikorian

Media Development Manager: Laura VanWinkle

Media Development Supervisor: Richard Graves

Editorial Assistant: Amanda Foxworth

Cartoons: Rich Tennant (`www.the5thwave.com`)

Production

Project Coordinator: Regina Snyder

Layout and Graphics: Karl Brandt, Seth Conley, Julie Trippetti, Jeremey Unger, Mary Virgin

Proofreaders: John Tyler Connoley, John Greenough, Andy Hollandbeck, Susan Moritz, Angel Perez, Carl Pierce, TECHBOOKS Production Services

Indexer: TECHBOOKS Production Services

Special Help: Rebecca Huehls, Andrea Boucher

Publishing and Editorial for Technology Dummies

Richard Swadley, Vice President and Executive Group Publisher

Andy Cummings, Vice President and Publisher

Mary C. Corder, Editorial Director

Publishing for Consumer Dummies

Diane Graves Steele, Vice President and Publisher

Joyce Pepple, Acquisitions Director

Composition Services

Gerry Fahey, Vice President of Production Services

Debbie Stailey, Director of Composition Services

Contents at a Glance

Table of Contents

Introduction

・・・

*T*hank you for buying my book! I had a very enjoyable time writing it, so I hope you enjoy reading it. Web services is an incredible new technology. You'll find this out as you peruse the pages of the book. As with all new technologies, it takes a while to come up to speed. Web services is a very deep topic. I took care to make sure that I addressed the right amount and depth of material for someone who is just starting out with Web services or has some experience. If you are an experienced Web services developer, you are likely not going to get much out of this book.

I have described Web services to some people as a technology that "fixes every problem there ever was in software development." Of course, I'm exaggerating, but it shows how passionate I am about the topic. In fact, I formed a company (Transport:80 Incorporated) around it! You can visit us on the Web at www.transport80.com.

Nowadays, most computers are connected to the Internet. It stands to reason that the need to connect and share these computers together is great. However, what do *connect* and *share* mean? Do they mean file sharing or allowing printer sharing? Internet connection sharing? Database sharing? Do they mean something greater?

Connect and *share* actually mean all these things. Depending on the work that needs to be done and other factors, connecting two systems may be easier or harder. Most of the connectivity and sharing issues depend on many things, such as the following:

- Languages used to create applications and components
- Operating system/platform that applications and components are hosted on
- Type of devices the applications use, such as server, workstation, mobile devices (PDAs), or cell phones
- Type of connection used to tie systems together, such as fixed or continuous bandwidth or a temporary connection, such as a cell phone
- Speed of connection
- Security devices, such as firewalls, between computers

All of these points are addressed with the advent of Web services on the Microsoft .NET platform. This unique combination of technologies merges and spans the above list to make distributed computing language independent, platform independent, and device independent.

Distinguishing Web services technology from cheap knockoffs

What Web services technology is really depends on who you ask. Ask most people, and you'll get an incomplete (if not inaccurate) answer. So I'm going to make sure you get it straight. A company that offers services over the Web doesn't necessarily provide Web services.

In fact, this couldn't be further from the truth. To illustrate the point, suppose a company named XYZ Corp provides online training for college students to learn history. Okay, so this technology is Web-based and available online, but does that make it a Web service? Not necessarily.

To be a Web service, XYZ Corp must have a defined interface that allows for programmatic access using standard Internet technologies, such as XML and SOAP. Translation? You have to look under the hood in order to really know. This book focuses on Web services technology, and you will find out more about all of these standards as you read.

Although I don't cover each and every one of these topics in this book, you should certainly get your appetite whetted by reading this book. In here, you get the basics as well as some more-advanced topics. Then you can move on to a more-advanced book that explores topics like mobile application development.

About This Book

I've spent much time writing this book so that you can benefit from my years of experience. I present the material in an easy-to-read format that will have you up and running in no time. I've done my best to make sure that everything in the book, from text to screen shots, is accurate. Therefore, the screens and text may vary slightly from what you see on your screen — but it is unlikely.

One issue that I always face when I write is knowing when to quit! Most of the time, the publisher has to tell me not to cover a topic because it would just make the book too big. This one is no different. If I didn't cover a topic that you wanted me to, I'm sorry; but if I were to cover every possible issue relating to .NET and Web services in-depth, the book would be from 1,500 to 2,000 pages long.

I have multiple servers and workstations that I used in the creation of the text and screen shots in this book. You may see any of the following machine names, which are my machine names. Yours will be different. I used any of the following: HAWKEYE, POTTER, HOTLIPS, RADAR, TRAPPER, SPARKY, RIZZO, FLAGG, or FERRETFACE. If you are a *M*A*S*H* fan, you'll notice a trend.

I wrote this book to be equally useful to beginners and intermediate users alike, especially in light of the fact that most people are new to Web services. I don't cover many advanced topics, such as mobile device development — I just don't have the space in this book. In this book, however, I do show you how to:

- Discover XML and SOAP
- Understand how Web services can benefit you and your organization
- Create Web service projects by using Visual Studio .NET
- Discover how to test and debug your Web service projects
- Secure your Web services
- And much, much, more

With this in mind, I hope you enjoy reading the book as much as I enjoyed writing it.

Conventions Used in This Book

I use some terms throughout the book that you should know about:

Select: You highlight an item by clicking it. This usually affects an item in a list box, grid, or menu.

Click: This describes an action during which you press and release the left mouse button while the mouse is positioned over an area of the screen. For example, if I say, "Click OK," I mean that you must press and release the left mouse button while it is positioned anywhere over the OK button.

Double-click: You must click the left mouse button twice in rapid succession. This action either selects an item and closes a dialog box, or it expands an item in a hierarchical tree.

Right-click: This means the same as *click,* except that you click the right mouse button instead of the left mouse button.

Code and boldface: When text `looks like this`, I'm giving you a snippet of sample code. If I describe a markup element (or tag), it looks like this: `<element>`. Attributes, objects, namespaces, and specific filenames are also in `this` format. The only time that this isn't the case is when I'm telling you exactly what to type. When I'm giving you the goods as part of a numbered list, the text that you're supposed to enter looks like this: **Type this**.

Who Should Read This Book?

This book is intended for anyone who needs a good overview of *why* and *how* Web services are used on the Microsoft .NET platform. Although some competitive information does make an appearance in Chapter 1, this book is largely Microsoft-centric. If you are wanting to understand *why* to use Web services and *why* to choose the Microsoft platform for designing, constructing, and hosting your Web services projects, this book is for you. If this isn't enough, the book also shows you *how* to design, develop, test, and deploy your Web services projects by using Microsoft-based technologies. Again, if these are of interest to you or your organization, you've picked up the right book.

Organization Is the Key to Life

If you are thumbing through this book in the bookstore, you probably want to know how the book is organized before you take the financial plunge. If you already bought it, you can use this section as a quick reference.

Part 1: Web Services Overview

This section gives you an overview of the key tools, technologies, and history that surround Web services on the Microsoft .NET platform. I also cover brief introductions into XML and SOAP.

Part 11: Web Services Design and Construction

This section shows considerations and issues surrounding the design of Web services. It also shows how to construct, test, and debug Web services projects by using Visual Studio .NET.

Part 111: Web Services Usage

In this section, I show you how to use Web services that were written by you or someone else. Using Web services is also known as *consuming* a Web service. I show you how to consume Web services by using Visual Studio .NET and also how to locate Web services (in the Microsoft UDDI registry) that are available for consumption.

Part IV: Advanced Topics

After you have a good handle on constructing, testing, and consuming Web services by using Visual Studio .NET, you need to grasp some more-advanced topics before implementing Web services throughout your organization. This part takes a look at these critical issues (such as software and hardware configurations) as well as security.

Part V: The Part of Tens

As with all *For Dummies* books, this book contains Part of Tens chapters. This section contains valuable information about the ten best resources for use with Web services. In addition, you find ten reasons to construct Web services on the Microsoft platform.

What About All Those Icons?

To help you identify key pieces of text, I put these icons in the margins throughout the book:

This icon indicates a tip that I give you, based on my experience. Paying attention to this icon can save you lots of time; but if you ignore this icon, it won't adversely affect your projects.

You should keep the key information you find alongside this friendly reminder in mind as you proceed because the info will help you.

This information is of a more in-depth technical nature than other information presented in the chapter. This information is very interesting, but not necessary to understand the overall discussion in the chapter.

I use this icon to point you to other book resources that can give you more detailed information about specific standards or technologies used in .NET and Web services.

Where to Go from Here?

Are you ready to get going with Web services on the Microsoft .NET platform? If so, I suggest reading the book beginning with Chapter 1 and ending with Chapter 15. Although each chapter stands alone, if you're new to this whole crazy world of .NET Web services, you might want to read from start to finish (just don't do it all in one day).

You'll find that the discussions on XML (see Chapter 3) and SOAP (see Chapter 4) seem quite involved. They are, but I promise, I cover only the most essential pieces of these technologies in order to have the rest of the book and your understanding of Web services make sense.

If you want to contact me with comments, suggestions, and questions, I can be reached at `tmann@transport80.com`.

Happy reading and thanks again for buying the book!

Part I
Web Services Overview

The 5th Wave   By Rich Tennant

"Can't I just give you riches or something?"

In this part . . .

You get an overview into the tools and technologies that make Web services possible on the Microsoft platform. Chapter 1 gives an overview as to why Web services are needed, as well as an overview into the different technological terms that Microsoft uses with respect to its technology. Chapter 2 demystifies the .NET platform, showing its pieces and parts. Chapter 3 gives an in-depth look into XML. Building upon the foundation of XML, Chapter 4 shows you how SOAP works. Both XML and SOAP are what make Web services possible.

Chapter 1

Introducing Web Services

*W*eb services promise to be the next major frontier in computing. Up until the advent of Web services, interoperability and integration (the exchange of data among computer systems) were extremely limited or cumbersome. Prior to Web services, limited integration took place with numerous technologies, vendors, obstacles, and formats that prevented the sharing of data. But then Web service technology came along and changed all that.

Web services is a promising new technology that solves virtually all the problems that have existed in traditional distributed computing. Web services are programmable and platform-independent. All you need is network connectivity that understands how to transmit HTTP requests and you're in business.

Microsoft has generated an exceptionally comprehensive platform for designing, developing, testing, and deploying Web services-based applications, but has taken this concept one step further and made its tools language-independent as well. In this chapter, I give you an overview of Web services: why they are needed, what they do, how they are used, the players involved, and the technologies involved.

At this time, I advise you to grab a cup of coffee, sit back, take off your shoes, prop up your feet, and dive right in!

What in the World Are Web Services?

No doubt you have heard of Web services. You can't exactly avoid them if you have any job function in information technology (IT) today. If you are a CEO, CTO, project manager, software architect, or developer, you have at least listened to some of the hype about Web services.

If I had to give you an oversimplified definition of the term *Web services,* I would say that Web services encompass the technology that's used in allowing data to be transmitted across the Internet by using a familiar programming methodology. To avoid any confusion about what Web services transmit over the Internet, I want to emphasize the fact that *only data* is transmitted using Web services technology. Web services do not have a visual interface, such as text boxes, radio buttons, and the like.

For example, a Web service may be offered in a B2B (business to business) scenario whereby Company A provides a currency conversion Web service and Company B, in turn, uses this Web service to provide the currency conversion functionality to its customers. The Web service offered by Company A can also be used by Company C in a different capacity. For example, Company C may combine Company A's Web service with other functionality and offer it as a Web service to other companies. In both scenarios, specific functionality is developed and made available as a programmable Web service that can be accessed by other companies over the Internet.

Of course, Web services are technically a lot more complicated than my oversimplified definition states. Try asking ten of your co-workers what a Web service is; you're likely to get ten different answers. So, who's right? Most likely, all of them. Everybody has their own definition because they describe how it affects their own personal lives.

Really, you need to decide for yourself (with the help of this book) what Web services are and how they affect your business. The term *Web services* means something different to each person, depending on his or her interest. Executives are likely to not understand exactly how the Web services technology can simplify development, but they are going to understand the high return on investment *(ROI)*. Conversely, developers and architects will likely understand that the Web services technology can help shorten development time and drastically make connectivity easier, but they won't grasp the immediate benefits of high ROI. Typically, developers and architects simply want to implement the coolest solution and use the latest and greatest technologies. With Web services, everyone can have his or her wish!

Web services is a technology for transmitting data over the Internet and allowing programmatic access to that data using standard Internet protocols. The term *Web service* is not used to represent a company that simply offers services on the Web, such as a banking Web site. Although this company that offers a service over the Web, it doesn't necessarily make its service available by using a programmatic interface that allows two applications to be integrated. In fact, a Web service allows a developer to include functionality into a program without needing to "reinvent the wheel" and without needing to know anything about the business or complexity of the Web service that he or she is using.

Web services as a technology is strictly related to the transmission of data over the Internet or your company's intranet (local network). ROI comes into play when you start analyzing what Web services can do for your organization or how effective they are to implement or create. I discuss how Web services affect your business throughout this book, but specifically in this chapter and in Chapter 2. I show you how to create Web services in Chapter 6.

Microsoft supports Web services with something called the *.NET Framework.* I cover the .NET Framework in the "Parts is parts: Putting the .NET pieces together" section, located later in this chapter. I discuss how the .NET Framework impacts your organization in Chapter 2. Together, all tools and technologies that support Web services are collectively referred to as the *Microsoft .NET platform.*

What Web Services Do for You

Web services is a broad term that represents all the technologies used to transmit data across a network by using standard Internet protocols, typically HyperText Transfer Protocol (HTTP). An eXtensible Markup Language (XML) format is used to represent the data, which is why Web services are sometimes known as *XML Web services.*

You can think of an individual Web service as a piece of software that performs a specific task (also known as a *function*), and makes that task available by exposing a set of operations that can be performed (known as *methods* or *Web methods*) with the task. Additionally, each of the methods exposes a set of variables that can accept data passed into the method. These variables are known as *parameters* or *properties*. Together, the properties and methods refer to a Web service's *interface*. For example, Company A creates a Web service that provides currency rate functionality, which may expose a method called GetRate. Company B is then able to pass a parameter called CountryCode into the GetRate method. The GetRate method takes the CountryCode parameter, looks up the appropriate currency rate in a database, and returns the rate back to the program that requested it.

In this example, which database did Company A use to access the currency rate information? What was the name of the database server? What communication mechanisms and security mechanisms were used to access the database server? The answer to all of these questions is "I don't care." The beauty of a Web service is the concept of *encapsulation.* Encapsulation allows the complexity of retrieving the actual currency rate to be completely self-contained within the company that created the Web service (Company A). The only thing that Company B knows is that they called a Web service to get a currency rate and it was given to them.

A little something about ASP

If you're using the Microsoft platform, the Web server used to host Web services is, of course, Internet Information Server (IIS). If you've done any Web development at all on the Microsoft platform, you know IIS intimately. IIS is used to host Active Server Pages (also known as *ASP*). Active Server Pages were developed to allow dynamic programming and scripting within the Web execution environment. However, ASP presented some technical issues and, just like all software, grew into something else: ASP.NET. ASP.NET has countless advantages over ASP; these advantages are covered in Chapter 2.

Where does ASP.NET come from? How does it get installed? The answer to both questions is the .NET Framework. I briefly discuss the .NET Framework later in this chapter (in the section "Parts is parts: Putting the .NET pieces together"), and I discuss it in even more detail in Chapter 2.

Web services are made possible by placing the programs, or applications, on a Web server, such as Microsoft Internet Information Server (IIS). Because the application resides on a Web server, it can be called, or *invoked,* from any other computer on the network by using HTTP. The Web service provides seamless distributed computing across the entire network, as long as both sides know how to use a Web service. If you've been in business for a while, you probably know that providing distributed services has always been a challenge in the past.

One major advantage of invoking or creating Web services over HTTP is that if the Web server is on the Internet, the network administrators on both ends of the data transmission don't have to open any additional ports in their firewalls. All transmission of data is sent across port 80 (typically) by using HTTP. Port 80 is always open in a firewall because it is the same port used to browse the Internet. The fact that the network administrators don't need to open additional ports means that you face virtually no additional security risk in using Web services.

Another major advantage in Web services is that (because Web services conform to open standards) a Web service written on one platform (such as the Microsoft platform) can call another Web service written on another platform (such as Linux).

Because of their innate flexibility, Web services make the notion of *software as a service* a real possibility. And because Web services provide integration between two systems, *software as a service* refers to the possibility of not having to install software on workstations or servers, but rather, being able to use it from across the Internet. In fact, Web services can change the way you use all your computing resources by doing the following:

- ✔ **Save hassle:** Imagine you need to install Microsoft Office. If Microsoft decides that they want to make Office available as a Web service, you don't have to go out, purchase the software, and install it out of the box to all the computers in your network. Instead, you can get the full functionality of that piece of software across a Web interface without any installation at all.

- ✔ **Save money:** Imagine renting or leasing software instead of buying it. You can "break your lease" when and if the applications aren't working for your organization, which can save you lots of money.

- ✔ **Stay ahead of the game without even trying:** Imagine not having to keep up-to-date with the latest version. The latest version is always available from the vendor who provides the software as a service.

All of these things are possible when using software as a service. What you're really doing when you use software as a service this way is *outsourcing* functions that you used to perform within your organization. Many businesses already outsource software products as a service, including my company, Transport:80. For more information, visit the Web site at `www.transport80.com`. Microsoft (and other companies) may, in the future, make their products available as a service.

Using Web Services on the Microsoft .NET Platform

To understand the benefits of Web services on the Microsoft platform, you have to examine the problems of distributed computing in the past. *Distributed computing* is the notion of having multiple computers in different locations individually provide computing power for the purpose of processing information. To help illustrate distributed computing in action, consider the following scenario. You develop a Web-based application that enables your customers to do the following:

- ✔ Create and manage user accounts

- ✔ Pay bills (this includes credit card processing)

- ✔ Look up prior bills for the past three years

- ✔ Support hundreds of simultaneous users

All these processes involve complex Web activity, real-time database activity, and historical database activity. In a typical networking environment, multiple complex applications can't be hosted on a single server. Therefore, the applications must be distributed across multiple servers. If all of the servers that you use for these applications are physically placed next to each other and are on the same platform (that is, Microsoft), you will have few challenges communicating among servers.

On the other hand, if some of the servers are located in other buildings, across the Internet, or on different platforms, you face major challenges trying to get the machines to talk to each other. Web services solves all the problems that occur with traditional distributed computing. You'll see this throughout the rest of this book.

Parts is parts: Putting the .NET pieces together

Many parts and terms make up or describe the Microsoft environment that support Web services. This section outlines those parts.

Having some familiarity with these parts and terms is helpful before you move on to subsequent chapters in this book.

Microsoft uses the following parts in the support of Web services:

- ✔ **.NET:** This is Microsoft's vision and surrounding technologies for making applications available any time, any place, on any device. For .NET to be realized, Microsoft put a tremendous amount of thought into the architecture of .NET. Microsoft also thoroughly planned all of the .NET tools, technologies, and subsystems that comprise the .NET platform. Saying that Microsoft is *betting the farm* on .NET is not an understatement. Because of Microsoft's power and standing in the industry, .NET is assured of being a great success.

- ✔ **.NET platform:** This is Microsoft's entire suite of tools, technologies, and services that support Microsoft's vision of connected applications being made available any time, any place, on any device. Web services is a large part of that vision. The .NET platform encompasses the .NET Framework and other components that are outlined in Chapter 2.

- ✔ **.NET Framework:** This is Microsoft's set of services that is used to support Web services. The specific services that comprise the .NET Framework, such as the Common Language Runtime (CLR), Base classes, and so forth, are discussed in Chapter 2. Web services would not work without the .NET Framework. You'll see when you get to Chapter 2, so hold your horses!

✔ **Visual Studio .NET:** This is a development tool that is used to create applications for the .NET platform, including Web services. Using Visual Studio .NET is easier than you may think. I show you how to use Visual Studio .NET (also known as *VS.NET*) in Chapter 6.

Understanding the standards that make Web services happen on the .NET platform

Web services are limited only by the creativity of the developers who create them and the software architects who design them. With the rise in popularity and flexibility of markup languages and other technologies, along with the fact that these technologies aren't restricted by platforms, many standards are used in making Web services function on the .NET platform.

The terminology surrounding those standards can be confusing, so I want to make sure that you have a brief understanding before you get to the later chapters that dive deeper into those terms. Because these terms are so interrelated, getting a handle on them now is important. Here are the major terms:

✔ **eXtensible Markup Language (XML):** *XML* is a format that is used to describe and format data. XML is formatted into a series of hierarchical tags that structures data based on the way it makes sense to your company. The XML data, known as an *XML Document,* is typically stored in a text file with an .xml extension. This XML data can be transmitted over the Internet using Web service technology. As you can see, XML is unbelievably flexible and capable of crossing platforms *and* even applications. XML is discussed further in Chapter 3.

✔ **XML Stylesheet Language (XSL):** Because XML is used to describe data only, it contains no instructions for how that data is to be presented on the screen (font size, font color, and so on). That's where XSL comes in. *XSL* is a format that describes how XML should be translated into HTML for display on the Web.

XML only describes data, not how the data is to be displayed. For example, suppose that you have an XML file that describes a banking transaction. The file contains the data related to the transaction itself, such as the account number, the amount of the transaction, and so on. The XML file does not contain any information about fonts, placement of the data on the screen, or anything else; that's where XSL comes in. XSL enables you to indicate how to format the XML so that it can be displayed on the Web.

A brief history of data transfer before Web services

Prior to the advent of Web services, many technologies promised to overcome the hurdles of transmitting data between distributed systems. You are probably familiar with many of these technologies:

- **File Transmission Protocol (FTP):** People use FTP to send and receive files, but FTP is very difficult to automate. FTP is also not geared towards being programmable; it simply transfers files.

- **Electronic Data Interchange (EDI):** This has proven to be quite useful in the transmission of data but does have a couple of problems. First, it is quite rigid. Documents must conform to a specific format. For example, all purchase orders are transmitted with the same format, which may sound like a good thing, but what if you wanted to add custom fields to your purchase orders? That's where EDI starts to fall apart. Second, EDI is notoriously expensive to implement. EDI files are text-based, but to process those text files requires expensive software and hardware.

- **Distributed Component Object Model (DCOM):** This one is based on the Microsoft standard, Component Object Model (COM). COM is a model for compiling code into programmable objects. COM is a great technology, but it works only on a single computer. When you start to get into distributed computing, DCOM is supposed to fill the gap. DCOM is programmable and distributed but has two major problems: DCOM is difficult to implement, and it is dependent on the Microsoft platform.

- **CORBA:** Even though this sounds like a new dance step, it actually stands for Common Object Request Broker Architecture. CORBA is similar to DCOM, but works on a UNIX platform only.

- **Floppy disk/CD-ROM/e-mail:** Sending files by floppy disk, CD-ROM, or e-mail are all still popular ways of sending files because these methods don't require network authentication or permissions. However, these methods of transmitting data are not programmable. They simply replace FTP.

- **XML Schema Description (XSD):** *XSD* is a document (file) that describes the *schema* (also known as the *format*) of an XML file. XSD files are used to test that an XML file conforms to the format specified in the XSD file. XSD is discussed in detail in Chapter 3.

- **Document Object Model (DOM):** *DOM* is a programmable object model that represents the contents of an HTML browser. For example, if a browser contains two text boxes, three radio buttons, and a button, the DOM allows you to access in your code the properties associated with these graphical elements.

- **XML Document Object Model (XMLDOM):** *XMLDOM* is a programmable object model for an XML document. XMLDOM allows for the querying, updating, inserting, and deleting of elements or nodes within an XML document. I tell you more about elements and nodes in Chapter 3.

- **Simple Object Access Protocol (SOAP):** *SOAP* is a standard protocol used to transmit XML data over a network, such as the Internet. Web services define the interface of a programmatic object, but SOAP allows a call to a Web service to be routed to the proper location over the Internet. SOAP is discussed further in Chapter 4.

- **Universal Description, Discovery, and Integration (UDDI):** *UDDI* is a standard for registering Web services that are available over the Internet. It is the *yellow pages* or *white pages* of Web services. Just because you have a Web service available doesn't mean that anyone will be able to find it. That's where UDDI comes in. UDDI allows someone to search a database and find your company or your services. UDDI is discussed further in Chapter 9.

- **Web Services Description Language (WSDL):** *WSDL* is a standard format for describing your Web service interface that you expose to applications that want to use, or *consume,* your Web service. WSDL is covered in Chapter 9.

We Are Not Alone

Most of the discussion and advertising (some call it *hype*) around Web services is related to the .NET platform (Microsoft's platform). However, just because Microsoft is the *loudest* doesn't mean that it is the only company that supports Web services. Plenty of other companies have jumped on the bandwagon.

You may wonder how other companies can support Web services. The answer is simple. Creating the concept of Web services and related technologies was not an effort by Microsoft alone. It was a joint specification developed by Microsoft and other companies and submitted as a standard for passing data over the Internet to the World Wide Web Consortium (known as the *W3C*). The specification was adopted by the W3C, which makes it an open, publicly available standard. Although I don't discuss the details of the standard per se, everything I discuss in this book is Microsoft's interpretation of this standard and how it chose to implement those standards. That's what the whole buzz around .NET is about.

Except for this section, this book is dedicated entirely to Web services on the Microsoft .NET platform. However, discussing what the competition is up to is only fair, even though I don't provide a review or an opinion on any of the other vendors' products. I've listed the other vendors in alphabetical order, so as to not show favoritism.

HP

HP has a Web service platform, called *HP Web Services Platform* (Version 2.0 at the time of this writing), that can be used to generate Web services. It was formerly known as *e-Speak*. Its platform is built around exposing Java and J2EE (Java 2 platform, Enterprise Edition) objects as Web services.

The HP Web Services Platform consists of the following tools that enable you to build Web services:

- **HP-SOAP:** Application server that processes SOAP messages
- **HP Registry Composer:** Enables the registration of Web services to public and private registries
- **HP Service Composer:** Development tool for graphically creating Web services

You can obtain more information about HP Web services at `www.hp.com/go/webservices`.

IBM

IBM fully embraces the concept of Web services and is integrating it into many of its products. In fact, IBM has worked with Microsoft to create applications that prove interoperability between platforms. IBM's answer to Web services is to provide a platform consisting of the following:

- **WebSphere Application Server:** A server that supports and hosts Web services on the IBM platform
- **WebSphere Studio:** A graphical environment for creating Web services, servlets, Java Server Pages (JSP), and JavaBeans
- **WebSphere SDK for Web Services (WSDK):** A toolkit that provides everything a developer needs to create Web services on the IBM platform, including samples, examples, architectural documentation, scripts, Java SDK, and even a scaled-down version of its WebSphere product
- **Web Services Toolkit (WSTK):** A toolkit that provides documentation and prototypes of how to develop Web services on the IBM platform

You can obtain more information about IBM Web services at `www3.ibm.com/software/solutions/webservices`.

Novell

Novell's strategy for implementing Web services is called *one Net.* one Net is a vision for allowing all networks to communicate with each other. This includes intranets, extranets, wireless networks, and more. To support this vision, Novell acquired SilverStream, apparently for their exteNd Web Services Platform.

The eXtend Web Services Platform consists of the following:

- **exteNd Composer:** A visual integration server, allowing connection to legacy systems
- **exteNd Director:** This enables developers to define personalization, workflow, business rules, and more
- **exteNd Workbench:** This enables the rapid development of Java/J2EE Web services applications
- **exteNd Application Server:** This provides runtime environment for Novell's Web services

You can obtain more information about Novell's Web services at `www.novell.com/webservices`.

Oracle

Oracle was a straggler in announcing a Web services strategy. However, it is supporting Web services on its Oracle9iAS Web Services Platform. The platform consists of:

- **OC4J:** The runtime environment for Oracle's Web services
- **Oracle9i Jdeveloper:** A graphical development tool for creating Java/J2EE-based objects and Web services
- **Oracle Enterprise Manager:** A management console for administering Web services
- **Oracle9iAS UDDI Registry:** This enables the publishing of Web services into UDDI and allows searching with UDDI

You can obtain more information about Oracle's Web services at `http://otn.oracle.com/tech/webservices/content.html`.

Sun Microsystems

Sun has supported the Web services standards by embracing them into its ONE *(Open Net Environment)* architecture. Sun also provides some tools to help with the development and support of Web services on the Sun platform:

- ✔ **Sun ONE Studio:** A graphical environment for developing Web services on the Sun platform

- ✔ **Sun ONE Web Server:** A Web server for hosting Web services

- ✔ **Sun ONE Application Server:** A server for serving J2EE-compliant applications and hosting Web services

You can obtain more information about Sun Microsystems Web services at www.sun.com/webservices.

Chapter 2

Preparing for Impact

. . . .

. . . .

*I*mplementing Web services in your organization is not necessarily easy or straightforward. In other words, the only thing you can be sure of is the fact that Web services *will* have an impact on your organization in one way or another. That may have something to do with the large investment in time, resources, money, and perhaps aspirin you'll need to make in order to plan and implement these services.

Unfortunately, you can't just flip a switch and have a new system up and running on the .NET platform. It takes planning. Planning means that you have an understanding of the overall philosophy, concepts, architecture, and time commitments required in making the switch from the way you currently do software development to the new concepts behind Web services and their design, development, and deployment.

In this chapter, I point out some of the things that you must take into consideration before taking the plunge into Web services. The following sections focus on the .NET architecture, installation requirements, and personnel requirements. After reading this chapter, you should have a good idea of how switching to .NET will affect your organization. Be prepared: This is a pretty hefty chapter, but I simplified it as much as possible. It may seem, at times, that this chapter goes into quite a bit of depth, but I included only the minimum amount of information necessary (featuring discussions of the Microsoft .NET platform) for you to understand the impact of implementing Web services in your organization.

A Short Course in the Web Services Revolution

The fact that you're reading this book signifies that you're interested in finding out more about .NET and how it fits into the whole Web services picture. Chapter 1 gives you an inkling about what .NET is, as well as what Web services can do for your business. Here's the basic skinny:

✔ **Web services:** The term *Web services* is used as a blanket term to describe a cross-platform, language-independent technology that allows applications to interoperate across the Internet. Web services applications can be written using Microsoft Visual Studio .NET and are hosted (or run) from a Web server (Microsoft Internet Information Server — IIS).

✔ **Programming interface:** A Web services application has operations that can be performed on it and parameters that can be sent to it programmatically. These operations and parameters are known collectively as the Web service *programming interface,* or simply an *interface.* An example of a Web service is an application that provides currency rate conversion over the Internet.

If you're writing a separate application that needs currency rate conversion, you can use, or *call,* the Web service application from over the Internet.

✔ **.NET:** .NET is a Microsoft initiative aimed at making Web services possible on the Microsoft platform. Because Web services are based on an open standard, Microsoft Web services are interoperable with Web services hosted on other platforms. .NET uses a variety of programming technologies to enable you to create Web services that work for your business environment.

I admit that there are a few new concepts that you need to get straight before taking the plunge into Web services. However, your challenge isn't insurmountable. In fact, this chapter has all of the basics that you need to start building an understanding of Web services on the .NET platform.

Crib Notes: The .NET Platform Architecture

The *.NET platform* is a set of tools, technologies, and services for developing robust applications for any type of device (computer browsers, mobile devices, cell phones, and so on) in any .NET supported language. (A *.NET-supported language* is a programming language that can be hosted on the .NET platform.)

Any programming language that can be supported within .NET is said to *target* the .NET runtime or the Common Language Runtime (CLR). The CLR is de-geekified in the following section.

The architecture behind the .NET platform is extremely complex, so enormous a topic that I can't begin to do it justice in this book. So, I focus specifically on the architecture that makes Web services possible. To start understanding what the .NET platform is, refer to Figure 2-1.

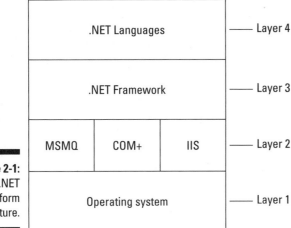

Figure 2-1:
The .NET platform architecture.

The architecture of the .NET platform is comprised of many key technologies:

 ✔ **Operating system:** Use Windows 2000 or later.

 ✔ **Miscellaneous services:** Sitting on top of the operating system is a set of miscellaneous services, such as message queuing (MSMQ), object handling (COM+), and a Web server (IIS).

 ✔ **.NET Framework:** Interacting with miscellaneous services is the concept of the .NET Framework, which is discussed in the next section.

 ✔ **.NET languages:** None of the .NET platform would be possible if developers couldn't use a programming language to write .NET code, so on top of the whole stack are .NET languages.

.NET Framework

The *.NET Framework* is a part of the .NET Platform and contains a set of object-oriented services and programs that are used to provide a robust runtime environment. This environment (called a *runtime environment* because it is used while programs are running) is responsible for executing programs that are written for the Microsoft .NET platform in any programming language that is supported within the .NET Framework.

The *.NET Framework services* provide an environment from which code is managed and executes within the operating system. *Object-orientation* refers to a set of functions grouped into logical, hierarchical, and programmable units called *objects*.

Objects can be reused in your code and inherited so that the programming interface (discussed earlier in this chapter) can be altered in objects that are lower in the object hierarchy. Inheritance is a great thing because it promotes code reuse by allowing an object to inherit functionality from a parent object that is higher in the hierarchy (or perhaps I should say *higher*archy). The top level of the object hierarchy is known as a *namespace,* which is discussed throughout this book, but is concentrated in this chapter and in Chapters 3 and 4.

In addition to being part of the platform architecture, the .NET Framework has its *own* architecture. This architecture is essential for you to understand, especially if you're an architect or software developer. If you're an IT manager, you should also pay attention here, because understanding the Framework can help you understand the resource needs from both an equipment and personnel standpoint. Figure 2-2 shows the .NET Framework architecture.

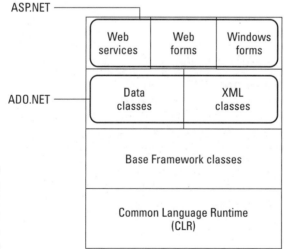

Figure 2-2:
The .NET
Framework
architecture.

Although the .NET Framework is just one piece of the .NET platform (refer to Figure 2-1), it is the most important piece.

The .NET Framework is made up of the following architectural subsystems, each of which plays a very important role in the overall picture (and are discussed in further detail in later sections):

✔ **CLR:** At the very core of the .NET Framework is the Common Language Runtime, or *CLR.* The CLR is a set of services that guarantees a consistent execution environment regardless of the programming language used to write an application or Web service. The CLR is described in the next section, "Common Language Runtime." Within the CLR is a set of *datatypes,* called the common type system or *CTS.* CTS can be used in all languages.

A *datatype* is an indicator to the .NET compiler that specifies what type of data will be stored in a variable, such as a string or an integer (which doesn't allow characters). CTS and datatypes are discussed later in this chapter in the section, "Common Type System."

✔ **Base classes:** Sitting on top of the CLR is a set of base classes, or services, that provide a consistent and basic level of functionality within the .NET Framework. These base classes are described in the "Class libraries" section, later in this chapter.

✔ **ADO.NET classes:** Above the Framework classes is another set of classes for accessing data by using ADO.NET. *ADO.NET* stands for ActiveX Data Objects on the .NET platform. ADO.NET is a programmatic set of classes used specifically for accessing data from a database. I discuss ADO.NET in more detail later in this chapter.

✔ **ASP.NET classes:** Above the ADO.NET classes are ASP.NET classes, which provide services that handle both Web services and Web forms.

This book does not cover Web forms or Windows forms. Because I know you're just dying of curiosity, Web forms and Windows forms are used for constructing familiar graphical interface applications and components, like menu bars, buttons, check boxes, forms, and so on. By contrast, Web services applications can be used to create components also, with two main differences. The first difference is that no graphical interface is part of a Web services application. The second is that Web services are constructed to be usable and callable over the Internet or on your local Intranet. ASP.NET is discussed later in this chapter, in the "ASP.NET" section, and throughout most of this book.

Common Language Runtime

The Common Language Runtime, or *CLR,* is responsible for managing the execution of code. CLR is a set of services that is core to the concept of the .NET Framework. All code that executes in the .NET Framework is run through the CLR. A CLR's ability to process all the code that .NET runs is what's called *managed execution.* Managed execution means that the process of executing code is completely managed by the CLR and gives little or no control to the programmer over certain functionality, which you'll see shortly.

Some overhead is associated with the CLR, but the benefits far outweigh the overhead. *Overhead* is resources, such as memory, network bandwidth, disk space, extra CPU processing time, and so on. Most systems that provide automatic functionality do so at the expense of some additional overhead.

The CLR uses some additional overhead because of all the functionality it provides, but the CLR provides these major benefits:

- **Guaranteed garbage collection:** Unused objects and other poorly coded procedures have little or no effect on server resources because this *garbage* is automatically cleaned up and fixed.

- **Memory management:** The allocation and cleanup of memory and making it available to other processes is handled automatically by the CLR.

- **True cross-language compatibility and integration:** One of the major benefits of the CLR is the capability to write objects and libraries in any desired programming language (as long as it is supported in the CLR). Additionally, objects written in one language can be inherited and reused in another language.

- **Common security mechanisms:** Any security-related functions and tasks that are available in one programming language are also available in any other programming language because the security of compiled code (objects, applications, and so forth) are handled within the CLR.

- **Common environment:** The programming environment for all types of projects (Web services, stand-alone applications, Web applications, and others) yields a consistent experience for the programmer. Also, because all code is managed by the CLR, a consistent behavior can be expected when code is executed in any language.

Because the CLR is built into the .NET Framework (and cannot be removed), any language that supports, or *targets,* the CLR is guaranteed to give you the benefits shown in the preceding list. In other words, any Web service application will play nice with CLR — right out of the box — if the application is created by using one of the following Microsoft programming languages:

- Visual Basic .NET

- Visual C++ .NET

- Visual C# .NET

- Visual J++ .NET

But wait, that's not all. There's more, folks. Lots of companies are writing languages to target the CLR. Some time in the future (if not by the time this book hits the shelves), you'll be able to write Web services and other .NET applications by using such languages as COBOL, Pascal, SmallTalk, and others.

Imagine writing a DLL (Dynamic Link Library) in COBOL that can be used by Visual Basic. Even better . . . imagine inheriting functionality in Visual Basic from a DLL written in COBOL. Are you starting to see the benefits?

Common Type System

The Common Type System, or *CTS,* defines, at the .NET Framework level, a set of datatypes that are shared across all languages that target the .NET Framework and CLR. (Say *that* five times fast.) A *shared datatype* allows for a consistent programming environment as well as interoperability. A shared datatype allows for consistency because it's shared across all languages that are supported by the .NET runtime.

For example, an integer in Visual Basic .NET is the same as an integer in Visual C++ .NET. An integer occupies the same amount of memory and stores the same range of values in all .NET languages. This was not the case prior to .NET, so interoperability was limited.

The CTS was needed in the old days because strings used by a C++ application were different than the strings used by a VB application. If you wanted to invoke a C++ DLL from a VB application, you'd have to do some conversion. (And maybe a little magic — pulling a rabbit out of a hat would be nice.) The same is true for some numeric datatypes, arrays, memory references (pointers), and more. The list goes on and on. Compatibility was a major pain, and conversion and jumping through hoops was the law of the land.

Class libraries

The .NET Framework provides an extremely extensive set of objects (made up of classes) from which you can write custom .NET applications, called *class libraries*. These class libraries, also known as *Base Framework Classes* or simply *Base Classes,* are a very rich set of services to ease your programming challenges. The base classes are organized into a series of hierarchical units. The top unit is known as a *namespace.* You can use the base classes in your own Visual Studio .NET projects to provide common services, such as database access.

Namespaces are a new concept in .NET. A *namespace* is simply a unique name given to a specific category of .NET objects. For example, the mother of all .NET object categories (the one at the top of the hierarchy) is called system. The system namespace provides a set of fundamental classes (including methods, properties, and events) that yields base-level services for .NET.

The system namespace contains a slew of other namespaces that extend quite deeply into the namespace hierarchy. For example, a system.data namespace provides the basis for data access in .NET, system.drawing provides basic graphics capabilities, and system.runtime provides runtime services for compiled .NET applications. Each of these sample namespaces is one level down in the system namespace hierarchy.

All in all, you can see thousands of classes in the .NET class library. For more information about these classes, as well as language-specific classes, point your browser to msdn.microsoft.com/library/default.asp?url=/library/en-us/cpref/html/cpref_start.asp.

.NET Enterprise servers

Microsoft has a whole slew of servers that support its .NET strategy. The .NET strategy is Microsoft's vision for interoperability among systems and is built upon the .NET framework, XML, and Web services. Of course, the operating system has to support .NET, but so do the individual servers that run businesses. These servers need to be interoperable.

To be a .NET Enterprise server (for the most part), the server must natively support XML and Web services by targeting the .NET Framework. These products are .NET Enterprise servers from Microsoft:

- Application Center
- BizTalk Server
- Commerce Server
- Content Management Server
- Exchange Server
- Host Integration Server
- Internet Security and Acceleration Server
- Microsoft Operations Manager
- Microsoft Project Server
- Mobile Information Server
- SharePoint Portal Server
- SQL Server
- Windows 2000 Server
- Windows 2000 Advanced Server
- Windows 2000 Datacenter Server

For more information about SQL Server 2000, check out my book, *Microsoft SQL Server 2000 For Dummies* (Wiley Publishing, Inc.).

The upcoming server operating systems from Microsoft, called Windows Server 2003, are part of a family of operating systems that are scaled for a specific role in the business enterprise. For example, the following editions are available:

- ✔ **Web Edition:** Basic operating system that is specially designed (and priced) to be used as a Web server. Typically, an organization will have numerous Web servers, known as a *Web farm,* to process lots of simultaneous requests from the Internet. The Web Edition eliminates a lot of the overhead in the operating system by not providing functionality that really isn't necessary for a Web server. The Web Edition allows for up to two Gigabytes (2GB) of memory and up to two processors.

- ✔ **Standard Edition:** Basic enterprise-level operating system that allows for up to 4GB of memory and up to four processors. It also allows for basic networking functionality, such as Active Directory, Virtual Private Networking (VPN), and more.

- ✔ **Enterprise Edition:** Contains everything that the Standard Edition contains, but allows for up to 64GB memory and up to eight processors. Amazingly, it also supports a 64-bit processor, which is a brand-new feature for any of the Microsoft operating systems. The Enterprise Edition also allows for failover clustering. *Failover clustering* is an advanced topic and is not discussed in too much depth in this book, but for more information, see Chapter 12.

- ✔ **Datacenter Edition:** Contains everything that the Standard and Enterprise Editions contain, but also added support for operations that occur within a large datacenter. The Datacenter Edition allows for up to 512GB of memory and up to 32 processors, so you better have a huge line of credit for one of these monsters!

You don't need to have any of the operating systems in the Windows Server 2003 family to implement Web services in your organization. You only need to install the .NET Framework on Windows 2000 as a runtime environment and use Visual Studio .NET to create your Web services applications. See "Installation Requirements," later in this chapter.

How .NET Does What It Does

Before you can accurately assess the impact of implementing Web services in your organization, you must understand how the .NET platform operates and some of the concepts behind it. This section aims at explaining these critical issues so that you can begin to assess how much of an impact you'll face. Microsoft has been criticized over the years because its development tools and runtime environments run exclusively on Windows-based systems. Although the good people at Microsoft aren't exactly shouting from the rooftops that the .NET platform can run on anything other than Windows, it is theoretically possible. The reason for this is how .NET operates at the core. Here's a simplified version of how .NET does what it does:

1. **At the top level, a developer or member of the IT department chooses a language that targets the .NET runtime.**

   These are the languages that will be used to build a particular Web service, such as one which provides currency calculation or returns stock quotes.

   Visual Basic .NET and Visual C++ .NET are two of the languages that work with the .NET runtime right out of the box.

2. **The languages are used to compile code into what is called Microsoft Intermediate Language code, or *MSIL* (also known sometimes as just plain *IL*).**

3. **Code executes at the machine level, which is even lower than MSIL.**

   You may be wondering why the code isn't compiled all the way down to machine-level code. The reason code is only compiled to MSIL is that all .NET languages (including those supported by third parties, such as COBOL) are compiled, as far as technically possible, without having to consider what type of CPU the machine uses. Therefore, MSIL code establishes a baseline from which all .NET code can be consistent, regardless of CPU type. Then the compiler takes the MSIL code and compiles it further to machine-level, which takes into consideration what type of CPU the machine uses.

4. **For this second, machine-level, compilation to take place, the Common Language Runtime invokes a compiler called a Just-In-Time compiler, or *JIT*.**

   The JIT compiler takes the precompiled MSIL code and compiles it down to machine-level.

   Microsoft supplies the MSIL compilers as part of the .NET Framework, as well as supplying a set of base Framework classes that are common between all languages that target the CLR. That's a plus: You have a measure of consistency across all .NET languages that you wouldn't have in other environments.

If you can follow what I'm saying, you may have begun to extrapolate certain concepts. If not, I'll just go ahead and tell you: If you run the .NET Framework on a Unix (or Linux) machine (which isn't possible at the time of this writing), the CPU-specific JIT compiler could theoretically allow a VB programmer to write Unix/Linux applications. This may seem like a very strange thought, but this is quite similar to the way a Java application can execute on any system that has a Java interpreter installed, regardless of the platform it was first developed on.

The bottom line is that the .NET Framework allows for any programming language that understands how to interact with the .NET environment (also said to *target* the .NET runtime) to have a consistent programming environment and behavior. Such consistent behavior allows for many technical possibilities that weren't previously possible. Possibilities include cross-platform interoperability and the ability for developers to use any desired programming language (or even a mixture of languages) to develop applications, such as Web services. The ability to develop in a desired language means that developers don't have to be retrained in a new language that they are not familiar with; thereby increasing return on investment (ROI).

Understanding the Problems ASP.NET Solves

ASP.NET is the latest version of Active Server Pages (ASP). ASP runs within Internet Information Server (IIS) and has been available for years. ASP.NET is not simply an upgrade of ASP with a couple of new features. It is made available because of a major rewrite of IIS Version 4.0 and is released as IIS Version 5.0. In other words, you need IIS 5.0 if you want to run ASP.NET applications. IIS 5.0 is installed when you install the .NET Framework.

Active Server Pages enable you to programmatically and dynamically generate HTML. ASP pages send HTML to a Web browser by using scripting technologies, such as VBScript and JavaScript. The original ASP technology was innovative and has served the computing industry well. However, it was not without its problems:

- ASP doesn't allow for the separation of script code (in VBScript or JavaScript) and HTML. Scripts (which control the programmability of Web pages) and HTML (which controls the graphical nature of Web pages) need to be separated to be useful for Web services applications. Web services applications do not contain a graphical interface. Web services are based on data and programmability only.

- Development of Web applications could not easily used mixed-development tools, which made it difficult for multiple developers to work on a single Web page simultaneously. ASP.NET fixes all of these problems and more.

- The reason that you should even care about ASP.NET is that it is one of the technologies that makes Web services possible, because Web services must be hosted on a Web server.

Although ASP.NET is an important facet of the .NET Framework, this book is not about ASP.NET, per se. If you want to learn more about ASP.NET, refer to *ASP.NET For Dummies,* by Bill Hatfield, published by Wiley Publishing, Inc.

ASP.NET extends ASP by allowing for a completely robust platform with which to develop Web-based applications. Microsoft has tried to make ASP.NET as compatible with ASP as possible; but with some changes made in ASP.NET, developers will have to learn some new tricks. Some of the concepts will be completely new. The major changes to ASP and some of the special features available in ASP.NET are described on the next few pages.

Putting code behind pages

ASP combines server-side scripts, client-side scripts, and HTML elements all in one file. For example, with ASP, you could construct code in a file similar to that in Listing 2-1. This listing illustrates and begins to outline why ASP.NET with its Code-Behind pages are necessary for Web services to operate.

Listing 2-1 is used to show certain ASP elements to illustrate a point. It is not intended to be the most elegant or even complete code.

In Listing 2-1, notice that three main elements are within the same file:

- **Server-side scripts:** All server-side scripts are executed and converted to HTML before the Web server returns the HTML to the browser. Server-side scripts are always denoted in ASP as being between `<% ... %>` blocks.

- **Client-side scripts:** All client-side scripts are executed upon certain con-figured events that are specified in code and are executed completely by the browser. No round-trip to the server is needed when executing client-side scripts.

  A *round-trip* is network traffic where a request is sent from a browser, the Web server processes the request, and the results are returned back to the browser. The limitation of client-side scripts is that the browser must support the scripting language used for these scripts. Client-side scripts are denoted in ASP as being between two `<SCRIPT>... </SCRIPT>` tags.

- **GUI/HTML elements:** The Web page contains two GUI/HTML elements, a table and a button. The table contains results of a SQL Server stored procedure, and the button is used to submit the form back to the server.

Listing 2-1: ASP sample code file

```
<%"nguage = vbscript%>
<head>
    <title>ASP Sample Home</title>
</head>

<SCRIPT Language="VBScript">
 Sub cmdSubmit_Click()
```

```
        Form1.HiddenCommand.Value = "S"
        Form1.submit()
   End Sub
</SCRIPT>

<body>
 <!--#INCLUDE FILE="inc/vbscript_general.asp" -->
 <!--#INCLUDE FILE="inc/header.asp" -->
 <!--#INCLUDE FILE="inc/toolbar.asp" -->
 <%
     Dim oConn
     SET oConn = Server.CreateObject("ADODB.Connection")
     oConn.Open "DSN=TEST"
     Call CheckSecurity

 %>
 <form id="Form1" name="Form1" action="Default.asp" method="post">
     <input type="hidden" name="HIDDENCOMMAND" value="">
     <p align="center">
         <table id="TABLE1" cellSpacing="1" cellPadding="1" border="0">
         <%
             'get data from database and build table of results
             dim rsList
             set rsList = oConn.Execute("usp_GetAdmin")
             If not rsList.eof then
               Call ConstructTableForResultSet(rsList)
             end if
         %>
         </table>
         <input type="button" onclick="cmdSubmit_Click" value="Submit">
     </p>
 </form>
<%
 If request("HIDDENCOMMAND") = "S" Then
     Response.Redirect "Save.asp"
 End If
%>
</body>
<!--#INCLUDE FILE="inc/footer.asp" -->
<%
 oConn.Close
%>
</html>
```

One of the major design goals of ASP.NET was to separate the code in Web pages from the user interface (also known as a Graphical User Interface, or *GUI*).

With all three types of code on one page, it is not possible to separate the bits of code from the GUI elements. Why would you want to separate GUI from code? Simple: to create Web services. Web services are about transmitting *data,* not visual GUI elements. Therefore, you need to separate the two.

GUI and code separation is also necessary for other types of .NET applications, such as a Web application (not to be confused with a Web *services* application), because a graphical designer can work on GUI part of a Web page, and a developer can work on the coding part of the Web page all at the same time.

In ASP.NET, code is separated from GUI elements in what is referred to as Code-Behind page. The Code-Behind page (with a .vb file extension for Visual Basic .NET code for example) contains your server-side and client-side code, while the ASP.NET page (with a .aspx file extension) contains GUI elements, such as text boxes and radio buttons. ASP.NET functionality is covered in more depth throughout this book because it is what makes Web services possible on the Microsoft platform.

Using configuration files

Another area that will impact your understanding of implementing Web services is related to the area of configuration of those Web services. In Web applications that were created prior to .NET, configuration of those applications was largely performed in code. In other words, a developer had to understand and code into the compiled application security issues, database connection settings, and so on.

In .NET (specifically ASP.NET), configuration of a Web server is done in files. These configuration files are, like most other things in .NET, XML files. XML is covered in depth in Chapter 3. Configuration files enable you to store configuration information, such as folder locations, database connection strings, and other application-level data. What's more, configuration files can be inherited from a folder higher in hierarchy to a child folder that is lower in the hierarchy. On the other hand, a child folder can also have its own configuration file if needed.

ASP did not allow for configuration files. You only had one choice for configuration information. It was in a global file at the application level, which was called global.asa. However, this file wasn't well suited for configuration. It was designed to configure only application and session-level settings, not settings at an individual folder level.

Configuration files in ASP.NET are named Web.Config. They can exist at any folder level of an application. For example, if you have a root folder and an Admin subfolder under the root folder in the hierarchy (known as a *child* folder), each folder can have its own configuration information. However, this is not a requirement. Configuration files are inherited. Therefore, if you have a configuration file in the root folder but no configuration file in the Admin subfolder, the Admin subfolder inherits the configuration settings from the configuration file in the root folder.

Likewise, the root folder of your application doesn't require a configuration file either. You can have all Web applications inherit from a configuration file on the server, also known as the *machine level.* In this case, and only this case, the file is not named `Web.Config`; it's named `Machine.Config`. There can also be a `Remoting.Config` file, which configures .NET Remoting. See the section, "Remoting," later in this chapter.

Listing 2-2 shows the XML structure of a `Web.Config` file. Although you haven't gone through the XML chapter yet (see Chapter 3), it is important to at least understand, at this point, that understanding the configuration file concept will have an impact on how you design and develop your Web services applications.

Listing 2-2: XML structure of a `Web.Config` file

```
<?xml version="1.0" encoding="utf-8" ?>
<configuration>

  <system.web>

    <!-- DYNAMIC DEBUG COMPILATION
         Set compilation debug="true" to insert debugging symbols (.pdb
             information)
         into the compiled page. Because this creates a larger file that
             executes
         more slowly, you should set this value to true only when debugging and
             to
         false at all other times. For more information, refer to the
             documentation about
         debugging ASP.NET files.
    -->
    <compilation defaultLanguage="vb" debug="true" />

    <!-- CUSTOM ERROR MESSAGES
         Set customErrors mode="On" or "RemoteOnly" to enable custom error
             messages, "Off" to disable.
         Add <error> tags for each of the errors you want to handle.
    -->
    <customErrors mode="Off" />

    <!-- AUTHENTICATION
```

(continued)

Listing 2-2: *(continued)*

```
        This section sets the authentication policies of the application.
            Possible modes are "Windows",
        "Forms", "Passport" and "None"
-->
<authentication mode="Windows" />


<!-- AUTHORIZATION
        This section sets the authorization policies of the application. You
            can allow or deny access
        to application resources by user or role. Wildcards: "*" mean
            everyone, "?" means anonymous
        (unauthenticated) users.
-->
<authorization>
    <allow users="*" /> <!-- Allow all users -->

        <!-- <allow     users="[comma separated list of users]"
                        roles="[comma separated list of roles]"/>
             <deny       users="[comma separated list of users]"
                        roles="[comma separated list of roles]"/>
        -->
</authorization>

<!-- APPLICATION-LEVEL TRACE LOGGING
        Application-level tracing enables trace log output for every page
            within an application.
        Set trace enabled="true" to enable application trace logging.  If
            pageOutput="true", the
        trace information will be displayed at the bottom of each page.
            Otherwise, you can view the
        application trace log by browsing the "trace.axd" page from your web
            application
        root.
-->
<trace enabled="false" requestLimit="10" pageOutput="false"
        traceMode="SortByTime" localOnly="true" />


<!-- SESSION STATE SETTINGS
        By default ASP.NET uses cookies to identify which requests belong to a
            particular session.
        If cookies are not available, a session can be tracked by adding a
            session identifier to the URL.
        To disable cookies, set sessionState cookieless="true".
-->
<sessionState
        mode="InProc"
```

```
                    stateConnectionString="tcpip=127.0.0.1:42424"
                    sqlConnectionString="dsn=test"
                    cookieless="false"
                    timeout="20"
        />

        <!-- GLOBALIZATION
             This section sets the globalization settings of the application.
        -->
        <globalization requestEncoding="utf-8" responseEncoding="utf-8" />

    </system.web>

</configuration>
```

By default, seven special XML elements are contained within the Web.Config file. These elements are used to configure your Web applications in ASP.NET. XML elements are covered in Chapter 3. The seven special XML elements are:

- ✔ <compilation>: Controls compiler options when compiling ASP.NET applications. Compilation options are covered further in Chapter 7.

- ✔ <customErrors>: Controls the errors that are displayed on ASP.NET Web pages. CustomErrors options are covered further in Chapter 7.

- ✔ <authentication>: Controls how users are authenticated in ASP.NET applications.

- ✔ <authorization>: Controls the users/groups that have access to ASP.NET applications.

- ✔ <trace>: Controls logging within a ASP.NET application..

- ✔ <sessionState>: Controls how session state is managed in ASP.NET applications. *Session state* identifies and tracks a user within a Web application. In ASP, this was a difficult chore because there was no robust provision for handling session state, so programmers had to come up with a mechanism for tracking session state if needed by an application. ASP.NET can track it automatically.

- ✔ <globalization>: Controls the settings that are local to a particular region or country.

When you create a new Web service (which I cover in Chapter 6), a Web.Config file is automatically created for you and contains the XML configuration elements I just mentioned. However, it is possible to have more level of control over the customization by specifying additional configuration elements. The following additional configuration elements can be contained in the Web.Config file (but are not automatically created for you):

- ✔ `<browserCaps>`: Controls the settings for browser-specific components.
- ✔ `<clientTarget>`: Controls aliases of user agents.
- ✔ `<httpHandlers>`: Controls and maps specific incoming URL requests to custom classes, known as *iHttpHandler*.
- ✔ `<httpModules>`: Controls the HTTP modules that are within a .NET application.
- ✔ `<httpRuntime>`: Controls and configures the HTTP runtime settings within IIS.
- ✔ `<identity>`: Controls the identity of a Web application.
- ✔ `<machineKey>`: Configures keys used for the encryption/decryption of cookies when they are used for authentication.
- ✔ `<pages>`: Controls page-specific configurations.
- ✔ `<processModel>`: Controls process model settings within IIS.
- ✔ `<securityPolicy>`: Controls the mapping of security levels to policy files contained within the domain or server. Security policies are covered in Chapter 11.
- ✔ `<trust>`: Controls the trust permissions of a Web application.
- ✔ `<webServices>`: Controls Web services-specific settings within ASP.NET.

Caching

ASP.NET applications are automatically cached in memory so that subsequent accesses to Web pages are faster. When you update your Web application pages, the cache is automatically refreshed. What could be easier?

Debugging the compilation glitch

Prior versions of IIS that ran ASP did not compile Web pages. The pages were interpreted at runtime. With ASP.NET, however, applications are compiled to make them run faster. Although you do get speed with ASP.NET, you should also be aware that ASP.NET applications are more difficult to debug than ASP applications. For more information about debugging ASP.NET applications, see Chapter 7.

Handling multiple browsers

In ASP (the predecessor to ASP.NET), if you couldn't guarantee that your users would have a specific browser, you had to manually code for different browsers — namely, Internet Explorer (IE) and Netscape Navigator. Netscape doesn't like VBScript; IE can use either VBScript or JavaScript. You had to consider whether the scripting code runs on the server or the client (because most Web-based programs do both).

Because many developers like VBScript better than JavaScript, the server-side scripts are written in VBScript (because these scripts are evaluated and turned into HTML before they're sent to the browser). The client-side scripts are largely written in JavaScript (because JavaScript works well with either browser). Furthermore, you need to consider some other potential browser problems as you plan your Web service. For example, the Document Object Models (DOM) are different between the two, so fancy coding has to be done two different ways for the two browsers.

ASP had no specific support for multiple browsers. In ASP.NET, you still can't guarantee what type of browser someone will be using, but you no longer care (even though IE is gaining ground over Netscape every day). ASP.NET relieves a developer of the burden of multiple browser coding. Because ASP.NET runs within IIS 5.0, which is installed as part of the .NET Framework, a developer can simply choose a desired language — and stick with that language. ASP.NET takes care of the burden of needing to code around specific browser issues.

Diving Deeper into .NET

Although your head probably hurts, you're almost through this chapter. I'd be remiss in my duties if I didn't mention a few more things about .NET. These additional items, while diving deeper into how .NET works, are imperative to understand (at least on the surface). If you don't understand how .NET works, the impact on your organization could be great. To minimize the impact of implementing Web services in your organization, simply read on.

Object orientation

ASP.NET and all other aspects of the .NET platform are fully object oriented. Object orientation (abbreviated as *OO*) is a very efficient programming model that bypasses old silo or monolithic programming (so called because these programming languages generally create one big application with lots of spaghetti code that cannot be reused in any way). Monolithic applications can't be reused amongst applications residing on a single server, let alone a distributed application amongst multiple servers. Using the monolithic approach, obviously Web services are out of the question. Therefore, if your software architects or developers are not familiar with an object-oriented approach for software development, the impact on your company's ability to implement Web services could be significant.

An object-oriented approach to programming means that all bits of code are packaged into *objects* that other applications or processes can reuse. Objects are programmable .NET units, called *classes,* that are constructed in logical and functional units. Object-oriented programming must comply with these criteria:

- **Encapsulation:** Allows you to hide the complexities of code and business processes. For example, say you create a credit application program. The complexity of the business process that goes into the credit decision is completely hidden from the user of the business process. The term *encapsulation* is very closely linked to *abstraction.*

- **Abstraction:** Allows you to expose a simple interface to the outside world for the encapsulated logic. In the preceding example, an exposed interface might be as simple as a single object that needs to be passed, such as a Social Security number. This Social Security number is then used with the complex application process to determine credit risk. The term *abstraction* is very closely linked to *encapsulation.*

- **Polymorphism:** Allows you to use the same defined object interface for multiple purposes. The term is derived from the root words *poly* (meaning multiple) and *morph* (meaning change). Why would you need polymorphism? You would likely need to define common interfaces, such as New, Close, Save, and so on. However, the specific implementation of these interfaces is different within the objects that are implementing the interface.

- **Inheritance:** Allows a child interface to inherit its interface characteristics from its parent.

The basic unit of OO is the class. A basic class can contain methods (actions), properties (arguments), and events (code that runs when specific actions happen). You can explore OO and creating classes in Chapter 6.

Assemblies

An *assembly* is a basic compiled block of code that is executed on the .NET platform. An application is made up of one or more assemblies. Each assembly is made up of one or more classes.

An assembly is compiled into either a `.dll` file or an `.exe` file. For example, you may have a Web service that is made up of five Visual Basic .NET source code files that are all compiled into a single `.dll` file, known as an *assembly.* You may be wondering how this is different from the way applications have been compiled ever since Windows came out. Well, on the surface, the compilation process isn't much different. Under the covers, however, there's a huge difference.

Remember the discussion about how .NET works at the beginning of this section? Well, the assembly contains all compiled code and resources, along with object metadata. *Metadata* is data that describes the objects, such as their interface. However, it contains only MSIL code. That's where the .NET Framework and CLR take over. The .NET Framework and CLR take the MSIL code and compile it at runtime, called Just-In-Time compilation, or JIT compilation. So, you see, `.dll` and `.exe` files prior to .NET were compiled down to machine-level code, which did not allow for the benefits achieved by the CLR, such as garbage collection.

Assemblies can be either private or shared. A *private* assembly is one that is used just for a specific .NET application. A *shared* assembly is one that multiple .NET applications can use. The majority of the .NET objects and namespaces, such as `system` and `system.data`, are shared assemblies. How does an application know that a .NET assembly is shared? Simple: It is in a global catalog called the GAC, or *global assembly cache.*

Security

When the folks at Microsoft designed .NET, they put security at the top of the consideration list. .NET applications, including Web services, can be made as secure as they need to be. Of course, you can also make them open to vulnerabilities. Security is affected by the settings of your Web services application, your network settings, security on your Web server itself, and even security settings within the .NET Framework. Security is covered in Chapter 11.

Remoting

Many times objects (also known as *components*) are not stored on a local server within a single domain. The server that contains the objects could be anywhere, on any domain, on any platform, with different security credentials. If you wish to access these objects, you must use .NET Remoting, which allows you to access remote objects wherever they happen to reside.

You're probably quite confused at this point, because everything I just described about remoting also describes what Web services are supposed to do. However, .NET Remoting isn't just a new term for the same thing. There is a subtle difference.

Web services are designed to communicate over HTTP using SOAP and WSDL. SOAP is described in Chapter 4. WSDL is described in Chapter 9. Web services are extremely easy to construct, deploy, and consume. That's what this book is all about.

.NET Remoting is a little more versatile than Web services are and serves as a viable alternative in certain circumstances. The main advantage of .NET Remoting over Web services is that .NET Remoting supports additional transports and payloads when used on the .NET Framework. .NET Remoting components can be transmitted by using a variety of protocols, such as Transmission Control Protocol (TCP), HTTP, HTTPS, and more. It can also transmit XML, binary, serialized, and other types of files. In addition, .NET Remoting supports the control of the lifetime of the object as well as multiple instances of the object.

.NET Remoting can be complex to set up, and configuring .NET Remoting objects as Web services requires extra work. Although .NET Remoting is beyond the scope of this book, I want you to know that it does exist.

ADO.NET

Most applications today, including Web services applications, need to access data from a database. This is not earth-shattering news! However, you should know that if your organization is not familiar with ADO.NET, there is a learning curve involved in getting up to speed with this technology because you'll need it to access data from your Web services.

Obviously, this learning curve can have quite an impact on your organization's ability to implement Web services, so I mention it in this section. After reading this section, you won't know everything there is to know about ADO.NET, but you'll have a good handle on what it is and how it is used.

Prior to the .NET Framework being released, application developers used ActiveX Data Objects, or *ADO,* which is a set of objects, in order to efficiently access data from a database or other storage mechanism, such as text files. Although ADO was not without its problems, like most things in .NET, ADO was redesigned to fix virtually all problems and to work in the .NET environment. Therefore, the new version is called *ADO.NET. ADO.NET* is a set of objects that are built on the .NET platform for the express purpose of accessing data. They are contained within the `system.data` namespace.

In this section, I outline the basic concepts of accessing data in ADO.NET. Although numerous books on the market cover the topic of ADO.NET in depth, this section shows the information that you need to grab data from databases for use with your Web services and leads to an understanding of how the basics of ADO.NET limit the overall impact to your organization of implementing Web services. I've divided ADO.NET into four categories to make tasks easier to understand.

If you're looking for more in-depth information about ADO.NET, check out *Programming ADO.NET* by Richard Hundhausen (published by Wiley Publishing, Inc.). Beware, though — this book isn't for the faint of heart!

This section shows how to use the basic functions of ADO.NET so that you can access your databases with your Web services projects. These examples are certainly not the only way to perform actions in ADO.NET. Also, all examples shown in this section are written in Visual Basic.NET.

Making connections

Before you do anything at all with ADO.NET, you must make a connection to your data source. Connections in ADO.NET are not that much different from ADO connections. You must provide at least the following information for a connection to be made:

- **Provider:** The technology used to connect to a specific data source. For a few years now, fast connections were possible with the OLEDB data provider. Now, Microsoft has come up with an even faster provider, but it works only with SQL Server. It is called SQLClient (or SqlConnection), and it works with SQL Server 7.0 and later.

- **Data source:** The server that contains the database to which you wish to connect.

- **User ID:** The user name that is used to log in to the server.

- **Password:** The password that is used to log in to the server.

- **Database:** The database to use for the given user name. This does not actually need to be specified if the server is configured to have a default database for the user. The database is also known as the *initial catalog*.

ADO.NET observes a disconnected model. A *disconnected model* means that ADO.NET does not require a continuous connection to a data source, such as SQL Server. This follows the paradigm of how Web services work on the .NET platform; the Web services and other applications that you write know nothing about where, when, or how a request was made. The Web service simply knows that a request *was* made.

To create a connection, as you might expect, you use a connection object. There are two types of connections, SqlConnection and OleDbConnection. The SqlConnection object is used to connect solely to SQL Server. The OleDbConnection object is used to connect to any OLEDB data source. The syntax of the commands is virtually identical, except for one thing: Because SqlConnection works only with SQL Server, you don't have to specify a provider. However, you do for OleDbConnection because it works with any OLEDB provider, so you must specify which one you intend to use.

The SqlConnection object is found within the System.Data.SQLClient namespace.

TIP

If you don't want to qualify object names with the complete namespace that contains them, in Visual Basic.NET, you can use the Imports keyword to specify the namespace that contains objects you wish to use. In fact, in this chapter, the code fragments shown assume that you have used the Imports keyword for each distinct namespace that contains the objects used, but these aren't shown in the code. For more information about the Imports keyword, see Chapter 6.

To connect to a database with the SqlConnection object, use this syntax

```
Dim var_connection As SqlConnection = New
        SqlConnection(connstring)
```

where the following substitutions can be made:

- ✔ var_connection is the name of your new connection object that is to be created.
- ✔ connstring is the connection string that contains the attributes necessary to make the connection to the database. The connection string that you use consists of a string of keywords and variable assignments. The keywords are very specific, although most of them are optional. Table 2-1 shows the possible keywords that you can use in your connection string.

Table 2-1	Connection String Keywords
Keyword(s)	*Description*
Addr	Same as the Data Source keyword.
Address	Same as the Data Source keyword.
Application Name	The name of the application that will be used and registered with SQL Server.
AttachDBFilename	Name of an attachable database.
Connect Timeout	Number of seconds to allow for a SQL Server connection to take place before aborting. The default value is 15 seconds.
Connection Lifetime	Number of seconds that a connection should be kept alive before it is destroyed instead of being returned back into the connection pool when the connection is closed. The default value is 0 seconds, which indicates infinite lifetime.

Keyword(s)	Description
Connection Reset	Connection should be reset when the connection is requested from the connection pool. The default value is True.
Connection Timeout	Same as the Connect Timeout keyword.
Current Language	The name of the current language that SQL Server uses.
Data Source	The name of the server that you wish to connect to.
Database	Same as the Initial Catalog keyword.
DSN	The name of the preconfigured data source name that has all relevant connection string information embedded within it.
Enlist	If True, will use the current transaction context of when the connection was created. The default value is True.
Extended Properties	Same as the AttachDBFilename keyword.
Initial Catalog	The name of the database that you wish to connect to inside the Data Source.
Initial File Name	Same as AttachDBFilename.
Integrated Security	If True, will connect as the currently logged on user, instead of specifying an explicit User ID and Password. The default value is False.
Max Pool Size	Maximum number of connections that are allowed in the connection pool. The default value is 100.
Min Pool Size	Minimum number of connections that are allowed in the connection pool. The default value is 0.
Net	Same as the Network Library keyword.
Network Address	Same as the Data Source keyword.
Network Library	The communications library that is used to make the connection with SQL Server. The default is dbmssocn, which is the name of the library for TCP/IP.
Packet Size	The size of the network packets. The default value is 8192.

(continued)

Table 2-1 *(continued)*

Keyword(s)	Description
Password	The password to use when logging into SQL Server if the Integrated Security keyword is set to False.
Persist Security Info	If True, will return security-related information in the connection string. The default value is False.
Pooling	If True, will use connection pooling. The default value is True.
Pwd	The same as the Password keyword.
Server	Same as the Data Source keyword.
Trusted_Connection	Same as the Integrated Security keyword.
User ID	The login name to use when logging into SQL Server if the Integrated Security keyword is set to False.
Workstation ID	The name of the workstation that is registered with SQL Server. The default value is the actual name of the workstation that makes the connection.

Here's an example of creating a connection string with the bare minimum number of arguments:

```
Dim oConn As SqlConnection = New SqlConnection("Data
        Source=DB1;User
        ID=ReportUser;Password=ReportUser1;Initial
        Catalog=Presidents")
```

In the preceding code, a new SQL Server connection is made to server DB1, database Presidents, with the User ID of ReportUser and Password of ReportUser1. The connection is made and assigned to the object variable oConn, so that the connection can be used later in code.

Now that the connection is declared, it simply has to be opened with the following line of code:

```
oConn.Open()
```

Now that the connection is open, you can access data in any way that is possible, based on security settings of the user within SQL Server. For example, if the security context (User ID and Password) of the open connection does not allow for updates to a table, you cannot issue an UPDATE SQL statement.

Issuing commands

After you establish a connection to the database, you can issue SQL commands to the database. These commands can be any SQL statement that the current security context has privileges to execute. The database itself handles these privileges, not ADO.NET.

Issuing commands is done with the `SqlCommand` object. Like the `SqlConnection` object, the `SqlCommand` object is found within the `System.Data.SQLClient` namespace.

To issue a command with the `SqlCommand` object, use this syntax

```
Dim var_cmd As SqlCommand = New
        SqlCommand(command[,var_transaction])
```

where you make the following substitutions:

- ✔ *var_cmd* is the name of your new command object that is to be created.
- ✔ *command* is the SQL command that you wish to issue to the database server. The command can be any valid SQL, such as a `SELECT` statement or the name of a stored procedure.
- ✔ *var_transaction* is the optional `SqlTransaction` object in which this command should take place.

For more information about transactions, check out my book, *Microsoft SQL Server 2000 For Dummies,* published by Wiley Publishing, Inc.

Here's an example of creating a `SqlCommand` with the `SqlConnection` object created in the preceding section:

```
Dim oCmd As SqlCommand = New SqlCommand("SELECT TOP 10 * from
        President", oConn)
```

The preceding statement selects the top ten rows of data from the `President` table. Of course, the `President` table must exist in the database that was opened with the `SqlConnection`, as well as the security context that opened the connection must have permissions to execute the `SELECT` statement.

The statement is now declared, but not actually executed. Before you can do that, you must instruct SQL Server as to what kind of statement this is. You give this instruction by setting the `CommandType` property for the

`SqlCommand` object that you just created. The `CommandType` property has this syntax:

```
var_cmd.CommandType = CommandType.type
```

You can make the following substitutions:

- ✔ *var_cmd* is the name of the new command object that you just created.
- ✔ *type* is type of command that you wish to issue against the database. The command type can be
  - `StoredProcedure`: The command entered for the `SqlCommand` object is the name of a valid stored procedure.
  - `TableDirect`: The command entered for the `SqlCommand` object is the name of a table that you wish to access. However, this is not valid if you are using the `SQLClient` data provider, which is what I'm assuming in these examples.
  - `Text`: The command entered for the `SqlCommand` object is a free-form SQL statement that will be evaluated when the command is issued to the database.

As an example, if you are trying to enter free-form SQL statements, your code would look like this:

```
oCmd.CommandType = CommandType.Text
```

Likewise, if you are executing a stored procedure named `usp_GetPresidentByLastName`, your code would look like this:

```
Dim oCmd As SqlCommand = New
        SqlCommand("usp_GetPresidentByLastName", oConn)
oCmd.CommandType = CommandType.StoredProcedure
```

However, what if your stored procedure accepts arguments? In the preceding example, based on the name of the stored procedure, you might infer that the stored procedure accepts an argument that is a full or partial last name. Doing this in code is quite simple as well. Add the parameters to the `SqlCommand` object that you declared earlier.

The `SqlCommand` object has a parameters collection. Within this collection, you can add or remove members. Because you just created the `SqlCommand` object earlier, there are no parameters, so you can simply add them. Adding parameters follows this syntax

```
var_cmd.Parameters.Add = ("@Param_Name", "Param_Value")
```

where you can make the following substitutions:

- ✔ *var_cmd* is the name of your command object.

- ✔ *@Param_Name* is the name of the parameter as declared in your stored procedure. Your SQL Server stored procedures must begin with the "@" sign.

- ✔ *Param_Value* is the name of the value you wish to pass for the parameter.

So, to retrieve all last names that begin with the letter *M* by passing this value to the ←stName parameter, use this code:

```
oCmd.Parameters.Add("←stName", "M")
```

If you have multiple parameters to add, simply add more statements, such as the preceding one, substituting different parameter names and values. Each statement adds to the Parameters collection.

After you have entered the SQL that you wish to execute and added the parameters (if you are executing a stored procedure), you're ready to execute the command. You can execute your SqlCommand object by using one of these four methods:

- ✔ ExecuteNonQuery: Executes a command without expecting data to be returned. However, this method does return the number of rows that the query affected.

- ✔ ExecuteReader: Executes a command and returns results into a SqlDataReader object. SqlDataReader objects are covered in the "Retrieving data" section later in this chapter.

- ✔ ExecuteScalar: Executes a command and returns a single value into a variable instead of a SqlDataReader object.

- ✔ ExecuteXMLReader: Executes a command and returns results into a XMLReader object. XMLReader objects are also covered in the "Retrieving data" section later in this chapter.

Use the ExecuteNonQuery method, like this:

```
Rtn = oCmd.ExecuteNonQuery
```

The command is simply executed and does not return any results, except the number of rows that the query affected (for INSERT, UPDATE, and DELETE statements only). Likewise, the ExecuteScalar method is just as easy:

```
Rtn = oCmd.ExecuteScalar
```

The ExecuteScalar method returns a single value into a variable, which must be declared as the same type that is returned from SQL Server.

Retrieving data

Retrieving data is also quite simple. If you execute your SQL commands using either the `ExecuteReader` or `ExecuteXMLReader` methods, data is returned in what is called a `DataSet`. A `DataSet` is exactly what it sounds like: a set of data! It is an in-memory representation of data that is returned from a database.

You may know of the term *recordset* in prior versions of ADO. A `DataSet` is somewhat similar but can contain multiple recordsets. It can also contain metadata about the data in the `DataSet`, such as relationships and tables that the data came from. This allows for disconnected editing of data that you can then resynchronize with the database at a later time.

Two types of `DataSet` objects are `SqlDataReader` and `XMLReader` objects. The `SqlDataReader` and `XMLReader` objects are exceptionally efficient. They are also forward-only, which means that after a data row is read, the `SqlDataReader` and `XMLReader` objects must be repopulated to perform work on an earlier row.

To use the `SqlDataReader` object, you must have executed the `ExecuteReader` method on the `SqlConnection` object, as shown in the "Issuing commands" section of this chapter. You also must have declared a `SqlDataReader` object with this syntax:

```
Dim var_reader As SqlDataReader
```

where *var_reader* is the name of your new command `SqlDataReader` object that will be created. Therefore, to create a `SqlDataReader` object called `oReader`, use this code:

```
Dim oReader As SqlDataReader
```

After the object is declared, you can loop through all records in the `DataSet` and take some action by issuing multiple calls to the `Read` method, like this:

```
Do While oReader.Read()
    Response.Write(oReader.Item("LastName") & "," &
           oReader.Item("FirstName") & "<BR>")
Loop
```

The preceding code writes out the last name and first name of every person that is contained in the `SqlDataReader` object. If you remember, the `SqlDataReader` object was populated earlier in this chapter based on a search conducted with the `usp_GetPresidentByLastName` stored procedure and passed the search parameter of ←stName. Of course, for this code to work, the stored procedure must return columns named LastName and FirstName or the preceding code will fail.

As you may recall, the ExecuteXMLReader method of the SqlCommand object creates an in-memory representation of an XML document that comes from SQL Server. However, the way you manipulate the XMLReader object is slightly different.

First, you must declare an object of type XMLReader. The XMLReader object is contained not within the System.Data.SQLClient namespace, but the System.Xml namespace. Therefore, you can declare an XMLReader like this:

```
Dim oReader As XMLReader
```

Although the XMLReader object contains properties and methods that aren't available in the SqlDataReader object, the looping code shown earlier still works, as long as the data returned from SQL Server is in an XML format.

Closing objects

It is a good programming practice to close objects that you open, including DataSet readers and database connections, as soon as they are no longer needed. This releases resources, which frees them up for other applications.

You may have heard that opening and closing database connections is very expensive from a resource point of view. However, with ADO.NET, connections are automatically *pooled*. This means that SQL Server and ADO.NET maintain a group of connections in a pool and hand out those connections when an application requests them. Closing connections releases them back to the pool, making them available to other applications.

To close your DataSet objects (SqlDataReader and XMLReader), you use the Close method. Here's an example of closing either of the reader objects with the Close method:

```
oReader.Close()
```

To close your database connections, you also use the Close method for the SqlConnection or OleDbConnection object. Here's an example of closing a SqlConnection object with the Close method:

```
oConn.Close()
```

Installation Requirements

As I mentioned earlier in this chapter, all you need to run Web services in your organization is the .NET Framework, which Microsoft provides for free — Happy Days! Information about downloading the .NET Framework is available at msdn.microsoft.com/netframework.

The requirements for installing the .NET Framework are quite liberal. From a hardware perspective, you can run the .NET Framework on a server or a workstation (which some organizations use as the same machine):

- ✔ **Server:** Requires a Pentium-class machine with a clock speed of 133 MHz and only 128MB of RAM.

- ✔ **Workstation:** Requires a Pentium-class machine with a clock speed of 90 MHz and only 32MB of RAM.

As everyone knows, Microsoft applications can be quite, shall we say, memory intensive. Therefore, I absolutely recommend that these be the bare minimum of hardware specifications. If there's any way to get your boss to spring for more hardware resources, it will be worth it.

From an operating system perspective, .NET Framework requirements are also quite liberal:

- ✔ **Server applications:** Require Windows 2000, Service Pack 2. (Any edition will work — Professional, Server, or Advanced Server.)

- ✔ **Client applications:** Require Windows 98 (any edition), Windows Millennium, Windows NT (any edition with Service Pack 6.0a), Windows 2000 (any edition with Service Pack 2), or Windows XP (any edition).

If you intend to use ADO.NET with SQL Server, you must install Microsoft Data Access Components (MDAC), Version 2.7 or higher, but that is installed automatically with the .NET Framework. For more information about MDAC, visit the Microsoft Web site at www.microsoft.com/data.

If you intend to use ASP.NET, you must install Microsoft Internet Information Server (IIS), Version 5.0 or higher, but this is installed automatically with the .NET Framework. For more information about IIS, point your browser to

www.microsoft.com/windows2000/technologies/web/default.asp.

What this boils down to is that you can basically install the .NET Framework on virtually any box. You don't have to upgrade to fancy-schmancy, expensive hardware.

Personnel Requirements

Personnel requirements for moving to .NET and Web services is a difficult thing to quantify or qualify. The answer to this puzzle (and most other things) depends on your particular situation. I can't tell you how many people you need to implement Web services in your organization. I can only point out some issues to help you decide. It depends on at least these things:

✔ **Business need:** Does your business really need to use Web services, or are Web services just a nice shiny new toy that you want to play with? If the business needs to implement Web services, the number of people and their skill sets will vary. For example, if your company will gain new customers from connecting two systems together by using Web services, you have a business need. If implementing Web services is not going to increase time, productivity, customers, or revenue, you probably don't have a business need to implement Web services.

✔ **Business scope:** Does the entire organization have to use Web services, or only one department? Obviously, if the entire organization needs to implement Web services, it is going to have a greater impact on the organization, require more planning, and more resources (personnel and otherwise). In other words, if only the accounting department could use a neat little Web service that provides currency conversions, but no other need exists in your company, you can probably consume this Web service with very little impact to your organization. A small scope like this could help you get your feet wet without diving in head first. Consuming Web services is covered in Chapter 9.

✔ **Training:** Have your developers/architects been to training? Do they understand how to design and develop Web services to fit business needs? If so, great! If not, you may want to consider training. Classroom training works for some people, but not all people. Some people learn better with books (like this one), videos, or online courses.

✔ **Skill level:** Web services are a beautiful thing, but it can be quite complex to understand all the aspects of them, such as security, design, architecture, and of course, how they all fit together. In some ways, software development has become easier, and in some ways, it has become harder. Software development is easier because the CLR manages much of the tedious coding that surrounds pointers, memory, garbage collection, and lots of other topics. It is harder because there are simply more issues to consider. Five years ago, it was unlikely that most developers considered fault tolerance, security, interoperability, upgradeability, uptime, performance, and well . . . I could go on for hours. Today, an application is considered to be poorly designed or coded if *all* these things are not considered. If staff members don't have the aptitude to take in all this, you have to factor in more time and personnel resources.

Chapter 3

Priming the Pump with XML

*I*t is possible to develop Web services using Microsoft Visual Studio.NET and not have to deal with SOAP and XML schemas. It's also possible to not have to deal with XML at all. However, as you become more proficient in writing Web services and consuming Web services, you'll be forced to learn more about XML and its related technologies.

That said, I must make sure that you know that this chapter is quite the whopper! And I think it's required reading! Believe it or not, even though it may seem complex, I only dive into the very basics of XML and XML-related technologies, such as namespaces and schemas.

After all, the old way of doing business was all about location, location, location. The new mantra is that your business is all about XML, XML, XML. . . .

If you want to understand SOAP (which is discussed in Chapter 4) and the structure of many configuration files within Visual Studio .NET, you need to first have some of the basics down about XML. But you should know also that you don't have to completely master either of these technologies to create Web services with Visual Studio.NET. This is because Visual Studio.NET and the .NET Framework take care of most of these details for you by automatically generating code and configuration files. It will help, however, if you familiarize yourself with the concepts in case you need to alter these automatically configured files.

Excelling with XML: Extensibility Is Key

XML is the lifeblood of Web services, as you can see throughout this chapter. XML stands for eXtensible Markup Language. It is called a markup language because it uses a series of tags to describe the contents of the XML.

XML is a basic text file that is deciphered or interpreted at runtime. Does this sound familiar? If you know anything about Web technologies, you'll recognize that this sounds like HTML.

So, what's the big deal about XML? If it is interpreted at runtime and contains tags, just like HTML, why not just use HTML? Why learn something new? The answer is that they are not much alike beyond what I just described.

If you're familiar with the essence of HTML, you know that the markup language contains a set number of tags. These tags are always noted within ⟨ and ⟩ symbols, and are used to control the display of content on-screen. XML, too, uses tags, but instead of describing *data display,* XML describes *data* itself, and the number and types of tags you can use are limited only by your imagination.

As markup languages go, XML is just about as flexible (or *extensible*) as you could ever hope it to be. It leaves HTML in the dust because you can customize the markup to the needs of your project — not the other way around.

Table 3-1 compares HTML and XML. As you can see, HTML just doesn't stack up.

Table 3-1	HTML and XML Characteristics		
HTML	*Limitation*	*XML*	*Solution*
Uses tags.	The set of tags is limited and can't be customized.	Uses tags.	The tags can be customized. Customized XML tags are called *elements.*
Describes data display in Web browsers.	Tags make no differentiation between on-screen presentation and the data itself. They are both mixed together.	Doesn't worry about presentation.	Focuses on describing data so that it can be transferred across a variety of applications.
Document formatting.	No way to verify format and structure of HTML.	Uses *schemas.*	Schemas help you document complex formats to verify that the XML document conforms.

It's not impossible to describe data using HTML, but if you examine the code in Listing 3-1, you might get a good idea why you wouldn't *want* to.

Listing 3-1: Sample HTML code

```
<HTML>
    <head>
        <title>Registration</title>
    </head>

    <p><center><h1>Enter your registration information</h1></center></p>

    <body>
        <form id=Form1 method="post" action="postanswer.asp">
            <!-- BEGIN TABLE -->
            <table id="TABLE1" cellSpacing="1" cellPadding="1" border="0"
              align=center>

                <!-- ROW 1 -->
                <TR>
                    <TD>
                  <P align=right><FONT size=4>Name:</FONT></P>
                    </TD>
                    <TD>
                        <P align=left><FONT size=4><INPUT id=txtName
                name=txtName value=""></FONT></P>
                    </TD>
                </TR>

                <!-- ROW 2 -->
                <TR>
                    <TD>
                  <P align=right><FONT size=4>Company:</FONT></P>
                    </TD>
                    <TD>
                        <P align=left><FONT size=4><INPUT id=txtCompany
                name=txtCompany value=""></FONT></P>
                    </TD>
                </TR>
            </table>

            <p align=center>
                <input type=submit id=cmdSubmit name=cmdSubmit value="Submit">
            </p>
        </form>
    </body>

</HTML>
```

I'm not trying to badmouth HTML, but it wasn't designed for Web services.
Here's a list of the issues from the preceding listing:

✔ First of all, every tag that is shown is a known HTML tag, such as `<form>`, `<TR>`, `<TD>`, and the like. No provision is made for custom tags.

✔ But wait, there's more. The form that is rendered in Figure 3-1 enables the user to fill out the data fields and then post the data to a Web page, called `postanswer.asp` (listed in the `action` attribute).

I won't waste valuable pages to show you the code in the aforementioned Web page, but you can take my word for it that the code in `postanswer.asp` looks for the data that was filled out by the user; the code must be in that page.

Figure 3-1:
Browser
rendering of
Listing 3-1.

✔ Okay, so far so good. Well, not quite; there is one major issue. The `postanswer.asp` page must know the field names in order to get the information from the posted form. In other words, `postanswer.asp` must be *hard-coded* to know that two fields on the form, named `txtName` and `txtCompany`, contain data. If you decide to add a field called `txtAddress`, you must then code for it in both places.

✔ And still more problems: The graphical elements of the code are mixed together with the data itself. The text boxes that appear on the form, as well as the `Submit` button, are mixed in with the data (the actual values for Name and Company).

✔ In other words, upon clicking the `Submit` button, the data gets posted to `postanswer.asp`, which then must look for the data among the graphical elements that make up the form.

Wouldn't it be nicer if you had a better way to transmit data? What if you had a self-describing format that is not limited to specific tags, and the application that receives the data could magically know all the fields of data without having to recode every time something changes? I'll bet you can guess that I'm going to say this format is XML. You'd be right! XML solves all of these problems.

Overview of XML

XML can get quite involved. In fact, entire books have been written to cover the topic of XML, so there's no way I'm going to be able to condense an entire book into one chapter. I'm just going to hit the highlights. Even though I don't go into too much depth, if you are new to XML, this may seem a little overwhelming. Don't fret! Read this chapter slowly. It may even take a couple of times, but you'll get.

For more in-depth information about XML, check out XML For Dummies, 3rd Edition, by Ed Tittel, Natanya Pitts, and Frank Boumphrey (Wiley Publishing, Inc.).

In its basic form, an XML document is a collection of user-defined tags that describe data. The XML document is probably stored as a text file. The text file is easy for a computer program to read. For that matter, any human can access and read the file by using Notepad or any other text reader. The data defined and described in an XML document is made up of elements and attributes using the XML *syntax,* or rules.

Elements and attributes are case sensitive, so make sure that you pay attention as you are typing.

As the saying goes, necessity is the mother of invention. This is the basic driver behind XML. As you saw at the beginning of this chapter, HTML had its place a few years back; but the need to integrate systems together prompted the need for a newer, better way to describe data without confusing presentation on the screen with the data itself. Because XML enables the definition of custom, nested tags, known as *elements,* you can construct an XML document that contains and also describes your data in the way that *you* do business. This XML document can then be transmitted to any system that understands your document, thereby allowing for interoperability.

I'd like to take this description of XML one step farther. If you could take your XML document (which contains your data) and package it in such a way that you could send it across the Internet in a secure fashion, you'd solve many of the problems that exist with distributed computing today. Well, the packaging of the XML document is what SOAP (as described in Chapter 4) is all about.

Introducing elements

An *element,* sometimes referred to as a *node,* is a hierarchical tag that breaks up data into logical groups. All XML documents are comprised of these elements because they are used to break your data up into a logical structure. For example, look at this XML code fragment:

```
<ContactInfo>
    <FirstName />
    <LastName />
    <Company />
    <EMail/>
</ContactInfo>
```

There is one set of data within an element called `<ContactInfo>`.
Hierarchically, within the `<ContactInfo>` element are four other elements
that contain data related to it: `<FirstName>`, `<LastName>`, `<Company>`, and
`<EMail>`. The reason that these four elements are contained within the
`<ContactInfo>` element is illustrated with this expanded example:

```
<ContactInfo>
    <FirstName />
    <LastName />
    <Company />
    <EMail/>
</ContactInfo>
<BillingInfo>
    <FirstName />
    <LastName />
    <Company />
    <EMail/>
</BillingInfo>
```

Notice that the same files, `<FirstName>`, `<LastName>`, `<Company>`,
and `<EMail>` are used again, but they are now contained within the
`<BillingInfo>` element. This establishes a very clear hierarchy of data that
can easily be read by any computer system.

Every element tag needs to be opened and closed in XML. HTML was a little
more forgiving on this topic, but XML must be well structured so that receiving systems know exactly how the data is laid out.

Unlike HTML elements, which are predetermined and can't be customized,
you can do whatever you want with XML elements.

An XML element begins with the `<` sign, followed by the name of the element.
For example, `<ContactInfo>` is an element. Closing an element is done with
the `/` sign, followed by the name of the element.

In the following XML example, you notice a difference in the closing syntax
between the way `<ContactInfo>` and `<FirstName>` are closed — as well as
the other elements contained within `<ContactInfo>`. `<FirstName>` contains
the `/` sign but does not contain the name of the element. This is because it is
on the same line as the opening tag. Therefore, the name of the element is
optional when the closing tag is on the same line.

`<ContactInfo>` is not on the same line, so the code must specify the / sign followed by the name of the tag. Additionally, you could construct the XML document with explicit end tags, like this:

```
<ContactInfo>
    <FirstName></FirstName>
    <LastName></LastName>
    <Company></Company>
    <EMail></EMail>
</ContactInfo>
```

The first *element,* or *node,* is `<ContactInfo>`. Because this is the first element, it is also known as the *root element.* It contains four other child elements, called `<FirstName>`, `<LastName>`, `<Company>`, and `<EMail>`. This makes sense because contact information is made up of certain elemental members that we all use every day in business. I show only four of them here for the sake of space, but I think that you get the idea. Depending on your own application, you may need to describe your data differently. For example, would this make sense?

```
<ContactInfo>
    <Personal>
        <FirstName></FirstName>
        <LastName></LastName>
        <EMail></EMail>
    </Personal>

    <Company>
        <Name></Name>
    </Company>
</ContactInfo>
```

This code fragment takes the prior example and formats it to contain an additional level in the hierarchy. This may be more conducive to contact information because it allows you to further describe your data. The code shown breaks up the four elements into categories that are contained within the `<ContactInfo>` tag but divides these elements into the categories of `<Personal>` and `<Company>`.

To further illustrate the hierarchy of your elements in your XML documents, take a look at this:

```
<ContactInfo>
    <Personal>
        <FirstName></FirstName>
        <LastName></LastName>
        <EMail></EMail>
        <Phone>
```

```
        <Home>
            <Home1></Home1>
            <Home2></Home2>
            <Home3></Home3>
        </Home>
        <Fax></Fax>
        <Mobile></Mobile>
      </Phone>
    </Personal>
</ContactInfo>
```

As you can see, <ContactInfo> is the *root* element that contains a hierarchy of other elements, known as *child* elements. The next level is the <Personal> element, as you've seen from other examples in this chapter. The <Personal> element contains the elements that you've also seen earlier in this chapter: <FirstName>, <LastName>, and <EMail>. However, an additional structure starts with the <PHONE> element. The <PHONE> element contains other telephone-related elements; <Home>, <FAX>, and <MOBILE>. However, notice that <Home> is further defined into <Home1>, <Home2>, and <Home3> to allow for up to three separate home phone lines. This structure assumes that there can be only one fax number and one mobile number, but that could easily be changed if you wanted to.

Also notice that the XML examples presented thus far in the chapter contain only a structure, not actual data. Well, hold on to your hat because that's coming next.

Attributing everything to common sense values

Okay, great! If you're reading along, you've seen that *elements,* or *nodes,* break up the data into a logical structure, but you may have noticed that none of the code in the preceding section (which represented contact information) actually contained contact information. What gives? Where's the data?

The actual data values are contained within attributes. Again, in Listing 3-1, you have already seen what attributes are. For example, the <INPUT> element contains three attributes that describe the element: id, name, and value.

Much like the way HTML elements are predetermined by the W3C, so are the attributes that describe the elements. In XML, there is no limitation on the attributes that describe an element. You can go hog wild if you want to, customizing attributes like crazy.

Following my earlier example, the following code shows the XML elements with a `value` attribute filled out. Note that the `value` attribute was specified because it makes sense with respect to our example. It has no special meaning other than that.

```
<ContactInfo>
    <Personal>
        <FirstName value="Anthony"/>
        <LastName value="Mann"/>
        <EMail value="tmann@transport80.com"/>
    </Personal>

    <Company>
        <Name value="Transport80"/>
    </Company>
</ContactInfo>
```

One problem with the preceding syntax is that the program that receives the XML document must know about the `value` attribute to grab the data. This might be appropriate if you have an XML document standard that indicates the data is stored in these attributes. However, this syntax might be more appropriate for a general XML document where no attributes are used:

```
<ContactInfo>
    <Personal>
        <FirstName>Anthony</FirstName>
        <LastName>Mann</LastName>
        <EMail>tmann@transport80.com</EMail>
    </Personal>

    <Company>
        <Name>Transport80</Name>
    </Company>
</ContactInfo>
```

This syntax makes traversing the XML document, looking for all elements and the data values for the elements, quite easy.

Now That's a Well-Formed Document!

Most systems that use XML require that the document be well formed. A *well-formed XML document* means that the document (and all the elements and attributes in it) conform to certain basic rules:

- ✔ An ending tag must accompany each opening tag.
- ✔ Attribute values must be enclosed in quotation marks.
- ✔ The version of XML you're using must be included in the document.

✔ An XML document must have one (and only one) root element.

✔ An XML document must contain a namespace that identifies the location of the XML schema being used.

A *schema* is simply a definition of the structure of an XML document. A schema is used to test the format of an XML document to see if it conforms to a defined structure. For example, I can define the schema, or structure, of an XML file that will be used for contact information. Then, when the contact information is actually received from a computer system, it can be tested to see if the format conforms to the XML schema.

The following sections clarify these important rules.

Using proper tag etiquette

An ending tag must accompany each opening tag. In other words, you cannot have only an opening tag. The following code snippet is invalid because it has no closing tags for `<FirstName>`, `<LastName>`, `<EMail>`, and `<Name>`:

```
<ContactInfo>
    <Personal>
        <FirstName>Anthony
        <LastName>Mann
        <EMail>tmann@transport80.com
    </Personal>

    <Company>
        <Name>Transport80
    </Company>
</ContactInfo>
```

On the other hand, the following code snippet is properly tagged:

```
<ContactInfo>
    <Personal>
        <FirstName>Anthony</FirstName>
        <LastName>Mann</LastName>
        <EMail>tmann@transport80.com</EMail>
    </Personal>

    <Company>
        <Name>Transport80</Name>
    </Company>
</ContactInfo>
```

Using quotes effectively

Attribute values must be enclosed in quotation marks. All attributes must be contained within traditional quotation marks (""), not single ticks (' ') like you might find in SQL Server. This code is valid and well formed:

```
<Name value="Transport80"/>
```

while both of these lines are incorrect:

```
<Name value='Transport80'/>
<Name value=Transport80/>
```

Documenting XML versions

The version of XML you're using must be included in the document. Up until now, I've only been dealing with the structure of the data, and I haven't talked too much about the structure of the XML document as a whole.

For a system to process XML, it employs a piece of software called a *parser*. All major software vendors have a parser for XML that is used to implement that company's interpretation of XML specifications. Microsoft has an XML parser, called MSXML, that is normally automatically installed with Windows 2000 or Windows XP as well as Internet Explorer.

If for some reason, you don't have it installed, you can download and install it from the Microsoft Web site at www.microsoft.com/xml.

For the XML parser to know how to parse the document and to be considered well formed, the XML document needs to contain the version of XML that you are using. This is kind of a future planning issue because XML only exists in Version 1.0. To indicate the version of your XML document, simply place this line at the beginning of your document:

```
<?xml version="1.0"?>
```

The question marks indicate a special directive to the XML parser at runtime and indicate that the values that are between these marks are not part of your data. However, notice that the rest of the characters follow the concepts outlined so far in this chapter. In other words, XML is an element that has one attribute, called VERSION.

Remembering your root

An XML document must have one (and only one) root element. Only one root element can appear in a well-formed XML document, and the first element in any XML document is the root element. Listing 3-2 shows multiple root elements, which are invalid in a well-formed XML document.

Listing 3-2: XML showing invalid multiple root elements

```
<?xml version="1.0"?>
<ContactInfo1>
    <Personal>
        <FirstName>Anthony</FirstName>
        <LastName>Mann</LastName>
        <EMail>tmann@transport80.com</EMail>
    </Personal>

    <Company>
        <Name>Transport80</Name>
    </Company>
</ContactInfo1>
<ContactInfo2>
    <Personal>
        <FirstName>Alison</FirstName>
        <LastName>Mann</LastName>
        <EMail>alison@transport80.com</EMail>
    </Personal>

    <Company>
        <Name>Transport80</Name>
    </Company>
</ContactInfo2>
```

The code in Listing 3-2 is not well formed because it contains two separate root elements, `<ContactInfo1>` and `< ContactInfo2>`. To correct the not-well-formed code in Listing 3-2, you would have to place another level of hierarchy into the XML document. This level would be used to differentiate each person's data.

In fact, adding a level that identifies each person (I call the element `<Individual>` in Listing 3-3) makes the code valid.

Listing 3-3: XML showing corrected XML with a single root element

```
<?xml version="1.0"?>
<ContactInfo>
    <Individual>
        <Personal>
            <FirstName>Anthony</FirstName>
```

```
            <LastName>Mann</LastName>
            <EMail>tmann@transport80.com</EMail>
        </Personal>

        <Company>
            <Name>Transport80</Name>
        </Company>
    </Individual>

    <Individual>
        <Personal>
            <FirstName>Alison</FirstName>
            <LastName>Mann</LastName>
            <EMail>alison@transport80.com</EMail>
        </Personal>

        <Company>
            <Name>Transport80</Name>
        </Company>
    </Individual>
</ContactInfo>
```

If you didn't have the additional element called <Individual>, you would not be able to decipher which <Company> elements went with which <Personal> elements.

Identifying namespaces and creating namespace aliases

You need to specify how your XML document will be used by systems and applications — otherwise, it's pretty much useless. To make these specifications clear, you use a namespace.

Super. Now what in the world *is* a namespace? A *namespace* is a URL that identifies a unique location on the Web that will be used to define your XML document. Because the namespace location is unique, your XML documents become unique. The namespace URL is specified in your XML documents as an attribute of the root element. The attribute must be called XMLNS (*ns* for *namespace*).

A *namespace* points to a location on the Internet that defines a specification of how your XML document will be used. You might say that a namespace defines the scope of your XML document. Namespaces are used to avoid confusion with similar documents that are used for another purpose. In other words, the namespace helps to clarify that the XML document used to describe contact information is (for example) for vendors as opposed to suppliers.

As an example, I might use this URL to identify the location of schema files for my XML document:

```
http://www.transport80.com/xml/schemas
```

When you know the URL of your schema documents, you have to include a namespace in the root element with the XMLNS attribute — like this:

```
<ContactInfo xmlns="http://www.transport80.com/xml/schemas">
```

A namespace can be aliased. In the XML world, an *alias* is a word or letter that is used in place of the original name. For example, the namespace `<ContactInfo xmlns="http://www.transport80.com/xml/schemas">` might be aliased as the `t` or `tp`.

You have two good reasons to use aliases in your XML documents:

- ✔ **To eliminate confusion and error:** An alias is especially useful when you have multiple similar namespaces in an XML document (or even an XSD document, shown later in this chapter) and you're trying to eliminate confusion and error. *XSD documents* are used to verify the format of an XML document, which is itself, written in XML.

- ✔ **To save time and effort:** An alias is also useful if you need to qualify or validate an XML document with the schema located in a namespace, but you don't want to list the full namespace every single time because you don't have to.

To alias a namespace, use this format

```
xmlns:alias = namespace
```

where *alias* stands for your chosen alias and where *namespace* stands for the actual namespace. For example, I may alias a schema's namespace as *tp* with this code:

```
<tp:ContactInfo
         xmlns:tp="http://www.transport80.com/xml/schemas">
</tp:ContactInfo>
```

Notice in this code, not only is the namespace aliased with *tp,* but *tp* is also prefixed in the `ContactInfo` element.

Testing XML Documents

You may be interested to know that you can use a very simple test to find out whether your XML documents are well formed. Save your XML document into a file with an XML extension. Then, try to open it in Internet Explorer (Version 5.5 or later).

For example, Listing 3-2 showed multiple root elements. If you save that file as `wellformed.xml` on your hard drive, you can type **C:\wellformed.xml** in your browser's URL to reveal the error shown in Figure 3-2.

Figure 3-2:
XML
parsing
error for a
document
that is not
well formed.

Likewise, Listing 3-2 was well formed. If you corrected the document and showed it in Internet Explorer, you'd get a screen like that shown in Figure 3-3.

Figure 3-3:
A well-
formed XML
document.

If you want to understand the structure of your XML document, you can click the + sign to expand a level or click the – sign to collapse an entire level in Internet Explorer. Figure 3-3 shows only – signs just to the left of the text, because all levels are already expanded. If you collapse a level, all child elements contained under that level disappear. Small XML documents don't really benefit by using these features, but you'll be grateful if you are viewing a large XML document.

Using document definitions to test XML

Document definitions describe the structure (or *schema*) of a document. In case you are confused, check out this example. Refer to Listing 3-3. It shows a well-formed XML document. However, how do you know that it conforms to the structure that the receiving party of the document expects? Actually, as it stands, you don't.

You would know that an XML document is in the expected format if you provide the XML parser information about how to validate an XML document structure. That's where document definitions come into play. You must point the XML document to a document definition, which is, in itself, another file (written in XML), in order to ensure that the validity can be checked.

Because XML standards are changing all the time, multiple ways of defining XML schemas are out there; I focus on the latest standards:

- **DTD — Document Type Definition:** DTD is a W3C standard for describing an XML schema. However, it can be quite cryptic because it is not written in an XML format.

- **XDR — XML-Data Reduced:** This format was the first attempt at making a standard for describing XML schemas in an XML format.

- **XSD — XML Schema Definition:** This is the latest specification for describing XML schemas in an XML format. Microsoft actually provides a tool that migrates your XDR files to XSD; the tool is located at `http://msdn.microsoft.com/msdnfiles/027/001/539/Search.asp`.

Because XSD is the latest standard with respect to describing XML schemas, I discuss XSD in more detail in the following sections. However, I can't possibly show you absolutely every aspect of XSD. I'm just laying out the basic principles here.

XSD Overview

Ensuring a sound structure, or *schema,* in your XML documents is the single most important thing you can do. That's why XSDs are so important. *XSD,* which stands for XML Schema Definition, is a method of describing the format, or schema, that an XML document must conform to. This format is configured by you (or a vendor or trading partner) in an XML format itself. What a revolutionary thought! Describe an XML document by using XML? Sure, why not?

Just like any other XML document, an XSD document must conform to some (but not all) of the rules outlined for other XML documents:

- ✔ The XSD file must be well formed.
- ✔ The XSD file must contain beginning and ending tags.
- ✔ The XSD file must contain one root.
- ✔ The XSD file should contain a namespace to make it unique.

The one main difference between a data XML document and an XSD XML document is that a data XML document does not have to have any specific elements and attributes (unless constrained by an XSD). However, an XSD XML document must contain only certain elements and attributes that the XML runtime processor understands. Here's a look at these elements and attributes.

Introducing the XSD root element

Every XML document must contain only one root element, the first element in the document. This rule is true of XSD documents also. To keep things simple, though, you never have to worry about which element should be root. It's already predetermined: The root element is called `<schema>`. Just as you may have read about namespaces for XML documents earlier in this chapter, you should provide an XML namespace for the XSD document in the root element.

You do not *have* to include a namespace in your XSD schemas.

However, you can use the standard namespace, called a Universal Resource Identifier, or URI, as a generic namespace. Here's how you specify a root element:

```
<xsd:schema xmlns:xsd="http://www.w3.org/2001/XMLSchema">
...your XML schema definition goes here...
</xsd:schema>
```

Declaring elements

Declaring an element is done with the `<element>` tag. Seems simple enough, eh? (No, I'm not Canadian.) Well, there's a little more to it than that. Lots of attributes can be set on the `<element>` tag.

Some people prefer to use the prefix (also known as an *alias*) `xs:` instead of `xsd:`. The two are equivalent, as long as you use one or the other consistently throughout the XSD document. No mixing and matching allowed! In fact, you can use any prefix as long as it is aliased properly. See the section "Identifying namespaces and creating namespace aliases" earlier in this chapter.

Two important optional attributes for the element tags are

✔ `BLOCK`: Prevents certain types of values from being specified for this element. You must specify the type of blocking as *extension, restriction, substitution,* or *#all*.

✔ `FINAL`: (Specifies that the values must come from *extension, restriction, substitution,* or *#all*.

Here's what these values mean:

- **extension:** Enables elements in addition to the specified attributes or parameters of a schema definition.

- **restriction:** Restricts elements from the specified attributes or parameters of a schema definition.

- **substitution:** Enables a group of one or more elements to be substituted for another.

- **#all:** Includes all of extension, restriction, and substitution.

Declaring simple and complex types

The term *type* seems to be used for everything in XML. In this context, it is expressly used to describe the concept of simple types and complex types. These two terms are used to describe the limitations of your XML schema, as well as other information about it.

Simple types

A *simple type* is used only for the `xs:string` datatype. A *datatype* is used to indicate the type of data that will be stored within an element. For example, a string datatype allows characters and numbers, and a decimal datatype only allows numbers. A datatype is used either to limit the values of an element or to define other information used on attributes and elements within the XML schema. A simple type is specified with the `<simpleType>` element.

The <simpleType> element allows for the attributes shown in Table 3-2.

Table 3-2	Attributes for the <simpleType> Element
Attribute	**Description**
final	(Optional) — Prevents certain values from being allowed in the element. You can choose from list, union, restriction, or #all. See the text discussion following Table 3-2 to discover what these terms are all about.
id	(Optional) — Unique identifier within the XML document.
name	(Required) — The name of the simple type.

In Table 3-2, four terms were used to describe the list of values that you specify for the final attribute. These terms are:

✓ **list:** This specifies a distinctive list of values to be used to represent the defined simple type. You will specify the values in the list. If you use the *this* keyword, you can also specify the id of the list, along with *itemtype* (which is a one other simple type or a built-in datatype).

✓ **union:** This specifies multiple inherited simple types that will be used to represent the defined simple type. You indicate these simple types in the hierarchy. If you use the this keyword, you can also specify the id of the union along with the membertype (which is a list of other simple types).

✓ **restriction:** This specifies a range of values (as opposed to a list of distinctive values) to represent the simple type. If you use the this keyword, you can also specify the *base* (which is the datatype) and id of the restriction.

✓ **#all:** This includes all of *list, union,* and *restriction.*

Depending on how involved you get with your XML schemas, you may only use simple types. As an example, let's declare a simple type, called *"SalaryRestriction,"* that limits the value of someone's salary in an XML document to any value between 1 and 100,000. Here's how you do it:

```
<xsd:simpleType name="SalaryRestriction">
  <xsd:restriction base="xsd:integer">
    <xsd:minInclusive value="1"/>
    <xsd:maxInclusive value="100000"/>
  </xsd:restriction>
</xsd:simpleType>
```

Complex types

A *complex type* is similar to a simple type, except that it works with other datatypes besides the `xs:string` datatype, and it allows for more options (also known as *attributes*). It is also used to either limit the values for an element, or define other information used on attributes and elements within the XML schema. A complex type is specified with the `<complexType>` element.

The `<complexType>` element allows for the attributes shown in Table 3-3.

Table 3-3	Attributes for the `<complexType>` Element
Attribute	**Description**
abstract	(Optional) — If *true,* indicates that this is a schema to be used for reference and not to actually validate XML documents.
block	(Optional) — Prevents certain types of values from being specified for this element. You must specify the type of blocking as either *extension, restriction, sub stitution,* or *#all.* Refer to the text discussion in the section "Declaring elements" to discover what these terms are all about.
final	(Optional) — Specifies that the values must come from either *extension, restriction, substitution,* or *#all.* Refer to the text discussion in the section "Declaring elements" to discover what these terms are all about.
id	(Optional) — Unique identifier within the XML document.
mixed	(Optional) — If *true,* will allow text data to appear between child elements in an XML document.
name	(Optional) — The name of the element. This cannot be used if the `ref` attribute is used.

In addition to the attributes specified in Table 3-3, you can also specify these additional content elements to be nested within the `<complexType>` element:

- `<simpleContent>`: Contains no elements, but might contain attributes. This element also allows you to define an `id` attribute.

- `<complexContent>`: Contains only elements or is empty. This element also allows you to define `id` and `mixed` attributes.

✔ `<group>`: Contains elements defined in a group of sequence or choice elements. This element also enables you to define `name`, `id`, `maxOccurs`, `minOccurs`, and `ref` attributes.

✔ `<sequence>`: Contains elements that define a list in a particular order (or sequence) which specifies the XML document element values must be listed in that specific order. This element also enables you to define `id`, `maxOccurs`, and `minOccurs` attributes.

✔ `<choice>`: Contains elements that define a list, which specifies the XML document element value must contain only one value in the list of choices. This element also allows you to define `id`, `maxOccurs`, and `minOccurs` attributes.

✔ `<all>`: Enables any or all specified elements to appear in any order.

Here's how this works. Pretend that you have an XML element, called *Gender,* that you are defining the schema for. Therefore, you want the complex type to be called *GenderChoices.* You want the only possibilities to be *male* or *female,* and the data field must be required. You would define a complex type to look like this:

```
<xsd:complexType name="GenderChoices">
    <xsd:choice minOccurs="1" maxOccurs="1">
        <xsd:element name="male" type="xsd:string"/>
        <xsd:element name="female" type="xsd:string"/>
    </xsd:choice>
</xsd:complexType>
```

Using comments and annotations in your XSD documents

Comments are a good idea in any code. That includes XML. *Comments* are used to describe something to people who look at the XML in order to help them understand it. A comment is completely ignored by any compiler or XML processor. Comments are done in XML exactly the same way they are done in HTML. Comments follow this format:

```
<!-- YOUR COMMENT HERE -->
```

Pay close attention to each and every character in the comment tags. They do look a little strange because the left tag is not exactly the same as the right tag. Your XSD file might contain a comment like this:

```
<!-- Construct Gender Choices -->
```

You may even get a little fancy and do something like this:

```
<!--**** BEGIN Construct Gender Choices ****-->

<xsd:complexType name="GenderChoices">
    <xsd:choice minOccurs="1" maxOccurs="1">
        <xsd:element name="male" type="xsd:string"/>
        <xsd:element name="female" type="xsd:string"/>
    </xsd:choice>
</xsd:complexType>

<!--**** END Construct Gender Choices ****-->
```

Additionally, annotating your schemas is a very good idea. Okay, so you're thinking, "What's the difference between a comment and an annotation?" Quite simple. A *comment* is for the reader of the XML schema file (or any XML file for that matter). After the XML processor checks an XML document for conformance to the XSD schema, no person, system, or process knows anything about the comments.

Annotations, on the other hand, present a completely different story. Any application that understands how to read an annotation can return back to the calling program to give additional help about something in your XSD file. However, if you don't annotate, this can't be done.

Annotations are done with three separate elements:

- ✔ `<annotation>`: This defines the beginning of an annotation that follows with a nested `<DOCUMENTATION>` or `<APPINFO>` element.

- ✔ `<documentation>`: This defines the text of the annotation, but it is meant to be used by a person. This element also allows you to define optional `SOURCE` and `XML:LANG` attributes.

- ✔ `<appInfo>`: This defines the text of the annotation, but it is meant to be used by an application. This element also allows you to define an optional `SOURCE` attribute.

The following snippet of code shows you how this concept works. In the code, I created an annotation to describe the purpose of the XSD schema:

```
<xsd:annotation>
    <xsd:documentation>XSD Schema used to verify
            vendors</xsd:documentation>
    <xsd:appinfo>XSD Vendor</xsd:appinfo>
</xsd:annotation>
```

The `<documentation>` element is a more human-readable form than what would be read by an application in the `<appinfo>` element.

Tying XSD to an XML document

You have constructed an XML document. You also have constructed an XSD schema definition. Now you need to tie the two together. If you don't, the XML parser won't know that it needs to validate the XML document with the XML schema.

To associate your XSD with the XML document, you must reference the standard URL (called a URI) in the XML file root element: `www.w3.org/2001/XMLSchema-instance`.

Depending on whether you specified a namespace in your XSD definition, you must use one of two possible attributes to indicate the way to find your XSD file:

- ✔ `xsi:noNamespaceSchemaLocation`: This indicates that you did not specify a namespace in your XSD schema.

- ✔ `xsi:schemaLocation`: This indicates that you did specify a namespace in your XSD schema.

Here's how it works in your XML file:

```
<?xml version="1.0"?>
<ContactInfo xmlns:xsi="http://www.w3.org/2001/XMLSchema-
             instance"
             xsi:schemaLocation="http://www.transport80.com/xml
             /schemas/vendor.xsd">
...Your XML File Contents Here...
</ContactInfo>
```

Notice that I used the `xsi:schemaLocation` attribute because my XSD file contains a namespace declaration.

To see how all the pieces fit together. Listing 3-4 shows the XSD file that validates the XML file in Listing 3-3.

Listing 3-4: XML document with embedded XSD schema reference

```
<?xml version="1.0"?>
<ContactInfo
  xmlns:xsi="http://www.w3.org/2001/XMLSchema-instance"
  xsi:schemaLocation="http://www.transport80.com/xml/schemas/vendor.xsd">
    <Individual>
        <Personal>
            <FirstName>Anthony</FirstName>
            <LastName>Mann</LastName>
```

```
            <EMail>tmann@transport80.com</EMail>
        </Personal>
        <Company>
            <Name>Transport80</Name>
        </Company>
    </Individual>
    <Individual>
        <Personal>
            <FirstName>Alison</FirstName>
            <LastName>Mann</LastName>
            <EMail>alison@transport80.com</EMail>
        </Personal>
        <Company>
            <Name>Transport80</Name>
        </Company>
    </Individual>
</ContactInfo>
```

In Listing 3-4, notice the reference in the root element <ContactInfo> that points to the XSD file that was created in this chapter.

Validating an XML Document

You would think that if you can load an XML document into Internet Explorer and verify that it is well formed, you should be able to have it automatically validate the XML document against the XML schema.

Well, that would be too easy. Instead, you must write a program that accesses the Document Object Model (or DOM) that exists in Internet Explorer. You can use virtually any programming language that can *instantiate* (or *invoke*) the DOM. This can get a little tricky to do and is outside the scope of this book (because the book is not about programming languages as such). More information can be obtained on the Microsoft Web site at

```
http://msdn.microsoft.com/library/default.asp?url=/library/en
        -us/xmlsdk/htm/xsd_devvalidation_81x0.asp
```

Chapter 4

SOAPing Up XML

. . . .

In This Chapter

▶ Discovering how SOAP makes Web services possible

▶ Diving into SOAP Headers and Envelopes

▶ Finding out how Web services relate to XML and SOAP

. . . .

*I*n Chapter 3, I showed you the basics of constructing XML documents and XML schemas. You also found out that (at least theoretically) you may not need to know too much about XML if you are developing Web services for the Microsoft platform and using Microsoft Visual Studio .NET as a development tool. Many of the XML configuration files are generated automatically for you by the Microsoft tools.

Theoretically, I said. The truth is that someone in your organization had better be XML-fluent. If you ever have to alter these files, you must understand XML.

This chapter takes XML one step further and discusses SOAP, which stands for *Simple Object Access Protocol*. SOAP is a set of XML-based technologies that enable XML documents to be packaged and routed to a specific location somewhere out there on the Internet.

What is the *object* in SOAP? The object means a Web service. In other words, SOAP allows you to call a Web service over the Internet and, in turn, have the Web service return the requested data back to the calling program. Although the details are more complex, the concept is as simple as that. That's why it's called *Simple* Object Access Protocol.

Think of XML and SOAP like peanut butter and jelly: They're two great tastes that taste great together. On its own, peanut butter is pretty good. Same with SOAP. But together, on fresh bread with the crusts cut off, they're spectacular. XML documents specify *what* you are sending across the Internet. SOAP specifies *how* and *where* you're sending those XML documents. For example, suppose you have a Web service that provides financial calculations. That Web service has an XML interface (as all Web services do). You invoke that Web service from across the Internet to your Web site (www.xyzcorp.com for example) by using SOAP.

If you really want to understand how Web services work, you should read this chapter (and Chapter 3, for that matter), even though much of the data that I explain here is automatically generated for you by Visual Studio .NET. In addition, there are many aspects of SOAP that I do not cover in this chapter. I do, however, cover the basics of how SOAP works and relates to your Web services projects. For more detailed information about SOAP and Web services, check out *Java and XML For Dummies* by Barry Burd (Wiley Publishing, Inc.).

Introducing SOAP

Before diving into the nitty-gritty of Simple Object Access Protocol (or SOAP, for you clean freaks), consider this example. There are two companies, Alpha and Beta. Alpha Inc. wishes to *call* (or *consume*) a Web service that Beta LTD has written.

The Internet landscape between Alpha and Beta looks like this:

- There are at least two Internet firewalls (one for each company).
- There are lots of servers, routers, and other network devices.
- All this networking gear is in place to prevent unauthorized activity on a network.

Based on this information, you may think that in order to facilitate Alpha Inc.'s seamless consumption of Beta LTD's Web service, there's some wrangling to be done.

That's where SOAP comes in. SOAP is a data structure (created in XML, of course) that provides a universal way of packaging up an XML data document and sending it somewhere on the Internet using the HTTP protocol (see my earlier example about the Alpha and Beta companies). SOAP standardizes how XML data is routed over the Internet by using a series of special tags. These tags are described later in this chapter.

Rub-a-dub-dub: How SOAP makes XML possible

Because SOAP is a protocol for invoking objects and passing XML data through a distributed networking environment, it doesn't matter whether the distributed network is an internal network or a network that spans the Internet. In fact, without SOAP, Web services wouldn't be invoked over *any* network at all. Data, including Web services invocations, is formatted in XML, but SOAP steps in to instruct the XML where to go over the Internet. The actual transfer of data happens using the HTTP and SSL protocols.

Here are some SOAP facts to get yourself in a lather over:

- ✔ **SOAP specifications themselves don't contain any data:** The SOAP specifications are used to describe how to transmit XML data — any XML data, known as an *XML document*. The XML document becomes embedded within the SOAP *message*, sometimes called a *SOAP document*. The message contains instructions about how to route the XML document across a network, such as the Internet.

- ✔ **The information contained within SOAP is called a SOAP message:** SOAP messages consist of a Body and a Header.

- ✔ **SOAP is platform independent:** SOAP is an industry standard, so it doesn't matter which operating system or environment sends or receives SOAP messages. In other words, a SOAP message doesn't have to be sent and received solely from the Microsoft platform.

  SOAP is an open standard developed and adopted by many companies; you can learn more about the SOAP standard on the World Wide Web Consortium (W3C) Web site at `www.w3.org`.

- ✔ **SOAP uses standard Internet traffic ports:** SOAP messages transmit XML documents through standard port 80 (for unencrypted HTTP traffic) and port 443 (for encrypted, or SSL, HTTP traffic). This is a really nifty thing. The significance of these ports is that your firewall is likely to allow this traffic through your network because these ports are used for browsing the Internet. Built into the industry SOAP standard is the fact that you can use any operating system or environment to send and receive SOAP messages.

If you use Visual Studio (the predecessor to Visual Studio .NET), you need to use the SOAP Toolkit from Microsoft, which you can download at `http://msdn.microsoft.com/SOAP`.

Anatomy of a SOAP Message

Because they are platform independent, HTTP and XML solve the problem of running programs on different operating systems in a network. SOAP explains (by using XML) what data should be in an HTTP header, as well as what data should be in an XML body, so that an application in one computer can call an application in another computer and transfer information between the two.

All information needed by a Web server that works with the SOAP protocol is contained in a SOAP message, which consists of a SOAP *Envelope,* a SOAP *Header,* and a SOAP *Body.* Here are some specifics:

- ✔ **SOAP Envelope:** Think of the SOAP Envelope as the whole enchilada, the entire package of data that is being used to explain how information should be transferred.

- ✔ **SOAP Header:** As part of the SOAP Envelope, the SOAP Header contains information about the routing and delivery options for the SOAP message.

- ✔ **SOAP Body:** Also part of the SOAP Envelope, the SOAP Body contains the actual data. The actual data is the method (or operation) that you are invoking (or consuming) from the Web service, as well as any arguments (or parameters) that you send to the method. Consuming Web services is covered in Chapter 9.

Just to make things a little more confusing, the contents of a SOAP Envelope (the SOAP Header and Body) are written in XML as well. It makes sense, though, doesn't it? If XML is used to describe data, why not use XML to describe the data related to transferring XML data? That's why this chapter is located after Chapter 3, which covers XML basics. Additionally, SOAP is used to enforce system-independence because SOAP uses industry-standard protocols, but also describes the contents of the data in the SOAP Body.

Putting SOAP to work

Suppose you have a Web service called FinCalc that does financial calculations. You've tested your Web service and it resides on your Web server within your firewall. Now you have a client that needs to access FinCalc. Here's how your client gets access to the FinCalc Web service, which is sitting behind your firewall:

1. Clicking a button or doing something that seems equally innocent calls FinCalc from its remote location across the Internet.

2. If he or she is using Visual Studio .NET, the client can simply set a Web reference to the FinCalc Web service and be on his or her way! (Web references are covered in Chapter 9.)

   But what did this do for you behind-the-scenes?

3. In the background, Visual Studio .NET creates a SOAP Envelope, a SOAP Header, and a SOAP Body for FinCalc. The rest of this chapter is dedicated to showing you how the SOAP message works with a couple of different examples.

   The SOAP Header contains information about the location of the Web reference on the Internet. The SOAP Body contains the actual data to be sent across the Internet, such as the method that you are calling. An example method is called Calculate, which resides in the sample

`FinCalc` Web service. The method accepts two parameters, `Num1` and `Num2`. In summary, you would call the `Calculate` method of the `FinCalc` Web service and pass it two values, one value for the `Num1` parameter, and another value for the `Num2` parameter.

You may not ever need to create or modify a SOAP message (which includes the Envelope, Header, and Body) if you are using Visual Studio .NET, but in case you are using another development tool or a non-Microsoft operating system platform, you'll know what it's all about. Even if you are using Microsoft tools, it helps to understand what is being done for you automatically so that you can appreciate how useful the tools and technologies from Microsoft really are!

Anatomy of the SOAP Envelope

The *SOAP Envelope* is created using an XML syntax that indicates parameters and tags that describe everything about a SOAP document, including the Header and Body of the Envelope. If you want a quick refresher about XML, see Chapter 3.

The basic XML structure for the SOAP Envelope looks like this:

```
<SOAP-ENV:Envelope>
    ...envelope options...

    <SOAP-ENV:Header>
        ...header options...
    </SOAP-ENV:Header>

    <SOAP-ENV:Body>
        ...body options...
    </SOAP-ENV:Body>

</SOAP-ENV:Envelope>
```

Perhaps you noticed the XML syntax with the elements `<SOAP-ENV:Envelope>`, `<SOAP-ENV:Header>`, and `<SOAP-ENV:Body>`. These house the structure of the complete SOAP document. The next couple of sections outline the information that can be specified in the SOAP Header and the SOAP Body.

In each of the code examples presented throughout the rest of this chapter, I use an example where XML data is used to specify personal and company contact information. This contact information example is shown extensively throughout Chapter 3, so I continue it here in Chapter 4.

Introducing the SOAP Header

The SOAP Header, specified by the `<SOAP-ENV:Header>` element, contains information about what to do with the specifications in the SOAP Body (see "Introducing the SOAP Body," later in this chapter). It can also contain information about the return path after the server responds to this message.

The `<SOAP-ENV:Header>` element enables you to specify the attributes listed in Table 4-1.

The SOAP Header is not required in a SOAP message.

Table 4-1	Attributes for the `<SOAP-ENV:Header>` Element
Attribute	**Description**
`Actor`	(Optional) Indicates that the recipient specified in the namespace must act on one or more parts of the SOAP message. Note that (although it doesn't seem to make sense) the SOAP body may have a different `actor` than the header.
`MustUnderstand`	(Optional) If *true,* the recipient must understand how to process SOAP Headers.

A SOAP message may be delivered to more than one receiving party. As a matter of fact, it may be required to route to one party before another. The `actor` attribute, if specified, is used to indicate that one part (or more parts) of the SOAP message is for the recipient specified in the namespace. An example of how to use the `actor` attribute is listed under the next attribute, `mustUnderstand`.

The `actor` attribute, if used, is always set to a standard namespace URL, known as a Universal Resource Indicator (or URI). It is always listed as

```
ENV:Actor="http://schemas.xmlsoap.org/soap/actor/next"
```

The actual routing of the SOAP message is not specified in the `actor` attribute. The `actor` attribute only specifies the namespace used for `actor` attributes (at `xmlsoap.org`). The actual routing is specified in the `xmlns` attribute.

The `mustUnderstand` attribute is used as a flag to indicate whether the processing server must understand how to read and processes SOAP headers. If this value is *true,* the server must understand the header, or it shall return without processing. If this value is *false* or it is omitted, the server can ignore headers if the server doesn't understand them.

In the code fragment that follows, I give you an example of using both the `actor` and `mustUnderstand` attributes.

Here are a few things to know before you check out the code, though:

- The line numbers are for explanation only. Your file would not actually include these numbers.
- The tags in lines 1 and 8 outline the SOAP header.
- Line 3 contains the declaration of the namespace and aliases it with a prefix of *tp*.

  That's why, in line 2, you see a tag prefixed with *tp* (and the corresponding closing tag in line 7).

  So, where does the *vendorCheck* keyword come from? Simple . . . I made it up. I wish to encapsulate the `actor` attribute and namespace into one designation. This designation indicates that in line 6, there is a body element with an ID called *pID*.

  Within the code fragment that follows, line 5 indicates that the receiving server must understand how to process SOAP Headers.

```
1:<SOAP-ENV:Header>
2:    <tp:vendorCheck
3:
            xmlns:tp="http://dev.transport80.com/xml/schemas/v
            endor"
4:    SOAP-
            ENV:Actor="http://schemas.xmlsoap.org/soap/actor/n
            ext"
5:    SOAP-ENV:mustUnderstand="1">
6:        <tp:bodyID>pID</tp:bodyID>
7:    </tp:vendorCheck>
8:</SOAP-ENV:Header>
```

Introducing the SOAP Body

The SOAP Body, specified as the `<SOAP-ENV:Body>` element, contains the body of your actual SOAP message. The body looks mostly like any XML document that has been discussed thus far in the chapter.

Using the contact information example from Chapter 3, suppose you have an XML file that contains personal and company contacts. Listing 4-1 shows how you might insert, or *wrap,* contact information XML into a SOAP Body message. Bear in mind that the structure of the XML file can be anything. I provide just a simple example.

Listing 4-1:   XML wrapped into a SOAP Body

```
<SOAP-ENV:Body>
    <ContactInfo>
        <Individual>
            <Personal id="pID">
                <FirstName>Anthony</FirstName>
                <LastName>Mann</LastName>
                <EMail>tmann@transport80.com</EMail>
            </Personal>

            <Company>
                <Name>Transport80</Name>
            </Company>
        </Individual>

        <Individual>
            <Personal>
                <FirstName>Alison</FirstName>
                <LastName>Mann</LastName>
                <EMail>alison@transport80.com</EMail>
            </Personal>

            <Company>
                <Name>Transport80</Name>
            </Company>
        </Individual>
    </ContactInfo>
</SOAP-ENV:Body>
```

I should point out that in Listing 4-1, everything is wrapped in `<SOAP-ENV:Body>` tags (on the first and last lines of the listing). Within these tags is essentially a complete XML file, whose structure is likely defined by the Web service you are calling.

Also, I use the `id` attribute when I declare the `<Personal>` element. This `id`, called *pID,* is the identifier that I was referring to in the third bullet point in the earlier section, "Introducing the SOAP Header."

The SOAP Body has an additional child element, called a SOAP Fault, which specifies how to handle errors during the SOAP routing process. SOAP Faults are an advanced topic and are not covered in this book, but if you want to find out more, you can search the Microsoft Web site at `http://search.microsoft.com` or the W3C Web site at `www.w3c.org`.

Validating SOAP messages

After you generate your SOAP messages, you can validate them with a tool available from Microsoft, called the SOAP Message Validator (imagine that!). It's available at this URL (sorry about the length):

```
http://msdn.microsoft.com/down-
loads/default.asp?url=/downloads/
```

```
sample.asp?url=/msdn-files/027/
001/587/msdncompositedoc.xml&fram
e=true.
```

Because this tool requires compilation of source code files, it's an advanced topic and is not covered in this book.

Getting a Handle on SOAP

If you have read this chapter from the beginning, you learned the basics of how SOAP works and how XML is contained, or *wrapped,* within the SOAP message body. I'm going to take this lesson one step further and show how a specific call to a Web service is wrapped within a SOAP message. In this context, two specific transactions take place. One is a request by the program that calls a Web service and the other is a response from the Web service server. Each is described in the next two sections, with examples. Again, these sections are mostly informational for you to understand how SOAP works. If you use Visual Studio .NET, these SOAP calls are handled automatically for you when you call a Web service.

SOAP requests

The SOAP request is HTTP data (in an XML format) that is sent from a client to the server that handles requests to Web services. As you learned throughout this chapter, SOAP is a protocol that routes Web service requests through the Internet. It also identifies the method calls and parameters to the method calls. For example, if you have a Web service named User, with a method named Calc, not only does the SOAP request contain information about the parameters that are defined within the Calc method, but also information about the namespace and location of where the Calc method is on the Internet. (I cover namespaces in further detail in Chapter 3.)

To continue with the Calc example, the SOAP request for the Save method of the User Web service is shown in Listing 4-2. Remember that the SOAP request for a different Web service call with different parameters will appropriately reflect that specific Web service call.

Listing 4-2: Sample SOAP request

```
POST /external/user.asmx HTTP/1.1
Host: dev.transport80.com
Content-Type: text/xml; charset=utf-8
Content-Length: length
SOAPAction: "http://webservices.transport80.com/Save"

<?xml version="1.0" encoding="utf-8"?>
<soap:Envelope xmlns:xsi="http://www.w3.org/2001/XMLSchema-instance"
               xmlns:xsd="http://www.w3.org/2001/XMLSchema"
               xmlns:soap="http://schemas.xmlsoap.org/soap/envelope/">
  <soap:Body>
    <Save xmlns="http://webservices.transport80.com/">
      <UserID>1</UserID>
      <LastName>Mann</LastName>
      <FirstName>Anthony</FirstName>
      <Address1>123 Main Street</Address1>
      <Address2>Apt 33</Address2>
      <City>Portsmouth</City>
      <State>NH</State>
      <Postal>03840</Postal>
      <Country>USA</Country>
      <HomePhone>603-111-1111</HomePhone>
      <HomeEMail>sample  ail.com</HomeEMail>
    </Save>
  </soap:Body>
</soap:Envelope>
```

Notice in Listing 4-2 that the SOAP Envelope contains generic namespaces defined by w3c.org and xmlsoap.org. These namespaces define how SOAP messages are constructed and do not need to be changed. However, you'll notice that the SOAP Body contains information that is specific to the Web service that the example is calling. Notice the first line of code under the SOAP Body is the namespace location of the Save method. The Save method accepts eleven parameters, which are specified as the XML elements <UserID>, <LastName>, <FirstName>, <Address1>, and so forth. Each of the 11 parameters have values specified that will be passed into the Save method. For example, the Country attribute (shown as an XML element) contains a value of USA. After the Web service receives this request, it performs whatever action is defined by the Web service, and then returns a SOAP response.

SOAP responses

The SOAP response is sent back to the calling program, in XML format, when the Web server receives and processes your SOAP request message. The SOAP response for the Save method of the sample User Web service is shown in Listing 4-3.

Listing 4-3:   Sample SOAP response

```
HTTP/1.1 200 OK
Content-Type: text/xml; charset=utf-8
Content-Length: length

<?xml version="1.0" encoding="utf-8"?>
<soap:Envelope xmlns:xsi="http://www.w3.org/2001/XMLSchema-instance"
               xmlns:xsd="http://www.w3.org/2001/XMLSchema"
               xmlns:soap="http://schemas.xmlsoap.org/soap/envelope/">
  <soap:Body>
    <SaveResponse xmlns="http://webservices.transport80.com/">
      <SaveResult>1</SaveResult>
    </SaveResponse>
  </soap:Body>
</soap:Envelope>
```

Just as in the SOAP request, the SOAP response in XML format shows the result of calling the Web service within the `<SaveResult>` tags. This tag is so named because the called method was named `Save`, followed by a constant keyword `Result`. In other words, all SOAP responses will contain the method name, followed by the keyword `Result`. The `<SaveResult>` tags are contained within a `<SaveResponse>` set of tags. Again, the same naming convention also applies. These tags indicate that the actual response values for the `Save` method are contained within these tags. The `<SaveResponse>` and `<SaveResult>` tags in Listing 4-3 show the result of the `Save` method returning a value of 1.

Part II
Web Services Design and Construction

The 5th Wave   By Rich Tennant

"One of the first things you want to do before migrating to .NET is fog the users to keep them calm during the procedure."

In this part . . .

*B*efore you can use your Web services, you must construct and test a Web services project on the .NET platform. Chapter 5 discusses the considerations and strategies that you must contemplate before you can create your Web services projects. Chapter 6 shows how to construct your Web services projects by using Visual Studio .NET in both the Visual Basic .NET and Visual C# .NET languages. Chapter 7 shows how to test and debug your Visual Studio .NET Web services projects.

Chapter 5

Designing Web Services

*W*hen you design XML Web services, you really need to start gathering information and analyzing requirements because these requirements have design implications.

After all, how can you build something if you don't know what you're building? In addition, how do you know what questions to ask if you don't know all the ramifications of using new technologies? This chapter helps you to understand the answers to these very questions so that you can create the very best design for your Web services projects.

Web services projects require many considerations that affect and influence the design. Some of these considerations are security, complexity, requirements, and performance. Understanding what your client wants (even if that client is an internal department within your organization) versus the complexity of the application versus performance versus development time are difficult things to juggle. But you must take all of these things into consideration.

Because I can't tell you exactly how to develop your own Web services applications, this chapter presents considerations that you may not be aware of when designing your Web services applications. This chapter should be used to spark the imagination and to consider all of the aspects that directly and/or indirectly affect your Web services projects.

Gathering and Analyzing Requirements

Gathering and analyzing requirements for a Web services project is not much different from performing similar tasks for other types of projects — and it is absolutely necessary. Your high school science teacher was right: If you don't understand the requirements of a project, the project will likely fail. Just be glad that your Web services project isn't a replica volcano spewing orange slime all over the place.

Before you can gather any requirements from your client, you must first identify the following:

- ✔ A single *point person* (usually a project manager) to contact for all issues
- ✔ Key *stakeholders* (people who will determine and affect the success of the project)
- ✔ Factors that will identify and label the project as a success or failure (or somewhere in between)

This chapter refers to the term *client*, which may be a customer with whom you do business or even an internal customer, such as the accounting department. In other words, a client in this chapter's context is any person for whom you must develop a Web services project.

Identifying your single point of contact

Your single point of contact is usually a project manager. This is someone at your client's site who is responsible for overseeing all aspects of the project and coordinating activities internally within your client's organization. Having a single point of contact is a good idea because, quite simply, too many cooks spoil the broth. Communication is too difficult with multiple contacts.

Imagine a situation in which two developers are working on a project. When the developers have a question for someone in the IT department at your client's site, they simply make a phone call, solve the problem, and things move forward. Maybe. If some technical decision is reached but the project manager doesn't know about it, the decision is never documented. Next thing you know, the project is then three months overdue and nobody can explain why. Not only is there no record of any important decisions, but suddenly the project is implementing new features that were out of the project's original scope, a phenomenon known as "scope creep." Scope creep can mean the difference between being on time and on budget and a complete project disaster. Let this little story be a lesson to you: Make sure that you have a single point of contact on your end as well as on the client's side. The moral to the story isn't that the project manager does all the work (even though the techies would like for that to happen), but that the project manager encourages proactivity within all parties of the team.

Identifying key stakeholders

Would you ask a brain surgeon what's required for an e-commerce project? You might talk to the surgeon about the headache the project gives you, but this medical professional probably won't have a whole lot of advice (and almost certainly doesn't care) about your project. And that's why your local M.D. is not a stakeholder. A *stakeholder* is someone who has an interest in the project.

A *key stakeholder* is someone who not only has an interest in the project, but plays a key role in it, as well, usually helping to influence the direction of the project in some way. A key stakeholder can be a director that is sponsoring the project, a project manager that is making decisions on the project, an IT manager, or even a CTO, CFO, or CEO.

Identifying your project as a success or failure

What criteria will you use to judge whether the project is successful? What criteria will your client use? If you can't identify these concrete measuring sticks, it will be absolutely impossible to declare the project a success. The criteria can be based on any combination of the following:

- Project deadlines
- Project requirements
- Technical achievements
- Return on investment (ROI)
- Budgetary requirements

When you have identified these basic issues, you can begin with the details of your project. To determine the requirements of your project, you have two possibilities for action. The first is that your client provides you with a detailed requirements document. The second is that you must determine the exact requirements of your client to know exactly what you are building. It is very infrequent that a client has detailed requirements for you to build your application. Therefore, you must find out what your client needs by interviewing the key stakeholders.

Suppose that you design and develop the best system in the world. It has all the bells and whistles that the client wanted and met all the requirements. It's a very elegant, scaleable, and well-performing system. Your software developers are pleased. However, the project is a failure. Why? Simple. It's three months late. It was important for the client to have the project on January 1st, and you delivered it on April 1st (which is a bad sign on it's own). The lesson here is that you must understand what factors the client deems necessary for the project to be a success or a failure.

Gathering Requirements by Interviewing Clients

Unless you have some detailed requirements from your client, you must determine the requirements for your Web services (and other) projects on your own. You can go through a variety of processes to get requirements from your client, but they all fall under the heading of *interviews*. Interviewing the client can take any or all of the following forms (depending on the complexity of the project):

- ✓ Surveys
- ✓ Focus groups
- ✓ One-on-one interviews

Another advantage of interviewing clients is that it gets people involved. Nobody wants to use a new system that they had no input in designing. Of course, the users won't be doing software design, but they will be helping with system design. For the following sections, suppose that management is considering an automated report generation system, which may evolve into an Executive Information System *(EIS)* or a digital dashboard, where the user can see only the information that he or she cares about.

Conducting surveys

You may gather information from your client by surveying users and/or key stakeholders. The easiest way to survey is by using an online surveying tool that asks a series of questions and collects responses. Of course, the questions must be appropriately phrased in order to address your target audience. But, I'll get to that in a bit (see the section, "Choosing the right phrasing for survey questions").

Finding topic areas for surveys

Before you can begin surveying, you need to choose your topic areas, which — depending on the project — will focus on productivity and ease of use.

Here are some typical questions that focus on ease of use:

- ✔ What are the top five ways that your job can be made easier? (Enter up to five.)
- ✔ What is the hardest thing about your job?
- ✔ What do you expect the new system to do?
- ✔ Is it more important to you to have a new system in place that's quick or feature-rich? (Choose one.)

This last question is a trick because it applies to productivity as well. You can often get good results by killing two birds with one stone.

Here are some productivity-related questions:

- ✔ How can your job be automated?
- ✔ How willing are you to use a new system that automates job functions? (Use a scale from one to five.)
- ✔ How many hours per day do you spend running management reports for your supervisor? (Choose one.)

Choosing the right phrasing for survey questions

Of course, no matter what topic area you choose, the questions in your survey must be appropriately phrased in order to address your target audience, and you can use a variety of options for asking the same question. For example, a question that asks users what the hardest part of their job is could be phrased

What is the hardest thing about your job?

Or it could be phrased as follows:

Of the three following options, which is the most difficult and time consuming?

A. Creating presentations

B. Scheduling

C. Data entry

Or you could ask:

Do you find the current scheduling software easy to use?

Although the people who work with the system every day wouldn't be considered key stakeholders (ultimately, decisions will be made by a manager or other supreme power), they probably have a few opinions that could shed some light on the direction of your project. That's why you want to phrase your questions so that most of them are *open ended*. An open-ended question forces a response from someone that is more specific than a simple yes or no. In contrast, if you allow the participants in your survey to answer with a yes or no, or if you have many questions that allow participants to choose a response from a list of choices, you might miss out on valuable information.

A yes-or-no question is referred to as a *closed-ended question* (what a surprise!). Not all closed-ended questions require a yes or a no response; as long as the respondent isn't required to say more than a single word (without elaboration), the question is closed. Although at first glance it might seem that you want users to give as much information as possible, sometimes closed-ended questions are necessary — if not preferred:

- ✔ **Keeping it short:** Users don't want to feel like they are writing a dissertation; it's simply quicker to click a couple of radio buttons on a survey than it is to type out detailed responses.

- ✔ **Fast analysis:** Closed-ended questions are easier to analyze. If 20 out of 25 people answer the question "How many hours per day do you spend running management reports for your supervisor?" with the answer "Two," then it becomes obvious and easy to quantify how an automated system can help administrative assistants to be more productive. It also helps to prove return on investment (ROI) because the time associated with 20 people spending two hours a day also has a real, associated cost. If these people didn't have to run reports for their supervisors, they could be doing something else.

  On the other hand, if you asked an open-ended question, such as "How much time do you spend running management reports for your supervisor?" but provided a text box for an open-ended answer, you may get answers that are harder to analyze. You may get an answer such as "usually between one and four hours, but only when Chrissy is out of the office or my boss wants only some reports." This answer doesn't really help you to quantify what you are looking for. When you design your questions, keep in mind the type of answers that you will be receiving.

- ✔ **Less ambiguity:** You're likely to find less ambiguity when you analyze the results of a survey that has yes or no or other kinds of closed-end questions in it.

Be careful which questions you designate as closed-ended. What are you going to do if you ask the question, "What is the hardest thing about your job?" and respondents give answers like, "My salary," "My boss," or "Completing stupid surveys?"

As President/CEO of a Web services company, Transport:80 Incorporated (www.transport80.com), I know from experience that a good online survey can make a big difference in the success of a project. Figure 5-1 shows a survey created by Transport:80.

Creating focus groups

A *focus group* is a focused set of people who are either physically gathered together in a room or who use special software at workstations and are queried by a moderator to answer a specific set of questions. The moderators of focus groups are usually experienced in conducting this form of interviewing.

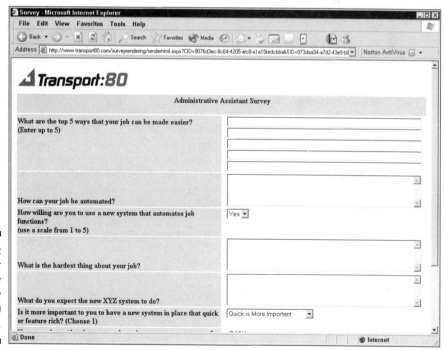

Figure 5-1:
Sample user
survey
provided by
Transport:80
Inc.

Taking notes in such a venue is usually difficult, so the entire session is typically videotaped or audio recorded. Obviously, it is important that the quality of these recordings be high. Additionally, analyzing the results of these audio and/or video recordings can be difficult. In fact, many times it takes an expert to analyze these findings into a quantitative report.

As you may expect, focus groups can be exceptionally expensive to conduct. The cost can be as little as $20,000 or as high as $150,000 or more. This option is generally too cost-prohibitive for most companies and is best used for finding out general attitudes of specific demographic groups.

Conducting one-on-one interviews

The one-on-one interview is a very common form of gathering information, and is an inexpensive, effective alternative. A one-on-one interview is transacted just as you would expect — someone interviews a client or user without the pressure and influence of others involved in the process.

With one-on-one interviews, you can start to draw a detailed picture of the "pain-points" that a client is feeling. Usually, because you are interviewing someone in the privacy of his or her own office or meeting room, he or she generally feels freer to discuss the real problems that are to be addressed by the project — not a sanitized version of them. One-on-one interviews can even be combined with surveys. If you want to further qualify answers that were received during interviews, perhaps you can generate a follow-up survey.

Interviews are generally a great forum for asking lots of open-ended questions, like "What is wrong with your current system?" or "How I can make your job easier?" With a face-to-face interview, you have someone as a captured audience, so they will be free to answer the question honestly. In fact, you might get more of a response than you ever expected — be prepared with lots of paper.

Another technique is to conduct an online survey and randomly interview a certain percentage of respondents. For example, if you survey 100 people, you might want to personally interview 10 percent of those respondents (or 10 people). Even though you may want to interview everyone, doing so can be time-consuming, so you may just have to do some sampling.

Analyzing and Using Requirements

As I've already stated, analyzing requirement results can be exceptionally difficult. You must take into account two forms of information during the analysis process:

- ✔ **Qualitative information:** Generally relates to the data that is collected during your interviews. Often, this is the data that's collected in a form that must be analyzed, such as open-ended questions and conversations.

- ✔ **Quantitative information:** Generally relates to the analysis of qualitative data. In other words, open-ended questions and conversations are analyzed in order to quantify some common theme or trend in the answers collected from your interviews. Additionally, closed-ended questions are considered to be quantitative because usually, not much analysis is needed for these questions.

Many companies specialize in doing nothing but analyzing data. You can certainly do a search in your favorite search engine to find one of these companies by searching on "Data Analysts," "Marketing Research," "Qualitative Research," and "Quantitative Research." On the other hand, if you know the subject area quite well and the number of people used during the interview process was minimal, you may be able to analyze the data yourself.

If you are analyzing closed-ended questions, spotting trends can be quite easy because the data is already qualitative. For example, you would know that 7 out of 10 people answered "Yes" to the question "Do you think the company needs a new software system to make your job easier?" Therefore, you can deduce that 70 percent of the people think that a new system is needed.

However, it becomes more difficult to understand the data when it's compared to other questions. Suppose that you had another question "Can your job be automated?" and only 2 out of 10 people answered, "Yes" to the question (or 20 percent). The fact that 70 percent of the people think that a new system is needed to make their jobs easier, but that only 20 percent feel that their jobs *can* be automated doesn't really make sense. In other words, why wouldn't everyone who thinks a new system is needed also think that their jobs can be made easier? Who knows! Maybe the questions are worded poorly and the survey-taker didn't understand one or more questions. On the other hand, maybe some analysis of the answers has to be performed to find out exactly what is going on. It might actually make sense. You might need to question the people who didn't seem to answer the questions consistently.

Constructing Use-Case Scenarios

When you finally get a handle on the specific requirements needed for the system that you're building, constructing use-case scenarios is a good idea. A *use case* is a documented scenario (known as a *use-case diagram*) that is based on every conceivable action that a user can take using a consistent, standard notation. Every possible path that a user can navigate through is generally considered. The different possible paths are based on the requirements that you gathered earlier in the process. For example, if you are constructing a use-case diagram for when a user enters a credit card number over the Internet, one path is what happens if the credit card is declined. Another path is when the credit card is approved. Do you think this is all? It might be, depending on the requirements. However, it also could be that you have to consider what happens if the user clicks the "Submit" button on a Web page more than once. Is the user going to be charged twice? Will you need to consider if the card being used is reported as stolen? All of these considerations are known as paths. You should only consider the paths that are related to your requirements. In other words, if your client doesn't care about stolen cards (they just come up as "declined"), then don't consider this scenario in the use-case diagram.

Use cases are documented by implementing a standardized graphical notation, called the Universal Modeling Language *(UML)*. UML is used to visually represent all conditions or paths that a scenario can follow. UML is a set of symbols and terminology that is used to document all aspects of a scenario. The following list details those aspects:

- ✔ **Actor:** A user or other system that is involved in the scenario in some way.

- ✔ **Scenario:** An instance of a use case that must be addressed and satisfied by the system requirements. The scenario generally starts with a verb to identify an action that is taken by an actor.

- ✔ **System boundary:** The area to which the responsibility of system functionality is constrained.

- ✔ **Main flow of events:** The normal everyday flow that is expected to happen. This is sometimes called the "happy day scenario" because it lists exactly what is expected to happen.

- ✔ **Exception flow of events:** This error condition is not expected to happen but must be considered.

This section is not intended to show you everything that you need to know about UML. UML is a complex topic and has been the subject of entire books. You can check out more about UML by pointing your browser to www.uml. org. Figure 5-2 features a very simple use-case diagram that shows how my company, Transport:80, processes surveys.

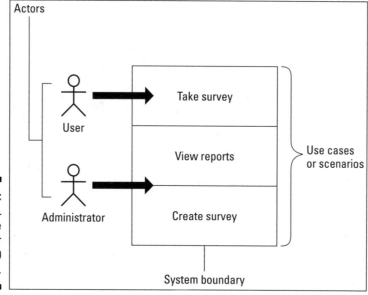

Figure 5-2:
Simple UML
use-case
diagram for
Transport:80
surveys.

In Table 5-1, I show the main flow of events (the "happy day scenario") for the
following scenario:

1. Administrator (who is an actor) logs in, creates a new survey, and makes
   it available to users, all within the system boundary.

2. User (also an actor) accesses the survey, completes it, and returns it
   within the system boundary.

3. Based on specially set properties, the administrator analyzes the survey
   results.

Table 5-1	Use Case Main Flow of Events
Use Case	**Description**
Create Survey	Administrator logs in
Create Survey	Administrator opts to create a new survey
Create Survey	Administrator configures survey properties
Create Survey	Administrator configures questions and answers
Create Survey	Administrator configures properties for all questions and answers
Create Survey	Administrator gets URL to new survey

(continued)

Table 5-1 *(continued)*

Use Case	Description
Take Survey	User logs in (if survey requires it)
Take Survey	User requests specific survey URL
Take Survey	User answers all required questions
Take Survey	User submits answers
Take Survey	System tests for required answers and all rules
Take Survey	Thank-you page is displayed
View Reports	Administrator logs in
View Reports	Administrator selects "Reports" option
View Reports	Administrator selects specific survey to report on
View Reports	Administrator selects type of report
View Reports	Administrator views report

Table 5-2 shows the exception flow of events that must be considered for the use cases shown in Figure 5-2 and represented in the "happy day scenario" in Table 5-1.

Table 5-2 — Use-Case Exception Flow of Events

Use Case	Description
Create Survey	Administrator login fails
Create Survey	Administrator creation of survey fails
Take Survey	User logs in incorrectly (if survey requires login)
Take Survey	User types-in the wrong survey URL
Take Survey	User doesn't answer all required questions
Take Survey	User has answers that are outside the acceptable range of answers
View Reports	Administrator login fails
View Reports	Administrator does not have a "Reports" option

Use Case	Description
View Reports	Administrator experiences a database error that prevents report selection
View Reports	Administrator selects type of report
View Reports	Administrator views report

Understanding every possible contingency and scenario helps you to verify that you have completely understood the requirements and have accounted for all possible contingencies.

You can use many tools to create use-case diagrams and object models (for designing Web services):

- ✔ **Visio for Enterprise Architects:** Offers a built-in tool for creating use-case diagrams and modeling your scenarios.

- ✔ **Enterprise Templates:** The task of creating object models is simplified with these templates, which are built into Visual Studio .NET, Enterprise Edition. Templates are good starting points to help you design and model your Web services projects.

- ✔ **Third-party Tools:** Other companies, such as Rational Software, also provide tools for designing use-case diagrams and object models. One such tool is called Rational Rose, which helps you to visualize your business processes. Visit the Rational Software Web site at www.rational.com.

Design Strategy Considerations

You should consider several strategies in order to better understand how you will design your Web services. Some of these strategies are listed throughout this chapter and the entire book. However, you must consider how you will *componentize* your code. In other words, how will you organize your code into projects, classes, methods, properties, and events? After you have determined exactly what your requirements are and which scenarios (through use-case diagrams) your application will need to handle, you can begin to design your application. You must construct your Web services projects into one or more objects that handle the functionality, which is validated in your use-case diagrams.

Understanding object modeling

Based on the business requirements, you must decide how to construct your components. Your components are then broken up into objects. The design of these objects is said to be an *object model.* The object model is broken up in any logical way that you want to show your components. For example, you can have one object model that is used for internal functionality and one for external interfaces.

With the use cases (based on requirements), you can begin to construct your object model by breaking out the logical objects that will satisfy your business requirements so they look something like the object model shown in Figure 5-3.

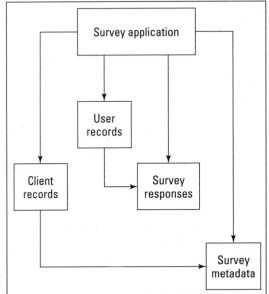

Figure 5-3:
Component-
ized object
model.

Dissecting the object model

To satisfy each of the use cases (refer to Figure 5-2, earlier in this chapter), the object model can be broken up into these major objects:

✔ **Survey application:** The program that is used to create the survey and contains client records, user records, survey responses, and also survey metadata (which is just the list of questions for a survey).

- ✔ **Client records:** Contains records for a client that administers a survey. How does the application know that someone is "allowed" to administer a survey? Simple, there is a client record for this person. As an example, suppose there are two people who work for XYZ Corporation; Mary and John. Mary is an administrator and is allowed to create questions for surveys. John is not an administrator. Mary would have a client record. John would not.

- ✔ **User records:** Contains records for users that take a survey. The user record is how the program "knows" who took the survey. If John Jones takes the survey, John Jones would have a user record.

- ✔ **Survey metadata:** Metadata is simply data that describes data. In other words, the survey metadata is an object that contains the questions for a survey. As an example, if there is a survey, named "requirements survey" with a question "What would you like to see this new system do for you?", this question would be part of the survey metadata.

- ✔ **Survey responses:** Contains the actual responses by a user that takes a survey. If a person answers the question, "What would you like to see this new system do for you?" with "Ease my workload," this answer would be stored as a survey response.

The basic object model contains objects that satisfy the requirements. You need to think about all of the properties, methods, and events that should comprise your objects. For example, you need methods for inserting, updating, and deleting records.

Assuring peak performance

As with any software project, you must take into account certain design considerations. Performance is one of the biggest issues. And so many areas affect performance. Some of the performance considerations are based on hardware, but some performance considerations are also based on software.

The next few sections outline the major areas to consider for performance.

Triple checking server memory — and then adding more

With memory, more is always better. However, how much is enough? It's best to follow the recommendations based on the requirements of the software manufacturer for each piece of software loaded on the computer. Then decide on a magnitude greater than that.

The easiest method for assessing the amount of memory needed is to determine the maximum amount of memory required if every application was in use at the same time. You also need to consider how many users you expect at any time.

Here are the main components to consider:

- ✔ **Operating system (OS) requirements:** That is, the amount of memory that the server needs to have in order to enable users to safely run the current OS and other installed software.

  For example, say you have two Web services that will be hosted on a Windows 2000 Server. Windows 2000 Server requires 128MB memory.

- ✔ **.NET framework requirements:** For example, say that the framework takes up 128MB of memory on the server.

  Together, the operating system and framework occupy a total of 256MB memory on your server, and that's without even considering the Web Services objects that you will be developing.

- ✔ **Users:** That is, the number of users who may be using a Web service at any given time. Suppose that you expect 100 users to need to use each of the two Web services objects at any time.

- ✔ **Web service requirements:** This is *very* difficult to estimate with any degree of accuracy, but at a minimum, add up all of the space that each of the datatypes will occupy. For example, suppose that one Web Service has two strings that can handle 50 characters each (or 100 characters/bytes total for this Web service). The other has three long integers, which take up 8 bytes of space each (or 24 bytes total for this Web service).

  If you multiply the first Web service space requirements by the number of expected users, you get 10,000 bytes or 10K. Do the same for the second Web service and you get 2.4K. This doesn't sound like much, but remember, this is only for the data storage.

- ✔ **Overhead associated with the Web service:** That is, the amount of memory your server should have over and above your initial estimates.

  If you estimate overhead of another 50K or so for each Web service, the memory starts to add up and compound.

Use the formulas shown here to help determine the system memory needed for best performance for the memory requirements I mention here.

First, determine the basic system requirements for a single server:

```
128MB (OS memory) + 128MB (.NET framework requirements)
```

Add 256MB to the answer of the following equations:

```
100 (Users) x (10K [Requirements for Web service #1] + 50K
          [Overhead])
100 (Users) x (2.4K [Requirements for Web service #2] + 50K
          [Overhead])
```

The answer, when all the calculations are complete (for 100 users of each of the two Web services), is 267MB. That's the bare minimum amount of memory your server will need.

If you account for some additional overhead, such as database connections, you are looking at 300MB just for these two small Web services and system requirements.

You have to make sure that you factor in everything that you haven't considered. Some people call it a *fudge factor*. Others refer to Murphy's Law. Whatever you call it, the worst thing you could do is *not* consider the fact that you forgot something along the way. Always overestimate the amount of memory you need. Then add to that amount. Heck, RAM is cheap!

It is absolutely necessary to go through the exercise of adding up the datatypes and multiplying the number of users. In fact, I recommend adding an additional overhead of 50 percent, just for good measure. I wouldn't be satisfied with 300MB if the example I presented here were my project. In fact, to ensure peak performance, I would not use less than 450MB memory. Because server memory is sold in increments of 128MB, the *bare minimum* memory that I would use is 512MB.

I wouldn't even consider anything less than 1GB RAM on your Web server. In fact, because memory is cheap, I suggest that you add as much as you can afford to account for growth (and the accompanying surge in your expected load). Indeed, it's not uncommon to have 2GB or even 4GB RAM on a Web server.

Double checking disk drives

Two major areas affect your server's disk performance: disk access time and disk configuration. Your server's disk drive(s) must also have enough free space, but that doesn't really affect performance. The only time that free space affects performance is if you don't have enough memory, and Windows has to do a lot of page swapping (from memory to disk). (Check out the preceding section, and don't say that I didn't warn you!)

Here's a rundown on how the major disk issues affect performance:

  ✔ **Disk access time:** Quite simply, the lower the access time, the better performance you get out of your hard drives. Access time (also known as *seek time*) is measured in milliseconds (noted as *ms*). Access time is a factor of how quickly the disk actually rotates on its spindle (revolutions per minute, or *RPMs*) and how quickly the armature can physically find the data that it's looking for on the hard drive. For example, a hard drive that has a 7ms access time is considerably better than one that has a 10ms access time. In fact, a 7ms hard drive is 30 percent faster than a 10ms hard drive.

✔ **Disk configuration:** Disk configuration refers to the number of physical disks in a server and the way in which they are laid out or configured. They can be configured in any number of ways that follow a certain RAID (Redundant Array of Inexpensive Disks) standard, called *levels.* The following RAID levels are typically used in network servers today:

- **RAID 0 (known as *disk striping*).** The operating system writes data blocks that are spread out across multiple drives at the same time, which is great for read and write operations because the work is being done by multiple physical disk drives. However, it doesn't provide for any fault tolerance. If one of the drives fails, you lose the data (at least all the data that's accumulated since the last backup).

- **RAID 1 (known as *disk mirroring*).** The operating system writes the complete data to one drive while making a separate physical copy on another drive. This doesn't help performance but is great for fault tolerance. If one drive fails, the other one has a perfect copy of the data.

- **RAID 5 (known as *disk striping, with parity*).** Disk striping occurs just as it does with RAID 0 but also calculates parity information, which is written to all disks in the array; this is known as a *striped set.* Parity information is a sort of checksum that can be used to recreate data if one of the drives fails. RAID 5 has the performance advantages of striping but also offers fault tolerance features in case a drive fails.

- **RAID 1+0 (known as *disk mirroring, with striping*).** RAID 1+0 is sometimes called RAID 10. (They are synonymous) RAID 10 is the best combination of performance with fault tolerance as well. The only problem is that you need twice as many disks as RAID 0 or RAID 5.

Considering networking issues for performance and security reasons

You may think that you don't have to do anything about networking. Your client uses networking, everyone has access to the Internet, and all is well. However, this is not necessarily the case. You need to be aware of many important aspects of networking regarding your Web services projects. Not only is networking important from a performance perspective, it is also important from a security and access perspective.

The performance of networking is affected by the following factors:

✔ **Network speed:** Network speed is an obvious issue, but one that commonly goes unaddressed. Many corporations have network segments that are only 10MB/Sec, or 10 megabytes per second. It can be expensive to upgrade to 100MB/Sec or even gigabit networks. I'm not suggesting that you recommend an upgrade to your client. but you should be aware of the issues that can affect performance.

✔ **Network bandwidth:** Network bandwidth is also a factor. If you are planning to have lots of traffic to your Web sites (using Web services), you must consider the network bandwidth. If you are only using ISDN, you only get 128KB/Sec per channel that you order. It is possible to combine channels to get more throughput, but this may be cost-prohibitive. You need to find out how much network bandwidth your client has or plans to have in place in order to host Web services. Many ISPs and some corporations have a T-1 (at 1.544 MB/Sec) or a T-3 (at 44.736 MB/Sec), or some fraction thereof.

✔ **Network appliances (firewalls, routers, switches, hubs):** Network appliances can slow down performance. Firewalls, routers, switches, and hubs are all necessary devices, but sometimes they aren't configured correctly, which hurts performance. For example, sometimes one switch goes into a hub. Then the hub is split and goes into another hub. The third hub is split and goes into another hub, and so on. This may seem to work. However, the number of *network collisions* (where data packets are not delivered correctly) increases with this configuration, thus slowing down performance.

A better way to wire your networks to avoid collisions is to have a hub or switch (which is more efficient than a hub) that can handle the correct number of nodes, and wire workstations directly to the source.

Firewalls must be configured correctly (with software), which can be tricky to do. If your client plans to place a Web server behind a firewall or between firewalls (known as a *demilitarized zone,* or *DMZ*), these network appliances must be configured correctly.

✔ **Connection protocols/technologies:** The connection protocols and technologies play a very important factor in network performance. If you are using a Virtual Private Network *(VPN)* to gain access to servers, it must be configured correctly, but it also must not become a bottleneck, either. Based on network traffic, your client may need a different approach or perhaps even multiple VPNs or greater bandwidth.

Something else that you must consider with regard to connection protocols and technologies is Dynamic Name System Resolution, or *DNS.* Because Internet technologies work with TCP/IP, DNS is responsible for translating a user-friendly name, such as `transport80.com` to a TCP/IP address. You must consider where the DNS server exists. If it exists with an ISP (as chosen by the company that sets up the domain name), then you don't have too many choices. However, you may be interested to know how long it takes to resolve the domain name to a TCP/IP address and find the server. You can do this by opening a command prompt. At the command prompt, type the following:

```
ping www.transport80.com
```

In the command prompt window, you can see how long it takes to access the Web server. Substitute any valid domain name for this example Web site. You also want to make sure that no requests time out. The `ping` command will send out four network pings. You want to make sure that you have 0 percent loss. If you have more than that, you may have a problem somewhere in the system.

✔ **Subnets:** Subnets are a factor in performance because two networking subnets are logically separated from each other. This is a security measure. However, even though it's possible for network segments to communicate with each other, translation can be slow. Be aware that this situation can be a factor, so you can find out more information from your client or internal IT department.

For more information about networking, check out *Networking For Dummies,* 6th Edition, by Doug Lowe (published by Wiley Publishing, Inc.).

Dealing with security issues

Security is one of the biggest topics in computing today. The fact that Web services are typically transmitted by using HTTP, the concern over security is great! In fact, any time that you transmit data over the Internet, security becomes a concern. This is such a big issue that Chapter 11 is dedicated entirely to the subject of security.

If any personal data — such as user names, passwords, addresses, credit card information, and so forth — needs to be transmitted over the Internet, it should be encrypted. If it isn't encrypted, anyone with hacking tools will be able to read the data being transmitted across the wire. The same is true on a corporate intranet or extranet. Therefore, encryption becomes a necessity.

Encryption is easily handled by Internet Information Server (IIS), which uses Secure Sockets Layer, or *SSL.* The only thing that you must do to use SSL is to install an SSL certificate that you obtain from a trusted third party. (See Chapter 11 for more on SSL certificates.) After the SSL certificate is installed, clients can access your Web sites or Web services by using the HTTPS protocol, instead of HTTP. (The *S* stands for *secure.*) This SSL certificate is known as a *server certificate.*

Just because you use SSL to encrypt your data doesn't mean that everyone should have access to your Web service. Access is controlled by an authentication scheme. Authentication is covered in more depth in Chapter 11, but just know that you can absolutely control who has access by allowing Active Directory to authenticate.

You also need to know how your Web Services should handle security. To know this, consider these questions:

✔ Can anyone or any system access the Web services?

✔ If access must be restricted, how will you restrict it?

✔ Should you use Active Directory to authenticate users?

✔ Should you use Passport to authenticate users?

✔ Should you limit Web services based on looking up valid users in a database?

The answers to these questions dictate how complex your Web services become. Certainly the easiest thing to do is to allow everyone access to your Web services, but this is not always practical. For example, what if you charge for your Web services usage through an Internet Service Provider (ISP)?

Ensuring interoperability

Interoperability is the concept that disparate computer systems need to be able to talk to each other. For example, if an Oracle database needs to work with a SQL Server database, you have to figure out how to make that happen. Likewise, if you know that your ERP (Enterprise Resource Planning) system has to talk with a CRM (Customer Relationship Management) system, you'd better get cracking.

Many of the interoperability issues that arise from disparate systems talking to each other can be addressed with a Microsoft product called BizTalk. BizTalk allows the mapping of disparate systems by allowing multiple protocols and formats. Internally, BizTalk uses XML to store mappings among these disparate systems.

TIP

Special considerations for Active Directory or Microsoft Passport users

If you're going to use Active Directory, you need to decide how you want to administer adding users and computers. For example, you should consider automating this task, depending on whether you plan to be signing up new customers/users very often. If you are going to use database lookups, you need to account for this functionality in your project plans and to determine the details of how this can work.

On the other hand, if you have Microsoft Passport do the authentication, you guarantee that a user is authenticated, but you don't have to store the user's information at your location. Remember that you need to look at security issues from every possible angle. Check out Chapter 11 for more on authentication.

Interoperability also has an impact on how different technologies have to work with each other. For example, does a .NET component need to invoke COM components? The two technologies are somewhat similar in concept, but not in technology. However, it is very possible to wrap COM components with .NET interfaces. This is called *COM-Interop*. COM-Interop is covered in more detail in Chapter 13.

Deciding What Your Users Have Access To

You must determine how much of your object model you wish to make available over the Internet, which is a concept known as *exposing*. It's important that you remember the concepts of a component, or object, that makes up your object model. You want to expose only an abstracted view of what is necessary to get work done and solve your use cases. Consider the following example.

You have a financial application that decides whether a mortgage should be granted based on specific criteria; you don't expose all the internal implementation details. That's your "secret sauce."

I say that the less you share, the better. Expose only the bare minimum number of objects, along with the bare minimum number of members (properties, methods, and events) needed in order to get work done. In my financial application example, you would expose only the interface that enables a user to create a new application, delete an application, or update an application (depending on its status). You may make the financial application as easy to use as providing a Social Security number only, or you may require a detailed account of all bills and income. But either way, the only thing users should see is the information that tells them what you need. You would not want to reveal anything in your object model that shows the outside world how your calculations are performed.

 By the way, you may be wondering how you would approve an application based on Social Security number only. Because the application approval process is quite involved, you would have to subscribe to other services (possibly Web services) that query all credit reporting agencies and other agencies that provide information, such as overdue alimony or child support. This may be quite difficult to implement, but think of how easy the mortgage application process would be if you only had to expose one Web service that expected only a Social Security number to be passed in. You'd have to fight customers off with a stick.

I discuss constructing your Web services interfaces in Chapter 6, and I show you how to expose those interfaces in Chapter 8.

Chapter 6

Constructing Web Services

· ·

In This Chapter

▶ Creating Web services projects with Visual Studio .NET

▶ Registering your assemblies with the global assembly cache (GAC)

▶ Compiling your Visual Studio .NET projects

· ·

*O*kay, you asked for it. This chapter contains the nitty-gritty information about how to create XML Web services by using Microsoft Visual Studio .NET. This chapter covers both Visual Basic and Visual C#. It is jam-packed with information.

Visual Studio .NET is a comprehensive development environment for designing, constructing, testing, and deploying your applications that target the .NET platform. This includes your Web services projects. Because you can perform all these activities within one program, as you might imagine, it can get quite complex. Not only do you have to know the environment, commands, and menus, but also the language that your Web services will be written in. Although there is much to creating an application that targets any environment, Microsoft has made it as easy as possible to create applications with Visual Studio .NET. This chapter shows you the basics of creating and compiling a Web services project in both Visual Basic .NET and Visual C# .NET. Remember that using multiple languages can be done all within the Visual Studio .NET development environment.

In addition, I show you how to deal with strong-names to enable placing your assemblies into the global assembly cache, or *GAC,* or to allow for the versioning of your assemblies. The GAC is somewhat of an advanced topic, but I cover it here for the sake of completeness.

I assume that you already have some experience in writing either Visual Basic or Visual C# code, but not necessarily for Web services. Unfortunately, because of the complexity of the topic, this chapter is just a drop in the bucket. If you're ready for more in-depth information about using Visual Studio .NET, you can consult many online services, such as the Microsoft Web site. Also, many good books are available on the subject, including *Visual Studio .NET All-in-One Desk Reference For Dummies* by Nitin Pandey and Senthil Nathan (Wiley Publishing, Inc.).

Introducing Visual Studio .NET

Visual Studio .NET is the best and easiest tool for creating all types of projects that target the Microsoft environment, regardless of the particular language you wish to develop in. In other words, Visual Studio .NET is your one-stop shop for development on the .NET platform.

The Visual Studio .NET suite comes in three flavors (with varying price tags):

- ✔ **Professional:** Allows you to create Web services that can be hosted in a Microsoft environment but can be accessed from any other platform. It also allows you to create Web-based, database (MSDE only — a desktop version of SQL Server), Windows, and thin-client applications, such as those for the PocketPC. The Professional edition also includes the Visual Basic .NET, Visual C# .NET, Visual C++ .NET, Visual J# .NET languages, and also includes support for additional third-party languages.

- ✔ **Enterprise Developer:** Has everything the Professional version has, plus the support needed for Enterprise-class development. Additional support includes Visual SourceSafe (for checking in/out code), Application Center Test (see Chapter 7), Enterprise templates (for rapid application development), and Visual Studio Analyzer (for identifying performance problems). Additionally, the Enterprise edition includes support for more than MSDE. It supports the full version of SQL Server.

- ✔ **Enterprise Architect:** Has everything that the Professional and Enterprise Developer versions have, plus special tools for designing applications. Such tools include Uniform Modeling Language (UML) application modeling tools (for designing applications with use cases), Visio database modeling (for visually creating database models), and a special version of BizTalk server (for integrating with trading partners). Additionally, you can create your own Enterprise project templates that allow you to share tried and true practices with your team.

So, what exactly does Visual Studio .NET do for you? Well, it does quite a bit. In its simplest form, Visual Studio. NET allows you to create Web services projects as well as other types of projects. But you knew that.

Here are a couple of examples of Web services that you can create with Visual Studio .NET:

- ✔ Create a financial calculator that can be used (or called) from across the Internet.

- ✔ Create a simple Web service that looks up user information (name, address, and so on) in a Microsoft SQL Server database, based on the user's ID and returns that information back to the calling program.

  Although this is a very simple example, it illustrates a few key points:

- How to create a function that encapsulates look-up functionality
- How to access a database using Visual Studio .NET
- How to expose a function to the outside world as a Web service

Throughout this chapter, I explain exactly how to create a Web services project to perform the look-up functionality that I just described. If that isn't enough, I show you how to create the Web services project not only in Visual Basic .NET but also in Visual C# .NET.

Getting Visual Studio .NET up and Running

All of the examples in this chapter require that Visual Studio .NET be installed and running on your computer. After you install Visual Studio .NET, you can run it by following these simple steps:

1. **To open Visual Studio .NET, choose Start➪Programs➪Microsoft Visual Studio .NET➪Microsoft Visual Studio .NET.**

2. **Click New Project.**

3. **Choose the desired language folder.**

   A dialog box appears, as shown in Figure 6-1. The folders that are presented depend on the languages that you selected when you installed Visual Studio .NET. Figure 6-1 shows two language folders: Visual Basic Projects and Visual C# Projects. This is because these are the only two languages that I installed. If you have installed other languages, such as Visual C++ .NET or Visual J# .NET, you'll see those language folders also.

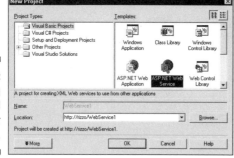

Figure 6-1: Choosing the desired language for the project.

4. **Click ASP.NET Web service.**

   This option is available for every installed language, including Visual Basic .NET and Visual C# .NET.

5. **Enter the location of your Web service.**

   The location is an HTTP Web address. All folders will be created automatically after you enter the name of the server and Web service name. By default, the last server that you have connected to will be displayed, along with a Web service folder called `WebService1`.

6. **Click OK.**

Anatomy of a Web Service Project

You should consider a couple of things when creating your Web service projects. First, you must consider the structure, or *anatomy*, of your Visual Studio .NET source code files. When you create a Web service project within Visual Studio .NET (in any language), some code is going to be generated for you automatically. YEAH! It is helpful to understand what the files that are automatically generated do and how/why you would alter them if necessary. Because many files are automatically created in your default Web services projects, you really should know what they are used for. After all, at least one of the files that is created automatically will need to be modified by you. Do you know which one? You will after you read this section.

You must also consider the configuration of the Web server itself. The configuration of the Web server affects the behavior of your projects even without code! Therefore, you must understand how these settings can be tweaked on the Web server to affect security, performance, and more. Because this chapter concentrates on constructing your applications, the Web server configuration is not covered here. You must visit Chapter 11 for more information on security and Chapter 12 for Web server configuration.

After Visual Studio .NET creates your Web services project, all folders and necessary files will be created for you. Again, this is true regardless of the language that you use to create your project within Visual Studio .NET.

Table 6-1 lists the files that are created by default with either Visual Basic .NET or Visual C# .NET. The *Web_Service_Name* shown in the table is the name that you give your Web services project when you create it.

Table 6-1		Project Files That Visual Studio .NET Creates Automatically
Language	*File/Folder Name*	*Description*
Visual C#	`AssemblyInfo.cs`	Contains information about how to build the compiled Visual C# assembly.
Visual Basic	`AssemblyInfo.vb`	Contains information about how to build the compiled Visual Basic assembly.
Visual Basic/ Visual C#	`Bin`	Folder that contains compiled output files.
Visual Basic/ Visual C#	`Global.asax`	Contains a pointer to the `Global.asax` code file (either `vb` or `cs`).
Visual C#	`Global.asax.cs`	Initialization code for the Visual C# Web service project.
Visual Basic/ Visual C#	`Global.asax.resx`	Contains general schema information about the project.
Visual Basic	`Global.asax.vb`	Initialization code for the Visual Basic Web service project.
Visual Basic/ Visual C#	`Service1.asmx`	Default Web service, called Service1, which contains a pointer to the `Service1.asmx` code file (either `vb` or `cs`).
Visual C#	`Service1.asmx.cs`	Visual C# file that contains the code for the Service1 Web service.
Visual Basic/ Visual C#	`Service1.asmx.resx`	Contains Web service schema information.
Visual Basic	`Service1.asmx.vb`	Visual Basic file that contains the code for the Service1 Web service.
Visual Basic/ Visual C#	`Web.config`	Contains configuration information about the Web service to be used by the .NET Framework at runtime. `Web.config` files are covered in Chapter 2 and Chapter 7.
Visual C#	*`Web_Service_Name.`* `csproj`	Contains information about the files that comprise the Visual C# project.

(continued)

Table 6-1 *(continued)*

Language	File/Folder Name	Description
Visual C#	Web_Service_Name.csproj.webinfo	Contains location information for your Visual C# project file.
Visual Basic	Web_Service_Name.vbproj	Contains information about the files that comprise the Visual Basic project.
Visual Basic	Web_Service_Name.vbproj.webinfo	Contains location information for your Visual Basic project file.
Visual Basic/ Visual C#file.	Web_Service_Name.vsdisco	Web service discovery DISCO files are covered in Chapter 9.

Getting Up Close and Personal with the IDE

After you understand what each of the default files do in your Visual Basic projects (as discussed in "Introducing Visual Studio .NET", earlier in this chapter), you're ready to take a peek at the Visual Studio .NET development environment, called the *integrated development environment,* or IDE. The Visual Studio .NET IDE is shown in Figure 6-2.

Getting to know IDE lingo

Here is a list of important IDE concepts:

✓ **Solutions:** Visual Studio .NET (and prior versions of Visual Studio) allow you to load more than one project at one time. All projects come together in the IDE into what is known as a *solution.* For example, a solution called WebServices may have two Web services projects loaded, one in Visual Basic and one in Visual C#. In fact, you can load into the IDE any number of projects that are built in any .NET language, and roll them into a single solution.

You accomplish the tasks of viewing, controlling, and managing the projects that comprise your solutions and projects in the area of the IDE called the *Solution Explorer.* Refer to Figure 6-2 to see what the Solution Explorer looks like with two projects loaded. Figure 6-3 gives you a closer look at the Solution Explorer toolbar.

Loaded files   Current file   Solution Explorer

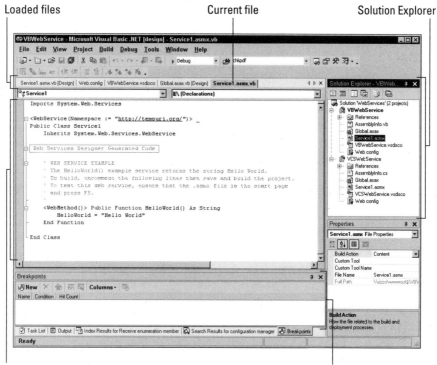

Figure 6-2:
Visual
Studio .NET
IDE.

Code and design area   Dynamic area (Output and breakpoints)

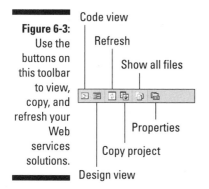

Figure 6-3:
Use the
buttons on
this toolbar
to view,
copy, and
refresh your
Web
services
solutions.

Code view

Refresh

Show all files

Properties

Copy project

Design view

✔ **Assemblies:** The basic unit of compilation and deployment in .NET is an
assembly. All of the code that you write is compiled into one or more
files that you can run, or *execute,* on the .NET Framework.

Assemblies appear in the form of DLL or EXE files. In Visual Basic and Visual C#, one project can have only one assembly. However, with Visual C++, you can create multifile assemblies. Assemblies can be either *private* or *global:*

- If an assembly is global, it's in a location called the *global assembly cache,* or GAC. Global assemblies are available machine wide, which is useful in sharing assemblies among multiple applications.

- If it is private, the assembly is located in the `bin` directory of your application.

✔ **Deployment:** To add an assembly to the GAC on a production computer, you must (or at least, you *should*) create an installation program, also known as a *deployment* (which is covered further in Chapter 8).

The reason that you should deploy with an installation program is that in order for Windows (all versions) to know when a shared library is no longer used, Windows keeps track of an internal counter that indicates how many programs need the shared library to function. Each installation that needs a shared library increases this counter by one. Each un-installation decrements this counter by one.

When the counter has a value of zero, the shared library is no longer needed and you can remove it. If you don't use an installation program to deploy your application, this counter won't automatically be incremented or decremented.

To register an assembly in the GAC on a development computer, you use the `gacutil.exe` program. The GAC is located in a folder named Assembly (imagine that!) under the folder where Windows is installed. On my Windows XP computer, my GAC is located in this folder:

```
C:\WINDOWS\Assembly
```

✔ **Strong-naming:** You must do one other thing before adding your assemblies to the GAC. They must be *strong-named.* You create a cryptographic pair of keys, which will be used to guarantee that the name of your assemblies are unique. Uniqueness avoids confusion and ambiguity in assembly names.

Adding an assembly to a GAC

To add an assembly to the GAC, follow this procedure:

1. **Create the cryptographic set of keys into a filename.**

   You create a cryptographic set of keys outside the Visual Studio environment; to do so, you use a program called SN.EXE. This program is installed with the .NET Framework software developer's kit (SDK). You can download the SDK from Microsoft at

```
http://msdn.microsoft.com/netframework/downloads/
         howtoget.asp
```

After you have the SDK installed, open a command prompt window and navigate to the `bin` directory of wherever you installed the SDK. Mine is installed at this location:

```
C:\Program Files\Microsoft Visual Studio
  .NET\FrameworkSDK\Bin
```

Then, create the pair of keys into a single file that you name with an SNK file extension (which stands for Strong-Named Key) using the SN.EXE program. This file will be used later in this chapter. Here's an example of how to generate the key pair file:

```
sn.exe -k KeyPair.snk
```

Figure 6-4 shows you what this looks like in a command prompt window.

Figure 6-4:
Command
prompt
window
showing
how to
create a
strong-
named
key pair.

2. **Choose a programming language and use it to assign the filename to the assembly.**

   Because this task is performed slightly differently, depending on the language that you use in your Web services projects, refer to the section "Strong-names" under the "Using Visual Basic .NET" or "Using Visual C# with Visual Studio .NET" sections.

3. **Build your project.**

   See the "Compiling Visual Studio .NET Applications" section, later in this chapter, to see how to build your project.

4. **Use the GACUTIL program to install your assembly into the GAC.**

   The GACUTIL program is located in the folder where the .NET framework is installed. On my computer, it is installed in this folder:

```
C:\WINDOWS\Microsoft.NET\Framework\v1.0.3705
```

Open a command prompt window and navigate to the folder where the .NET Framework is installed.

Type **GACUTIL /i** (the /i switch indicates that this is an installation) followed by the full path to where your compiled assembly is located, along with the filename. You can even use a UNC path, like this:

```
gacutil /i \\rizzo\c$\Inetpub\wwwroot\VBWebService\bin\VBWebService.dll
```

The preceding line installs the VBWebService assembly located on the server named rizzo in the VBWebService\bin folder on the Web server into the GAC.

Figure 6-5 shows you what this looks like in a command prompt window.

Figure 6-5:
The command prompt window showing how to register an assembly in the GAC.

If you wanted to remove an assembly from the GAC, you don't need the full path again; you only need the name of the assembly (without the file extension), but this time, use the /u switch, like this:

```
gacutil /u VBWebService
```

Creating multiple versions of assemblies

Built into all assemblies is a *manifest,* which lists critical data about the contents of the assembly. One such critical piece of data is *versioning* information. If you want to implement versioning of assemblies, you must create strong-names for them (refer to the discussion about strong-named assemblies earlier in this chapter).

Versioning allows for like assemblies to exist side-by-side in different versions. This is useful if you want to make sure that a version of the code is supported by an older application (this is called *backward support* or *backward compatibility*), but you also have to make many changes to it for newer versions.

Whenever an application or the operating system requests an assembly, it attempts to *bind* to a specific version of the assembly. (That is, it tries to make sure that it always opens the appropriate version of the assembly by default.) However, just like most things in .NET, you can configure the binding on your own. Multiple configuration files are involved in determining the resulting version of the file that will be bound.

The actual version number of an assembly that you compile is located in the `AssemblyInfo.vb` file (for Visual Basic projects) or `AssemblyInfo.cs` file (for Visual C# projects). Whether you use Visual Basic or C#, the file contains virtually the same information; in my example, I show you the Visual Basic version.

The `AssemblyInfo.vb` file already contains a reference to the Assembly classes that reside in the `system.reflection` namespace. *Namespaces* categorize groups of functions, known as classes, into logical classifications or libraries. Namespaces also ensure that like-named classes are guaranteed to be unique by providing a location or scope for the classes. Namespaces are discussed further in Chapter 3. The namespace reference enables you to configure the assembly version with a single line of code:

```
<Assembly: AssemblyVersion("1.0.*")>
```

The version of your code can be changed at any time and will be compiled into your assembly as part of the manifest. The format of this version number is:

```
Major.Minor.Build.Revision
```

The version numbers in a numbering scheme are shown as being more significant on the left *(Major)* and less significant on the right *(Revision)*. For example, Version `2.0.1.0` is a higher version number (and thus more significant) than `1.1.0.5`.

Revision numbers are sometimes called *builds.* The two terms can be used interchangeably.

You decide the numbering scheme for your own versions. After you do, enter the version number and compile your application.

If your organization doesn't use the build and revision parts of the version numbering scheme shown earlier, then simply place an asterisk in place of the build and revision numbers to indicate that you won't be using them. In other words, a valid version where you do not use the build and revision numbers would be `1.0.*`.

Then follow the rules for creating strong-named assemblies by referring to the discussion on strong-names earlier in this chapter.

Using code-behind pages

One of the great things about Web development with Visual Studio .NET is the ability to separate the visual elements of a form from the code elements. The creators of the Visual Basic programming language always had this concept in mind. For example, suppose that you had a file named `Form1.frm`. This form allows you to configure graphical elements, such as text boxes and images, in the Design view. It also allows you to open the form in Code view and start coding away.

However, there is one major drawback to plain-vanilla Visual Basic: The Visual Basic Code view and Design view are both stored in the same file, making it impossible for one person to work on code while another person works on the graphical elements.

Thank goodness for Visual Studio .NET. Problem solved. Because Visual Studio .NET allows any language to have a *code-behind* file, you can have your cake and eat it too. Even if you're on a diet or don't like cake.

So what exactly is *a code-behind page?* Basically, it's a separate file. You've got your graphical file, which simply contains a pointer to the code file. You create a pointer by using the `Codebehind` attribute.

If you create a new Visual Studio .NET Web service, named `WebService1` and open the `Service1.asmx` file in a text editor, you'll see this in Visual Basic:

```
<%@ WebService Language="vb" Codebehind="Service1.asmx.vb"
         Class="VBWebService.Service1" %>
```

Likewise, you'll see this very similar pointer in Visual C#:

```
<%@ WebService Language="c#" Codebehind="Service1.asmx.cs"
         Class="VCSWebService.Service1" %>
```

In either case, the `Codebehind` attribute points to another file that contains code, such as the ASMX file that's shown in the preceding code fragments.

Using Visual Basic.NET

The main file for your Visual Basic Web service is automatically created for you when you create a Web service project. By default, this file is called `Service1.asmx.vb`. Refer to Figure 6-2 to see this file in the `VBWebService` project.

When writing your Web services code, you have to be concerned with the following three areas in your code:

✔ Namespace

✔ Auto-generated code

✔ Custom code

The following sections discuss these three areas in greater detail.

Changing namespaces

A *namespace* is automatically generated the second you create a Web service. (A namespace is a unique online address for a file. Namespaces are written in XML.) The default namespace automatically entered is `http://tempuri.org`. However, this is only a placeholder. The first thing that you should do is change the namespace that's associated with your Web service.

I don't recommend that you use the temporary namespace in production because everyone who creates a Web services project will also have this namespace automatically entered. Namespaces allow you to uniquely define your Web service. In other words, if two Web services contain the same interface, they can actually be differentiated by having a unique namespace. My company uses the namespace `http://webservices.transport80.com` for its Web services. This way, no matter who creates any Web service, it is guaranteed to be unique. (I discuss namespaces in more depth in Chapter 3.)

As an example, if you create a Web service project in Visual Basic .NET, a file with an ASMX extension will be created automatically for you. Within that file is a shell of code, known as a *stub,* that defines the basic elements needed for a Web service. All you need to do is add the code specific to your own Web service. One of the bits of code that is automatically entered into the stub of code is the namespace declaration that you should change. Before you change it, the temporary namespace is used and looks like this:

```
<WebService(Namespace := "http://tempuri.org/")>
```

Then you change the default namespace to use your own, to look something like this (although this is my namespace — you must use your own):

```
<WebService(Namespace :=
        "http://WebServices.transport80.com/")>
```

Examining autogenerated code

Some initialization code is automatically generated for you when you create your Web service project. Generally, you don't need to alter this code, but it is useful to see what this initialization code does. The reason why you need to know about this initialization code is that you need to recognize where it is in the automatically generated file. If you think that this code isn't necessary and you delete it, your application won't compile . . . so you must know where the code is inside the file and its main purpose.

This area of code is not shown by default, even though it does exist in the file and does get compiled into your project. Code is divided into *regions;* you can expand or collapse regions so that you don't have to always view and scroll through all the code if it doesn't change very often or it is very long.

To view the region that contains autogenerated initialization code, click the plus sign (+) located just to the left of the region; this code is defined as Web Services Designer Generated Code. Clicking this sign displays the code shown in Listing 6-1.

Listing 6-1: Autogenerated Web services code

```
#Region " Web Services Designer Generated Code "

  Public Sub New()
    MyBase.New()

    'This call is required by the Web Services Designer.
    InitializeComponent()

    'Add your own initialization code after the InitializeComponent() call

  End Sub

  'Required by the Web Services Designer
  Private components As System.ComponentModel.IContainer

  'NOTE: The following procedure is required by the Web Services Designer
  'It can be modified using the Web Services Designer.
  'Do not modify it using the code editor.
  <System.Diagnostics.DebuggerStepThrough()> Private Sub InitializeComponent()
    components = New System.ComponentModel.Container()
  End Sub

  Protected Overloads Overrides Sub Dispose(ByVal disposing As Boolean)
    'CODEGEN: This procedure is required by the Web Services Designer
    'Do not modify it using the code editor.
    If disposing Then
      If Not (components Is Nothing) Then
        components.Dispose()
      End If
    End If
    MyBase.Dispose(disposing)
  End Sub

#End Region
```

If you are new to Visual Studio .NET, the code in Listing 6-1 may look complex. You should use caution when altering this code because it is necessary to create your Web services object when it is called by an external program or destroyed when it is no longer needed (to save system memory).

Creating custom code

When you create a Web service project, Visual Studio .NET automatically places very simple Web service code into the code editor and comments it out (so that if you compile the Web service, commented code isn't included):

```
<WebMethod()> Public Function HelloWorld() As String
  HelloWorld = "Hello World"
End Function
```

This code simply declares a function, called HelloWorld, and returns the string "Hello World" back to the calling program. This function takes no *arguments,* as noted by the empty parentheses. An *argument* is a value that is passed into a function and is used to perform some action or processing within the function. For example, if you have a function named Calculate, you may need to declare two arguments that are used within the Calculate function itself. Because functions that you create perform some action, they are referred to as *methods.* The very term *method* indicates some action will take place. Therefore, a Calculate function would be known as the method Calculate. If the function is called over the Web, it's known as a *Web method.*

If you have done any programming in Visual Basic (even as far back as Visual Basic Version 1.0), you notice that this is exactly the same way that you've always written your code, except for one thing — the <WebMethod()> directive.

The <WebMethod()> directive indicates to Visual Basic that a particular function will be made available as a Web service method. When you compile and run your application, you'll be able to call this function over the Web.

If you press F5 and navigate through the test page to invoke your new Web service, you arrive at a page similar to the one shown in Figure 6-6. The server name and Web service may be different, depending on the names of your files, folders, and server. (Testing your Visual Studio .NET applications is covered in Chapter 7.)

Of course, this test page is exceedingly simple. In practice, your Web services may be quite complex. However, the concepts remain the same. The difficult task of configuring all of the software, including XML and SOAP, is handled automatically by Visual Studio .NET. Read on to find out how to add more-complex functionality to your Visual Basic projects.

```
<?xml version="1.0" encoding="utf-8" ?>
<string xmlns="http://tempuri.org/">Hello World</string>
```

Done   Local intranet

Figure 6-6:
Web service
test shown
in Internet
Explorer.

Using base classes

One main advantage of writing your Web services applications on the .NET platform is being able to use the huge set of base classes that the .NET Framework provides. *Base classes* are a set of functions and interfaces that have been written by the good developers at Microsoft. Base classes automatically handle common tasks so that you don't have to. The following are examples of base classes:

✔ `System.Math` class: Contains common math and trigonometric functions, such as Sin, Tan, and Cos.

✔ `System.Data` class: Contains generic functionality needed to access databases, such as Microsoft SQL Server, Microsoft Access, and others.

✔ `System.Data.SQLClient` class: Contains specific functionality needed to access Microsoft SQL Server only.

✔ `System.Windows.Forms` class: Contains functions needed to manipulate forms within Windows.

Each base class is located within a namespace (see earlier discussion on namespaces). To access a desired base class, you must indicate to Visual Studio .NET where to find the functions and classes that you wish to access. In fact, you have two choices to indicate where your classes are located:

✔ Set a reference to the namespace with the `Imports` keyword. For example, if you need to use the functions contained within the `System.Data` class, you can use the `Imports` keyword like this:

```
Imports System.Data.SqlClient
```

Then, you can just call any of the functions within the `System.Data.SqlClient` class, such as `SqlCommand`, as if those functions were part of the development environment, like this:

```
Dim cmd As SqlCommand = MyDB.CreateCommand()
cmd.CommandText = "SELECT * FROM MyTable"
```

✔ Fully qualify the name of the base class that you want to use every time you use the base class in your code. When compared to the preceding code example, a fully-qualified base class name would contain the name-space, like this:

```
Dim cmd As System.Data.SqlClient.SqlCommand = MyDB.CreateCommand()
cmd.CommandText = "SELECT * FROM MyTable"
```

Notice that the same line of code uses a fully qualified syntax to reference the same `SqlCommand` function.

Thousands of classes are available through the .NET Framework set of base classes. It's best to consult the online documentation to find out which classes belong to which namespaces, along with arguments and usage. For more information about accessing data, refer to Chapter 2.

Calling other Web services

Okay, so you're writing a Web service that the public will use. Great! But what if your Web service depends on results from another Web service? You can do that with a *Web reference.* In other words, you call a Web service by using a Web reference.

To do so, you simply set a reference to another Web service and call it as if it was any function. Chapter 9 shows how to call, or *consume,* a Web reference.

Error handling

Error-handling capabilities in prior versions of Visual Studio were primitive. In Visual Studio .NET, error-handling functions are greatly improved. Visual Studio .NET uses the same type of error handling that has always existed in C++, which is sometimes referred to as a `Try...Catch...Finally` block — and which, incidentally, works really well. Error handling in Visual Studio .NET is so named because it is made up of `Try`, `Catch`, and `Finally` statements. The syntax for these statements is shown below:

```
Try
   [ TryStatements ]
[ Catch [ Exception [ As Type ] ] [ When Expression ]
   [ CatchStatements ] ]
[ Exit Try ]
...
[ Finally
   [ FinallyStatements ] ]
End Try
```

Where the following substitutions can be made:

✔ *TryStatements* is the set of code that you are testing, or trying to run without errors.

✔ *Exception* is an optional parameter that indicates which specific exception you want to handle. You can use multiple *CatchStatements.*

✔ *Type* is an optional datatype of the *Exception* parameter.

✔ *Expression* is an optional parameter that indicates the Catch block will only execute when certain conditions evaluate to True. This parameter makes for extremely versatile error handling.

✔ *CatchStatements* are one or more optional statements that are executed when the expressions specified in the Catch block are "caught."

✔ *FinallyStatements* are one or more optional statements that are executed after all other error handling is processed. The *FinallyStatements* are always executed, regardless of any specific error condition or lack thereof.

The Try...Catch...Finally statement block is used to handle certain conditions while the program is running in your production environment. It is not used to forgo testing. On the other hand, testing allows you to verify that your Try...Catch...Finally statement block is working correctly. To see an example of how to use the Try...Catch...Finally statement block, look at Listing 6-2, later in this chapter.

Strong-names

After you generate a key file that contains the cryptographic key pairs, you indicate to your project where this file is stored. In my example, I didn't move it from the default location, which is where the SN.EXE program resides.

In Visual Basic, open the project file AssemblyInfo.vb. Assign the AssemblyKeyFile attribute with the full path and name of the cryptographic key pair file that you generated. Make sure that you have an entry in this file that looks like this:

```
<Assembly: AssemblyKeyFile("c:\Program Files\Microsoft Visual
          Studio .NET\FrameworkSDK\Bin\KeyPair.snk")>
```

Of course, you have to substitute your path and filename to make yours work.

An Example Web Service Created by Using Visual Basic .NET

So far in this chapter, I've shown you how to do a bunch of things in Visual Basic; I've also referred you to other chapters where you can see how certain things, such as data access, are done. Listing 6-2 is an example of how to build a Web service, called WebService1, with a method called GetNameForUserID. This method takes one argument, which is the ID of the user, to look up in a database. The database name is db1, with a UserID and password both of LookupUser in a table (or initial catalog) called WS.

Listing 6-2: Using Visual Basic to create a simple Web service

```
Imports System.Web.Services
Imports System.Data.SqlClient

<WebService(Namespace:="http://tempuri.org/")> _
Public Class Service1
    Inherits System.Web.Services.WebService


#Region " Web Services Designer Generated Code "

    Public Sub New()
        MyBase.New()

        'This call is required by the Web Services Designer.
        InitializeComponent()

        'Add your own initialization code after the InitializeComponent() call

    End Sub

    'Required by the Web Services Designer
    Private components As System.ComponentModel.IContainer

    'NOTE: The following procedure is required by the Web Services Designer
    'It can be modified using the Web Services Designer.
    'Do not modify it using the code editor.
    <System.Diagnostics.DebuggerStepThrough()> Private Sub InitializeComponent()
        components = New System.ComponentModel.Container()
    End Sub

    Protected Overloads Overrides Sub Dispose(ByVal disposing As Boolean)
        'CODEGEN: This procedure is required by the Web Services Designer
        'Do not modify it using the code editor.
        If disposing Then
            If Not (components Is Nothing) Then
                components.Dispose()
            End If
        End If
        MyBase.Dispose(disposing)
    End Sub

#End Region

    <WebMethod()> Public Function GetNameForUserID(ByVal UserID As String) As
            String

    'Initialize return variable
        Dim sName As String = "Name Not Found"
        Try
            Dim oConn As SqlConnection = New SqlConnection("Data Source=db1;User
                ID=LookupUser;Password=LookupUser;Initial Catalog=WS")
```

(continued)

Listing 6-2: (continued)

```
        'open connection to database
        oConn.Open()

        'prepare SQL command
        Dim oCmd As SqlCommand = New SqlCommand("SELECT FirstName, LastName
          FROM [User] WHERE LoginID = '" & UserID & "'", oConn)

        'retrieve data into data reader object
        Dim oReader As SqlDataReader = oCmd.ExecuteReader

        'read results
        Do While oReader.Read()
            'assign results to sName variable
            sName = oReader.Item("FirstName") & " " &
          oReader.Item("LastName")
        Loop

        'close objects
        oReader.Close()
        oConn.Close()
    Catch
        sName = "Error"
    Finally
        'return data from Web Service
      GetNameForUserID = sName
    End Try

  End Function

End Class
```

Notice the error handler in the code. The `Try` block executes the code to access the database. The `Catch` block doesn't look for anything specific; it just catches any and all errors. If an error occurs, the name `Error` returns. For this Web service, it isn't important to return a detailed error message. The only thing that matters is that a specific name wasn't retrieved. The `Finally` block is always executed to ensure that a name is returned back to the calling application.

Using Visual C# with Visual Studio .NET

Using Visual C# is very similar to using Visual Basic except that the syntax is different. The concepts are basically the same. The main file for your Visual C# Web service is also automatically created for you when you created a Web service project using Visual C# as the language. It is called, by default, `Service1.asmx.cs`. This file is shown in the `VCSWebService` project shown earlier in Figure 6-2.

Because most of the concepts are basically the same, the detail shown in this section is not as great as was shown in the section "Using Visual Basic .NET."

Strong-names

To generate a strong-name in Visual C#, you need to use the SN.EXE program. Here's an example of how the `AssemblyKeyFile` attribute is used in Visual C# in the `AssemblyInfo.cs` file:

```
[assembly: AssemblyKeyFile("c:\\Program Files\\Microsoft
           Visual Studio
           .NET\\FrameworkSDK\\Bin\\KeyPair.snk")]
```

Notice that, within the pathname, the Visual C# syntax uses double backslashes instead of single backslashes like in Visual Basic. This is just a syntactical difference because Visual C# considers the backslash character to be an escape character for specialized functionality. That's why two backslashes are needed; two backslashes tell the compiler that it is not an escape character (such as \n, which is for a new line).

An example Web service created by using C# .NET

Now that you've seen how to create a sample Web service in Visual Basic .NET, how'd you like to see how to do the same stuff in Visual C# .NET? To illustrate the differences between the Visual Basic .NET project and the Visual C# .NET project, I show you the same Web service project for looking up user information in a database. Listing 6-3 is an example of how to build a Web service, called `WebService1`, with the same method, called `GetNameForUserID`. Again, this method takes one argument, which is the ID of the user, to look up in a database. The database name is db1, with a UserID and Password both of `LookupUser` in a table (or initial catalog) called `WS`.

I need to point out a few things that are different in the Visual C# code in Listing 6-3 as compared to the Visual Basic code in Listing 6-2. (Although if you compare the two listings, you see that the same fundamental objects are being used.) The following items are different with the Visual C# code:

- **Base class declarations:** Base classes in Visual Basic are declared with the `using` keyword and not the `Imports` keyword.

- **Case sensitivity:** Visual C# code is case sensitive, so a keyword, such as `Using`, is not the same as `using`.

- **Namespace declaration:** The namespace is automatically declared as the same name of the Web service.

✔ **Constructor/Destructor code:** The concept of the Constructor/Destructor code (which controls how the Web service is created and destroyed) is the same, but the implementation is slightly different because of language syntax. This code is between the #region...#endregion tags.

✔ **Comments:** Commented code is indicated with a double-slash (//) instead of an apostrophe (also known as a *tick*).

✔ **SqlDataReader:** The SqlDataReader object works basically the same in Visual C# as it does in Visual Basic, except that the data can't be accessed by using the Item method the way you used it in Visual Basic. Therefore, the GetString method is used instead.

✔ **Try...Catch...Finally:** Notice that the Finally block is omitted. This is because, in Visual C#, you can't return from a procedure within this block like you did in Visual Basic.

Listing 6-3:   Using C# to create a simple Web service

```
using System;
using System.Collections;
using System.ComponentModel;
using System.Data;
using System.Data.SqlClient;
using System.Diagnostics;
using System.Web;
using System.Web.Services;

namespace VCSWebService
{
  public class Service1 : System.Web.Services.WebService
  {
      public Service1()
      {
          //CODEGEN: This call is required by the ASP.NET Web Services Designer
          InitializeComponent();
      }

      #region Component Designer generated code

      //Required by the Web Services Designer
      private IContainer components = null;

      /// <summary>
      /// Required method for Designer support - do not modify
      /// the contents of this method with the code editor.
      /// </summary>
      private void InitializeComponent()
      {
      }

      /// <summary>
```

```
/// Clean up any resources being used.
/// </summary>
protected override void Dispose( bool disposing )
{
    if(disposing && components != null)
    {
        components.Dispose();
    }
    base.Dispose(disposing);
}

#endregion


[WebMethod]
public string GetNameForUserID(string UserID)
{
    //Initialize return variable
    String sName = "Name Not Found";

    try
    {
        SqlConnection oConn = new SqlConnection("Data Source=db1;User
          ID=LookupUser;Password=LookupUser;Initial Catalog=WS");

        //open connection to database
        oConn.Open();

        //prepare SQL command
        SqlCommand oCmd = new SqlCommand("SELECT FirstName, LastName FROM
          [User] WHERE LoginID = '" + UserID + "'", oConn);

        //retrieve data into data reader object
        SqlDataReader oReader = oCmd.ExecuteReader();

        //read results
        while (oReader.Read())
        {
          //assign results to sName variable
          sName = oReader.GetString(0) + " " + oReader.GetString(1);
        }

        //close objects
        oReader.Close();
        oConn.Close();
    }
    catch
    {
        sName = "Error";
```

(continued)

Listing 6-3: (continued)

```
        }

        //return data from Web Service
        return sName;

    }
  }
}
```

Compiling Visual Studio .NET Applications

If you have ever built Web applications with Visual InterDev, you know that all you had to do to make a change to an ASP page was to save it. Because ASP was an interpretive environment, you did not have to compile your pages. Internet Information Server (IIS, Version 5 and earlier) simply read the page at runtime when a user requested the page, and all was right with the world.

However, Visual Studio .NET is used to create applications that target the .NET runtime. Because the .NET runtime (along with IIS Version 6) now runs compiled code, you now must compile all changes in your Visual Studio .NET applications in order for them to take effect. Compiling an application is also known as *building* an application.

Like most things in Visual Studio .NET, compiling your application is quite simple. However, before I dive into that, you must understand the concept of configurations. A configuration is controlled and administered by the Configuration Manager.

Configuration Manager

A *configuration* is a concept that indicates which projects in a solution are to be included in a build. This allows you to easily control development, test, and production environments. To use the Configuration Manager, follow these steps:

1. **Open a Visual Studio .NET solution.**

2. **Open the Configuration Manager.**

   You can open this manager by choosing the Build⇨Configuration Manager menu. Doing so brings up the dialog box shown in Figure 6-7.

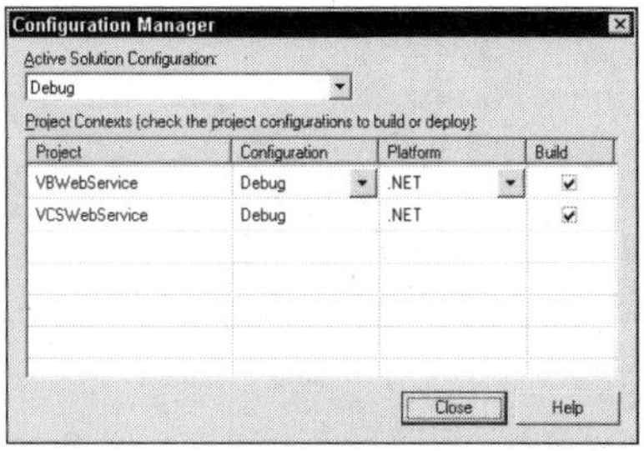

Figure 6-7:
Config-
uration
Manager
dialog box.

3. **Select the Active Solution Configuration.**

   In the drop-down list, you see the currently selected Active Solution Configuration. By default, you have the choice of Debug and Release.

4. **Select options for each project.**

   In the grid, for the Active Solution Configuration currently selected, you can choose from the following options, one for each project:

   - **Project:** The projects listed in this column are not configurable because each project in your solution is listed here.

   - **Configuration:** Although it may seem redundant to have the config-uration column within the currently selected Active Solution Configuration, it is not. It is possible that, for example, you want the Debug Active Solution Configuration, but for that configuration, one of the projects should be built using the Release configuration. However, this is not usually the case. Usually, each configuration will match the Active Solution Configuration.

   - **Platform:** Currently, one platform is available to be built, so it is automatically selected. It is the .NET platform.

   - **Build:** If checked, this indicates that the specific project in the solution should be built for the currently selected Active Solution Configuration.

5. **Click Close to save your changes.**

Project dependencies and build order

It is quite possible that you have multiple projects loaded into your solution. Additionally, it is also possible that you must build one project before the other because the second project relies on code that is in the first project. Therefore, you must indicate to Visual Studio .NET the order in which the projects must be built, and you must clarify the dependencies on those pro-jects. To indicate these dependencies and build order, follow these steps:

1. **Open a Visual Studio .NET solution.**

2. **Open the Project Dependencies dialog box by choosing the Project⇨Project Dependencies menu.**

   This menu brings up the dialog box shown in Figure 6-8.

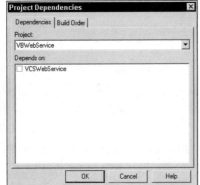

Figure 6-8:
Project
Depend-
encies
dialog box.

3. **Select the project that has dependencies.**

   In the project drop-down list, select the project that depends on other projects. After you choose this project, you see a list of the other projects in your solution.

4. **Check the dependencies.**

   If the currently selected project depends on one or more other projects in the solution, simply check the dependent projects.

5. **View the build order.**

   Click the Build Order tab. Clicking this tab brings up the dialog box shown in Figure 6-9.

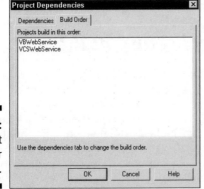

Figure 6-9:
Project
Build Order
dialog box.

You'll see a list of all the projects in your solution in the order that they will be built. If you want to change the order, you must change the dependencies. For example, `Project1` depends on `Project2`. `Project2` depends on `Project3`. You configure the dependencies as shown in Steps 3 and 4. Can you guess what the build order will be? It will be `Project3` and then `Project2` and finally `Project1`.

Building your project

After you configure the dependencies for your projects, building them is very simple. You have four options:

- ✔ **Build Solution:** Builds the entire solution, including all projects, but only compiles the pieces that need to be compiled.

- ✔ **Rebuild Solution:** Builds the entire solution, including all projects, but recompiles everything even if it didn't change since the last build.

- ✔ **Build *Project_Name*:** Builds only the currently selected project, compiling only what has changed since the last compilation.

- ✔ **Rebuild *Project_Name*:** Builds only the currently selected project, but compiles all parts of the project, even if they didn't change since the last build.

To build your project, simply choose the desired option from the Build menu in the toolbar. Output from the build, such as errors and warnings, appear in the dynamic area of the Visual Studio IDE, as shown earlier in Figure 6-2.

Chapter 7

Testing and Debugging Web Services

. . . .

In This Chapter

▶ Discovering how to test your Web services

▶ Debugging Web services

▶ Fixing Web service problems

. . . .

*I*n Chapter 6, you can find out how to construct XML Web services with Visual Studio .NET. However, just because you created a Web service doesn't mean that it works, right? Therefore, you need to test and possibly debug problems that occur with your Web services. Testing and debugging your Web services applications are exceptionally easy with Visual Studio .NET. This chapter shows how to do both testing and debugging in your Web services applications, with samples shown in Visual Basic .NET.

The samples shown in this chapter are quite simple, but if you have complex Web services applications to debug, you can use the same concepts. It's best to start small. The key is to keep things modular and logical. This helps you not only during design and development, but also during testing and debugging.

Using Built-In Test Pages

You aren't going to believe how easy it is to test your Web services applications. Microsoft has built into the .NET Framework two HTML test pages that present information and prompt for parameter values. The first HTML page is generic for the Web service ASMX file and shows all methods that are exposed to this Web service. To access this page, you must first compile your Web service project.

If you are unfamiliar with how to compile Web service projects, refer to Chapter 6.

You can bring up the built-in test page to query your Web service in one of two ways. The first way is to follow these steps:

1. **Open your Web services project in Visual Studio .NET.**

2. **Right-click the filename that represents your Web service.**

3. **Choose the Set As Start Page menu.**

4. **Press the F5 key.**

   The Web service is queried and opens in a browser window.

The second method is to simply open a browser and enter the URL to your Web service. My example Web service is `user.asmx`, which is located in a directory called `external`, so I type:

```
http://dev.transport80.com/external/user.asmx
```

Either of these methods brings up a Web service in a browser. Refer to Figure 7-1 for an example of what this Web service method looks like.

Methods   Web service file name

Web service class name   WSDL link

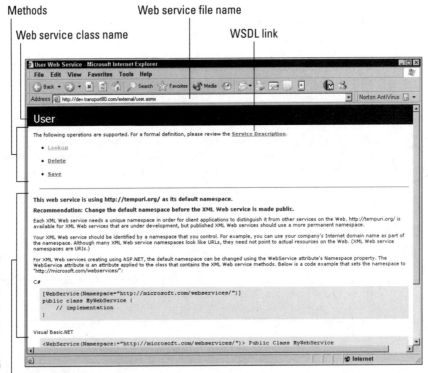

Figure 7-1:
Web service
test page,
showing
exposed
methods.

Errors and warnings

A short namespace primer

Essentially, namespaces give your Web services a scope. Just as you can't have two classes with the same name in the same project, you can't have two Web services with the same name in the same namespace. You should change the default namespace of `http://` `tempuri.org` to something that is germane to your organization. For example, my company uses `http://webservices.transport 80.com` as a namespace to define its Web services. To find out more about namespaces, check out Chapter 3.

Notice that Figure 7-1 shows the following information:

✔ **Web service filename:** This is the physical filename, with an ASMX extension, that's being accessed. The filename in Figure 7-1 is `user.asmx`.

✔ **Web service class name:** This is the class name that you created, which contains members (properties, methods, and events). This class name must be unique within a Web service. The class name in Figure 7-1 is `User`.

✔ **Service description:** A link to the WSDL file that describes your Web service. For more information about WSDL, see Chapter 9.

✔ **Methods:** The actions (usually represented as verbs) that can be called for a Web service. Figure 7-1 shows three methods for the `User` Web service; `Lookup`, `Delete`, and `Save`.

✔ **Error and warning information:** Displays information about any problems that occur with the Web service.

Figure 7-1 shows a warning message about needing to change the default namespace. This error won't stop the Web service from functioning, but you should change the default namespace prior to releasing the code to production.

If you click on one of the methods listed for a Web service, the .NET Framework automatically presents a list of all arguments that can be filled in to test the method. In my example (refer to Figure 7-1), clicking the `Save` method brings up a list of its arguments, which are shown in Figure 7-2.

To use this page, simply fill out parameters and click the `Invoke` button. The `Invoke` button performs whatever action has been coded into the Web service method. In my simplified example, clicking the `Invoke` button for the `Save` method tells the Web service to save the data specified in the parameters on the test page and also to return a status code, which indicates whether the save was successful (if it was, a value, in the form of the Employee's ID, is displayed), or not (if it wasn't, a value of 0 is displayed). Invoking a Web service method is also known as a *Web service call.* These results are shown in Figure 7-3.

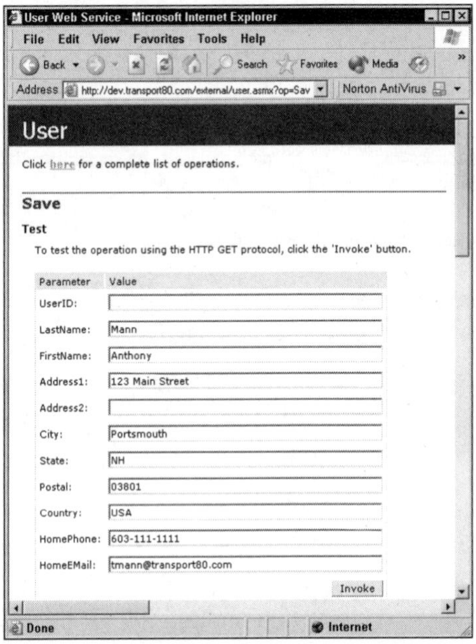

Figure 7-2:
Web service
test page,
showing
parameters
for a method
(filled in).

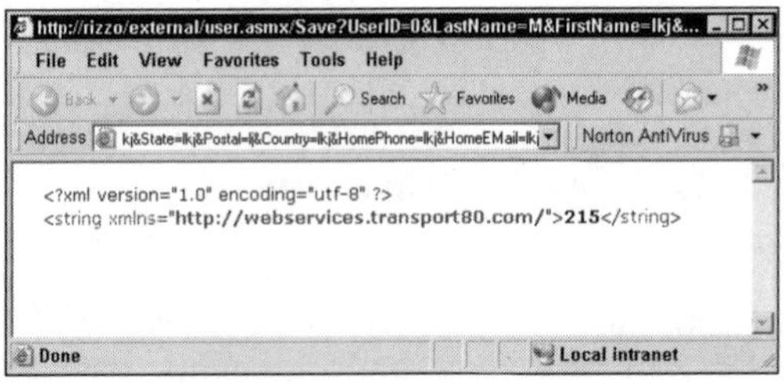

Figure 7-3:
Web service
test page,
showing
results of
invoking a
method.

In addition to the parameters shown in Figure 7-2, other information is available about your Web service call. This additional information is not shown in Figure 7-2 because of scrolling limitations of screen shots. The following sections outline the additional information shown on this screen.

HTTP Get, Post Requests, and Post Responses

Before diving into the testing of your Web services, it is important to understand how HTTP data is transmitted over the Internet. After all, Web services use HTTP to transmit information using SOAP (see Chapter 4), so a basic understanding of how HTTP data is transmitted is imperative.

Two types of HTTP messages are used to transmit HTTP data — Get and Post. For each type of message (which is explained in the following text), a request is issued. If the request is received, a corresponding response is transmitted back to the issuer of the request. This is exactly the way you would expect any transmission to work.

You really need to understand that HTTP information being transmitted over the Internet is done by a programmer or a program (such as a SOAP generator built into Visual Studio .NET). The programmer will implement the HTTP messages that have been designated by a software architect or designer. Whether you need to use a Get or a Post request is determined mostly by the type of application that you're developing and how the application needs to function. Here are the HTTP message types in action:

- ✔ The Get *request* is used to retrieve information from a URL. (Check out "HTTP Get request," later in this chapter, for details.) An example of a Get request is the method employed by Google.com. If you point your browser to `www.google.com` and perform a search, such as "Radio Parts," you'll notice that the URL contains the search terms. For example, the search for "Radio Parts" presents this URL after searching:

```
www.google.com/search?hl=en&ie=UTF-8&oe=UTF-
        8&q=radio+parts
```

  Notice that the terms "radio" and "parts" are in the URL. A program, such as the Google search engine, can look at these terms by using an HTTP Get request. In other words, a Get request occurs after the data is already present. Get messages are used when testing your Web service applications using built-in pages.

  Of course, if a Get request is issued, then a Get *response* is expected as well, which contains the actual values requested. (Check out "HTTP Get response," later in this chapter, for more information.)

- ✔ The Post message also gets information via HTTP but does it a different way. If you remember, a Get request looks for data that has been sent by a process. A Post actually *sends* the data via HTTP. Therefore, unlike a Get request (which expects the data to already exist over HTTP), a Post request sends the data; it doesn't expect the data to exist.

As an example, consider how one logs into most Web sites, such as Hotmail.com. The user is presented with a box to specify a username and a password. When the user clicks the button to log in, the information has to go somewhere! What happens, in most cases, is that instead of passing the data in the URL (such as in the case of a Get request), it is passed directly to another Web site or URL. One major advantage of using an HTTP Post is that the data can be encrypted with SSL. (SSL is covered in Chapter 11.) The Post request is discussed further in "HTTP Post request," later in this chapter.

Likewise, just as Get assumes a response, so Post implies that a response will be generated. (I discuss this topic in "HTTP Post response," later in this chapter.)

HTTP Get request

Get messages are great for asking for information from a Web site or other URL, but they are limited to only the fields that are specified in the URL.

Following the example that has been used so far in this chapter, the Get request for the Save method of the User Web service looks like this:

```
GET
        /external/user.asmx/Save?UserID=string&LastName=st
        ring&FirstName=string&Address1=string&Address2=str
        ing&City=string&State=string&Postal=string&Country
        =string&HomePhone=string&HomeEMail=string HTTP/1.1
Host: dev.transport80.com
```

If you used the preceding Get request in real life, the request would have values substituted for string after the field names in the Get request.

HTTP Get response

Every time a Get request is generated, a Get response is returned. The Get response for the Save method of the User Web service looks like this:

```
HTTP/1.1 200 OK
Content-Type: text/xml; charset=utf-8
Content-Length: length

<?xml version="1.0" encoding="utf-8"?>
<string
        xmlns="http://webservices.transport80.com/">string
        </string>
```

Just as in the case of the Get request in the preceding section, in real life, the Get response would have an actual value for the response value instead of the `string` placeholder.

HTTP Post request

A Post message first sends the initial call that starts the process of sending information. Post messages are used to send information to particular URLs.

Depending on your type of application, you may or may not need a Post message.

An advantage of using a Post message over a Get message is that you are not limited to only the fields that are specified in the URL. In fact, Post messages don't use URL parameters at all. You can get the value of any of the fields specified in the Web page. These fields are specified on a Web page, as designed by an architect, designer, or developer. You pass Post messages by using values or fields that are on a form. These fields can even be hidden fields, which hide some complexity from the user or even increase security. A Post message would be advantageous in a situation whereby one page has to send data to another page, such as a registration application. In such an application, many fields would be present on the screen, such as "First Name," "Last Name," "User Name," "Password," and the like. After these fields are filled-in, the page containing these fields must send the values to another page to do something with the values, such as save them to a database, check them for validity, or any other operation defined by the programmer. Therefore, these values are posted to another page.

The Post request in the running example I've used so far in this book for the `Save` method of the `User` Web service looks like this (where `string` is just a placeholder):

```
POST /external/user.asmx/Save HTTP/1.1
Host: dev.transport80.com
Content-Type: application/x-www-form-urlencoded
Content-Length: length

UserID=string&LastName=string&FirstName=string&Address1=strin
        g&Address2=string&City=string&State=string&Postal=
        string&Country=string&HomePhone=string&HomeEMail=s
        tring
```

HTTP Post response

If a Post request is issued, then a Post response is also expected. The Post response for the `Save` method of the `User` Web service looks like this:

```
HTTP/1.1 200 OK
Content-Type: text/xml; charset=utf-8
Content-Length: length

<?xml version="1.0" encoding="utf-8"?>
<string
          xmlns="http://webservices.transport80.com/">string
          </string>
```

The Post response would also have an actual value for the response value instead of the `string` placeholder.

Using Application Center Test

Application Center Test (or ACT) is an automated tool for testing Web-based applications, including Web services.

ACT comes with the Enterprise Architect and Enterprise Developer editions of Visual Studio .NET. The main concept of ACT is to record a series of HTTP requests (either Post or Get) and then play back those requests a specified number of times to simulate load on an application.

Understanding ACT lingo

Before you can use ACT, it's important to understand the general principles and vernacular that it implements:

- **Project:** The highest level within ACT is a *project*. In practical terms, all tests that you wish to perform are organized into one container, called *the project*. Because a project is a logical grouping, it can contain multiple tests, one for each method in a Web service, or perhaps even all Web services that are part of a larger project. You need to consider how to use an ACT project in your organization, but remember that the project is only a grouping of tests. You can have multiple ACT projects, but only one is available for testing at any one point in time.

- **Test(s):** A project can contain one or more tests. A test is a set of HTTP instructions that will be run numerous times to test stress loads. A test can be something like an individual call to a Web service, or even calls to multiple Web services, depending on how you organize your tests. When you perform a test, you run an individual test in its entirety. Therefore, if you want multiple Web service to be part of the same test, remember that you can't split them up during testing. In other words, if you have a Web service named CalcA and another named CalcB and the calls to these Web services are part of the same test (named TestAB), every time you run TestAB, it will always call CalcA and also CalcB. Therefore, it may make more sense to make CalcA and CalcB their own tests.

✔ **Stress:** One of the things that ACT tests for is *stress*. Stress is the ability of an application to perform until the point where it breaks (much like stress in people while they write books). An application breaking can be evident by the server not responding or not acting as designed.

✔ **Load:** ACT also tests for *load*. Load is a close cousin of stress. Load is the ability of an application (including your Web services) to perform well when multiple users are accessing your Web services simultaneously. When a software architect designs a Web service, it may perform perfectly well when one or two users access it. However, what happens when 100 or 1000 users access it? Well, to find out, you have to test for load. It is unlikely that you have 1000 users in your organization that can actually perform a test, so you have to let a tool, such as ACT, do it for you.

✔ **Users:** An ACT project can also contain users. If the Web service that you are testing requires security authentication, then the user's credentials can be set up in the Users folder within a project so that ACT can perform the test without manual user intervention. For example, suppose you need to test your Web service, named CalcA, but CalcA requires user authentication, you can enter that user's login name and password into ACT Users folder for use by ACT to test the CalcA Web service.

Setting up a simple ACT test

I can't go through every possible way to use Application Center Test, but to see the main functionality, follow these simple instructions:

1. **Open the Application Center Test program.**

   To do so, choose Start⇨Programs⇨Microsoft Visual Studio .NET⇨ Microsoft Visual Studio .NET Enterprise Features⇨Microsoft Application Center Test. This action brings up the screen shown in Figure 7-4.

2. **Create a new test.**

   Right-click Tests, and then click New Test. A wizard appears to guide you through the process.

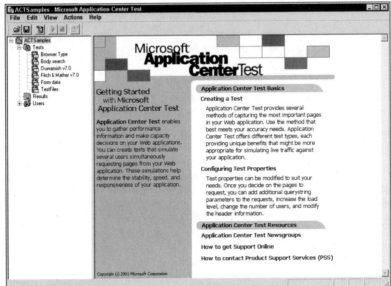

Figure 7-4:
Application
Center Test
main page.

3. **Click Next until you get to the Test Source step.**

   You have two options. The first allows you to create a new empty test. An *empty test* is just a shell that can be altered at a later time. The second option (and the one that you'll use in this step) creates a new test, but it will be filled with information that you will record. To record a new test, select the Record option, and then click Next.

4. **Choose Next to go past the Test Type step.**

   By default, only one script language is available to ACT, so VBScript is the only option.

5. **When you are ready to begin, click the Start recording button.**

   A new browser window appears to record your every single HTTP request.

6. **All you have to do is simply point and click every Web page and option that you want to record for later playback.**

   The output that is captured by the record process is too lengthy to mention here, but you can get an idea by checking out Figure 7-5.

7. **Click the Stop recording button after you are finished recording.**

   If you inadvertently clicked the Stop recording button, you can simply click the Start recording button again to continue where you left off.

8. **Click Next.**

Even though you can play back HTTPS requests (SSL-encrypted requests), the recording process doesn't allow you to record SSL requests. The likely reason for this is so that you do not store secure information in your ACT projects. Microsoft recommends turning off SSL on the Web browser during testing and then turning it back on after you are finished. However, this is not always possible.

9. **Enter a test name.**

Choose a name that's germane to the site you browsed for recording purposes. This test name will appear in the list of tests in the hierarchy of the main window. Click Next when you are ready to continue.

10. **Click Finish.**

Figure 7-5:
ACT
showing
HTTP
requests
after
recording.

Changing ACT test properties

After you have set up your initial test, you can change the testing properties. You may need to change properties if, for example, one URL in your test has changed but you don't want to re-record the entire test. Assuming that you just completed the set of steps in the previous section and have the ACT application running, follow these steps:

1. **Right-click the name of your test and choose the Properties menu.**

The dialog box shown in Figure 7-6 appears. The test that I used was called "Sample Test for Book," so that's shown at the top of the dialog box.

2. **The dialog box shows three main options to choose from.**

   • **Number of browser connections:** To simulate a real load, you most likely want to simulate a specific number of browser connections. Enter the number of browser sessions you can reasonably expect the application to receive, plus some reasonable factor over that value, such as 25 percent. For example, if you were expecting no more than 100 sessions, you would enter a number of 125 here (100 expected users plus 25 percent). The default is 1.

- **Run tests for a specified duration:** If you want to run tests continuously for a specific period of time, fill out the boxes in this section. You can enter days, hours, minutes, and seconds. In addition, you can specify a warm-up time in seconds. You will likely want to run a test for a specific duration if you want to determine whether your application performance will degrade over time. The nice thing about this option is that you can set a test to run before you go home at night and have it finish before you arrive the next morning.

A *warm-up time* is the time required by a server to cache data or perform some other initialization. Test results are not logged during this period. The default value for the duration option is five minutes, with no warm-up time.

- **Run tests a specified number of times:** If you want to run tests a specific number of times, select this option and enter the number of times you want to run your test. This number isn't related in any way to of the length of time that it takes to run your test. This option is advantageous if each test takes a very long time to run. In other words, if your test takes 15 minutes to run, you may want to run the test a specific number of times instead of specifying a duration using the previous option.

3. Click OK when you have entered all of your options.

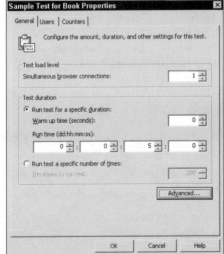

Figure 7-6:
Properties
dialog box
for test
named
"Sample
Test for
Book."

Running the ACT test

When you have recorded the test and made adjustments to the testing properties, you're ready to run the test. If you have a dedicated development or QA (Quality Assurance) environment, you can run the test at any time. On the other hand, if you must run your test in a production environment, do so at a point in time when traffic won't be impacted, such as the middle of the night. Don't forget that international users might be accessing your Web site when it is in the middle of the night for a U.S. time zone.

To run your test, follow these steps:

1. **Right-click the name of your test and choose the Start Test menu.**

   Alternatively, you can press the Ctrl and F5 keys simultaneously.

   The test runs, and the dialog box shown in Figure 7-7 appears, announcing the status of your test.

2. **When the test is complete, view the results.**

   Click the Results menu and find your test on the right-hand part of the screen. Drill down into your test to find the specific results that you want to view. You can choose from three types of tests: overview, graphs, and requests.

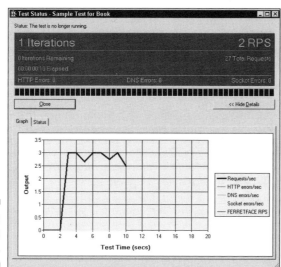

Figure 7-7:
Test Status
dialog box.

Analyzing ACT results and knowing what to do with them

Analyzing the results of running an ACT project can be a difficult thing to do. The ACT test results screen shows many bits of information (refer to Figure 7-7). To help you analyze results, here's a list of the data elements contained on the screen:

- **Status:** Lets you know whether the test is currently running or if it has stopped.

- **Iterations:** The number of times that your test has been run.

- **Iterations Remaining:** The number of iterations that you have specified, minus the number of iterations that have already run. If the test is finished, this value will be zero.

- **Elapsed:** The total length of time that the entire test took to run. This value is in the format of Days:Hours:Minutes:Seconds.

- **RPS:** Stands for Requests Per Second and measures the average number of requests per second. This number helps you to understand the *throughput* of your application. The throughput is a measure that helps you determine stress and load.

- **Total Requests:** The number of HTTP requests that were made across the network for the entire test.

- **HTTP Errors:** The number of HTTP errors that occurred during your test run. An HTTP error can be something like a URL that does not point to a valid location on the Internet or your local network. Likewise, a Web server that is not responding will result in an HTTP error.

- **DNS Errors:** The number of Dynamic Name System (or DNS) errors that occurred during your test run. A DNS error will occur if a URL cannot be resolved to a TCP/IP address. This number should be zero. If it is not, have your network administrator look into DNS problems.

- **Socket Errors:** The number of TCP/IP transmission errors that occurred during your test run. This number should be zero. If it is higher than zero, you should investigate network problems.

The graph area of Figure 7-7 (earlier in this chapter) visually shows the important metrics to help you analyze the results of your test. The graph shows the number of requests or errors (depending on the color on the graph) per second, over time. Take a look at Figure 7-7. It shows only one line, which is the number of requests per second because there were no HTTP, DNS, or Socket errors. This test was run only one time and only averaged two requests per second.

In your own tests, it would help you to know what the graph looks like for a single iteration, but then under extreme load as well. You need to determine how load and stress affect your applications using ACT. For example, you know in Figure 7-7 that there were no errors. However, suppose that you ran the test 100 times, and you found that you began to have errors after a few iterations, and the number of errors increased over time. This situation would likely show a memory leak or a memory-caching problem.

On the other hand, if you construct your test to simulate 1,000 simultaneous users and you find that the number of HTTP errors increases, it is likely that you Web server cannot handle the load. Therefore, you may have to go back to the drawing board. It may be that your Web service application simply cannot handle 1,000 users on a single Web server. You may have to use multiple Web servers and balance the load between those servers.

As you can see, covering all possible problems is impossible, but you should at least have an idea how ACT can help you to test your applications and do it more efficiently that your own testers can!

Debugging with the IDE

Debugging is a term used to describe the process of finding and fixing problems, or *bugs,* in your Web services (or any other software). *IDE* is a term used to describe the graphical environment within Visual Studio .NET, which is referred to as the Integrated Development Environment. Debugging a Web services project is the same as debugging any other .NET application (such as Windows applications and ASP.NET applications). This section covers debugging your Web services by using Visual Studio .NET.

You can debug your applications in a couple of ways. The first is simply to test the application (as demonstrated in previous sections in this chapter) and view the results.

Depending on the results of your test (refer to Figure 7-3), you may just be able to know where your problem is, fix your code, and recompile your application.

However, it is more likely that you would need to debug your applications by using the built-in debugger in Visual Studio .NET. Debugging with Visual Studio .NET is accomplished by following these steps:

1. Verify debug configuration.
2. Set breakpoints (and possibly watches).
3. Run application in debug mode.
4. Step through code.
5. Query or set values.

Each of these topics is covered in the following sections.

Ensuring debug configuration

The first thing that you must do is verify that your Visual Studio .NET project is in the Debug configuration. *Debug configuration* makes sure that all debug symbols and required information for debugging are built into the application when it is compiled. To ensure debug configuration, follow these steps:

1. **Open your Web services project in Visual Studio .NET.**

2. **Choose the Build⇨Configuration Manager menu.**

   Choosing this menu brings up the Configuration Manager dialog box, as shown in Figure 7-8.

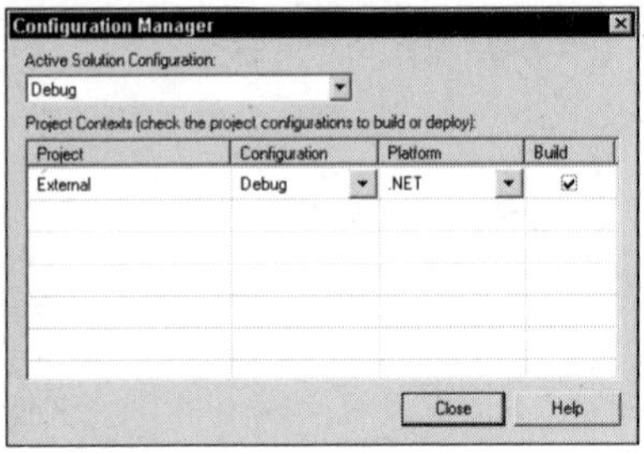

Figure 7-8:
The
Configu-
ration
Manager.

3. **Ensure that Debug is selected as the Active Solution Configuration.**

   The other option that you have, by default, is Release. The difference between Debug and Release configurations is primarily the overhead that is built into the application for debugging. That's why you don't want to deploy with a Debug configuration, although technically you could do so.

4. **Click the Close button.**

Note: Also review the compilation element discussed in the section "Debugging with Configuration Files," located later in this chapter.

Setting breakpoints

A *breakpoint* is an instruction that you give to Visual Studio .NET to indicate you want the code to break (or pause) execution when it gets to a certain point. When execution of code is paused, it is said to be in *break mode*. An example of a breakpoint would be the beginning of a function that you wish to debug in code. You would set the breakpoint on the name of the function. After doing so, if you start Visual Studio .NET in debug mode, the code will be paused every time the function (where the breakpoint is set) is called.

You use breakpoints to pause execution of the application so that you can check the values of variables. Another reason for setting breakpoints is to watch the application's execution step by step, as you move through your code. Breakpoints can be very helpful if you have lots of branching in your code. Suppose you have an "If-Then-Else" structure in your code. You can visually step through and watch as each line of code is executed, allowing you to see how your branching logic functions. This process may reveal that code you expected to execute never gets executed.

To set a breakpoint, simply place the cursor on the desired line of code and press F9. To clear a breakpoint, simply press F9 again. Visual Studio .NET simply toggles between setting and clearing breakpoints with the F9 key. A set breakpoint is indicated with a solid red line. It is quite possible (even likely) that you'll have multiple breakpoints in your application. Remember that code will be paused each and every time a line of code is reached that contains a breakpoint. Therefore, you don't want to have too many break-points, or you'll never reach the end of your code.

Your breakpoints get saved with the project, so you don't have to set them every time you open your project. As long as you start your application in debug mode, your breakpoints will function. Figure 7-9 shows what a break-point looks like in Visual Basic .NET.

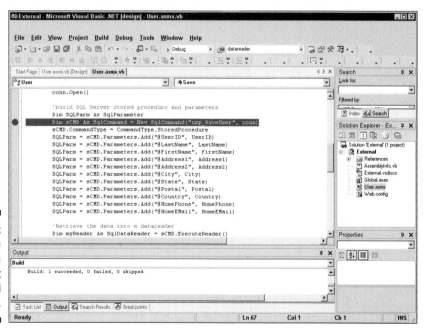

Figure 7-9:
Code
showing a
breakpoint
in Visual
Basic .NET.

A close relative to a breakpoint is a watch. A *watch* allows you to not only view the value of one or more variables, but it also allows you to set a *conditional* breakpoint. In other words, you don't actually place a breakpoint on a line of code, but instead you can, for example, pause execution when the value of variable V1 contains a value of 10. Setting conditional breakpoints is somewhat involved because there are so many possible options. Consult your favorite book on Visual Studio .NET or even the online help that comes with the product for more information on setting conditional breakpoints or watches.

Running the application in debug mode

To run your application in debug mode, follow these steps:

1. **Set a startup page.**

   I show you how in the section "Using Built-In Test Pages" earlier in this chapter.

2. **Press the F5 key, or choose the Debug⇨Start menu.**

   The application will start in debug mode, enabling you to step through code, view watches, and so on. However, before this can happen, your code will automatically be compiled first. After all, Visual Studio .NET cannot debug code that is not compiled. You will not be allowed to debug your code if your application doesn't compile first. In other words, if there are syntax errors or any other errors that prevent the compiling of your application, you'll have to fix those errors before you can debug.

   If your application compiles without errors, you see a new browser window magically appear, which allows you to access your Web services application by using a test page. You can enter parameter values in your test pages, as shown earlier in this chapter. When your breakpoint is encountered, code will break execution.

   Imagine, for example, that you would like to debug a Web service method named LookupSalesTaxRate. LookupSalesTaxRate is defined with a single argument, StateCode, which expects the two-character designation for a U.S. state. The Web service call will return the tax rate that gets looked up in a table; however, your code is not returning the correct tax rate. To rectify the situation, you set a breakpoint on the line of code where the Web service method LookupSalesTaxRate is defined. Now, when you test your application, whenever you make a call to the LookupSalesTaxRate Web service method, the code will break, allowing you to visually step through your code and watch how Visual Studio .NET branches though the code and also enables you to test values.

Stepping through the code

After your application is in break mode, you can step through the code. In fact, you have the following options for the execution of your code after a breakpoint is encountered:

- ✔ **Step Into:** Enables you to watch the execution of every line of code. If another subroutine or procedure is encountered, each of those subsequent lines of code will be stepped into, allowing you to visually see every single line of code as it's being executed. Step Into can take quite a lot of time to debug, because every line of code, including those contained in subroutines, will be executed one-by-one. To step into code, press F11, or choose the Debug⇨Step Into menu.

- ✔ **Step Over:** Steps into every line of code, except for subroutines and other procedures. If subroutines are encountered, they are still executed, but this does not allow you to see every line of code as it's executed. They are just executed and returned immediately. This can be a great timesaver if you don't care to see every line of code being executed in a subroutine. As an example, suppose you have a procedure, named ProcA, which calls ProcB only when the value of x equals 1, like this (shown in Visual Basic code):

```
Line 1: Sub ProcA (x as Integer)
Line 2:  If x = 1 Then
Line 3:     Call ProcB
Line 4:  End If
Line 5: End Sub
```

  If you have a breakpoint set on Line 1, after a call is made to ProcA, the execution of code is paused. Using the Step-over option will place the execution on Line 2. Using the Step-over option again will place the execution on Line 3 (assuming the value of x is actually 1). Using the Step-over option one more time actually executes ProcB but does not show every single line of code within ProcB. On the other hand, Step Into will actually step into ProcB and show every single line of code within that procedure. If this is a large procedure, it can take quite a bit of time to step into every line of code. Therefore, the Step-over option is perfect for this case (assuming that you don't need to debug ProcB). If you did need to debug ProcB, you would want to use the Step-into option.

  To step over code, press F10, or choose Debug⇨Step Over.

Querying or setting values

Visual Studio .NET provides for the ability to query and set variable values. Querying values allows you to test values that have been passed into your Web services and other variables. Setting values allows you to alter the path that your code takes by manually setting a value.

Both of these operations take place in the command window after you have already started your application in debug mode and a breakpoint is reached. You query values by typing a question mark (**?**) followed by the name of the variable to query. Alternatively, you can type the word **print** instead of using the question mark. You set the value by typing the variable name and assigning it a value with the equal sign (=) without the question mark. Refer to Figure 7-10 to see what the command window looks like.

Notice the Command Window in the bottom-right corner in Figure 7-10. It contains the following three lines of code:

```
?LastName
"Mann"
HomeEMail = "tmann@transport80.com"
```

The first line of code is used to query the value of the `LastName` variable. The value is retrieved after you type **?LastName** and press Enter. The value `"Mann"` was automatically placed in the Command Window by Visual Studio .NET. The last line of code was used to set the value of the `HomeEMail` variable. The value is set by entering a value (enclosed in quotes for strings) and pressing the Enter key.

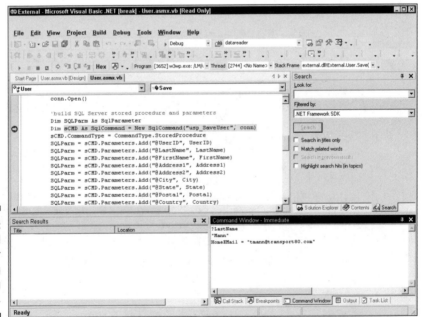

Figure 7-10:
Command window for querying and setting values.

Debugging with Configuration Files

One way to debug is to send detailed error messages to your Web pages, including Web services. Web-based projects can contain a configuration file called `Web.Config`. An application doesn't have to have this file, but if it doesn't, it will inherit the settings of the `Web.Config` file of its parent. The `Web.Config` file is formatted as an XML file and contains specific elements that the .NET framework looks for.

The following are the elements within the `Web.Config` file that affect debugging:

- ✔ `<compilation>`: Affects how your Web services project is compiled.
- ✔ `<customErrors>`: Affects the errors that are displayed within your Web services project.
- ✔ `<trace>`: Affects how detailed output is logged on each page.

The `<compilation>` element has a debug attribute, which must be set to "true" to allow for debugging symbols to be included in your project, although this is set to "true" by default. The compilation element looks similar to this:

```
<compilation defaultLanguage="vb" debug="true" />
```

The `customErrors` element has a mode attribute, which can be set to one of three values. "Off" indicates that custom errors won't be displayed and standard (ASP.NET) error messages will be displayed. "On" indicates that custom errors will be displayed. For this to work, you must enter the custom error messages. "RemoteOnly" is somewhere between the two. If this value is set, your custom errors will be displayed to remote clients (where requests are sent from a machine other than the Web server), and standard error messages will be displayed if the Web page or Web service is run from the Web server itself. The `<customErrors>` element looks like this:

```
<customErrors mode="Off" />
```

If no custom errors are defined, standard error messages will be displayed anyway. To define custom error messages, you must define an `<error>` element within the `<customErrors>` element, with two attributes: `statusCode`, which is the HTML error code that is passed by all Web servers, and the `redirect` attribute, which is the HTML page that should show a custom error. An example of an `<error>` element is:

```
<error statusCode="404" redirect="PageNotFound.htm"/>
```

TIP

Putting it all together, your `<customErrors>` element would look like this:

```
<customErrors mode="Off">
    <error statusCode="404" redirect="PageNotFound.htm"/>
</customErrors>
```

The `trace` element contains three main attributes that control a detailed output trace. The first is the `enabled` attribute. If it is set to "True," ASP.NET will log traces; it is set to "False" by default. The second is the `pageOutput` attribute. It is set to "False" by default, but if you set it to "True," the trace output will be placed at the bottom of a Web page instead of a log file (called `trace.axd`). The third attribute is `localOnly`. By default, this value is set to "True," which means that trace details are only logged when the Web requests are initiated on the Web server itself. If this attribute is set to "False," any request will show traces. An example of the `trace` element looks like this:

```
<trace enabled="true" requestLimit="10" pageOutput="true"
            traceMode="SortByTime" localOnly="true" />
```

Because I know that you're just as curious as can be, Figure 7-11 shows how much detailed information is returned when the `<trace>` element is enabled and is output to the page.

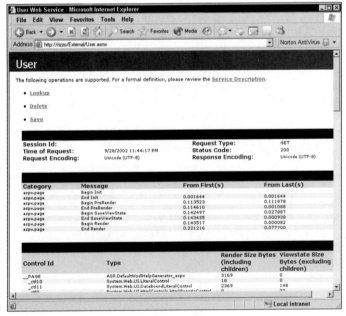

Figure 7-11:
Trace values being output to a page.

Part III
Web Services
Usage

The 5th Wave   By Rich Tennant

"We're here to clean the code."

In this part . . .

Part II showed you how to design, construct, test, and debug your Web services projects. Part III discusses using Web services after they are already constructed. Chapter 8 shows how to deploy and publish your Web services. Chapter 9 shows how to consume, or use, the Web services that you or someone else has already constructed. Chapter 10 discusses how to use building-block services that companies, such as Microsoft, make available to you out of the box.

Chapter 8

Deploying and Publishing Web Services

In This Chapter

▶ Deploying your Web services

▶ Publishing with UDDI directories

▶ Specifying Web services instance info

*B*efore your organization or your clients can use your XML Web services, you must deploy your Web services from your development or testing environment to your production environment. You perform this task by using Visual Studio .NET. After you deploy your projects into a production environment, you can publish them in a UDDI directory or registry. A *UDDI directory* is a centralized database that allows other to find your Web services.

This chapter explores how to deploy and publish your XML Web services by using Microsoft .NET. You see how to use XCopy deployment, how to use the Copy Project Wizard, and even how to create a setup project that will allow for easy installation of your Visual Studio .NET projects. This chapter also shows how you can register your company and list your Web services (known as *publishing*) in the Microsoft UDDI directory. Although the theory of registering and publishing to the Microsoft UDDI registry is easy, many details are involved. In this chapter, you see the steps involved in publishing to the Microsoft UDDI directory.

Deploying Web Services

If you're up to date on constructing and testing Web services, you need to shift your attention from development and testing to deployment. Time to go from the development and testing environment to the production environment. The truth is that you've done all the hardest work already; deploying your Web service may just be the easiest part of all.

DLL rhymes with. . . .

If you have been in the software industry for at least two years, you may recall the problems with what was widely known as "DLL Hell." DLLs, or Dynamic Link Libraries, required registration into the Windows registry, which was a central database for DLLs that resided on a computer. Registering DLLs was done by using an Application Programming Interface (API) during the setup process or by manual means (that means you did it all on your own). Registration was necessary because if the DLL just resided in a folder, Windows would not be able to find it. With registration, information about where to find the DLL could be found on the disk drive.

Registering a DLL manually involved using the REGSVR32.EXE program that resides in the System32 folder under the folder where Windows (all versions) was installed. Registering the DLL creates a 16-byte value that represents the ID of each object contained in the DLL. This value is called a Globally Unique Identifier, or *GUID*. It is also referred to as a ClassID. Registration seems easy enough, doesn't it?

Well, as you may imagine (by my building the scenario), registration caused many problems. The process could fail for lots of reasons. These things can go wrong during the registration process:

✔ Incorrect permissions to register the object.

✔ A different ClassID already exists for an object with the same name.

✔ The registry database is full.

In addition, the registry database causes many problems for IT departments to troubleshoot. For example, an application on two separate workstations is behaving differently. Ultimately, it can be because a third-party DLL has different versions between the two machines. You weren't even aware that one user downloaded the latest version. Perhaps the user wasn't either. I have seen problems like this take days and even weeks to find for large applications! .NET fixes all of these issues.

If you've been in the software industry, you may know a little bit about DLLs (Dynamic Link Libraries) and the havoc they can wreak when you need to update the Windows Registry. (If you want a little more information, check out the sidebar "DLL rhymes with. . . .") The good news? All the DLL problems are solved with .NET, so your deployment is simple. The next few sections describe the different scenarios for deploying your Web services applications.

Deploying Web Services on a Local Network

There is a difference between deploying your Web services applications locally versus remotely. A local deployment is one where the target server is on the same network as the *source server* (the one where you've done your development and/or testing). The only people who will be able to use the Web service are those who have access to your private network. Outsiders can't go there, so to speak.

All about XCopy

One of the best ways to deploy your Web service on the local network (and to prove the end of DLL Hell) is by allowing for XCopy deployment. XCopy is an old DOS command that instructs the operating system to copy a folder (which used to be called a *directory* in the old days) along with all the folder's subfolders. XCopy is available by using the Windows Command Prompt.

Even though you can copy folder structures by using Windows Explorer, you should use the DOS XCopy command instead because this command permits the verification of files. It also works with nonmapped network drives. To use XCopy, you must open a command prompt. Opening the command prompt is shown later in this chapter in the "Using XCopy to deploy a Web service locally" section. When the command prompt window is open, get help on the command by typing **_XCopy /?**.

The XCopy command may differ slightly in syntax, depending on the operating system you are using. The syntax in Windows XP is shown in Figure 8-1.

```
C:\WINDOWS\System32\cmd.exe                                          _ □ ×
Copies files and directory trees.

XCOPY source [destination] [/A | /M] [/D[:date]] [/P] [/S [/E]] [/U] [/W]
                           [/C] [/I] [/Q] [/F] [/L] [/G] [/H] [/R] [/T] [/U]
                           [/K] [/N] [/O] [/X] [/Y] [/-Y] [/Z]
                           [/EXCLUDE:file1[+file2][+file3]...]

  source       Specifies the file(s) to copy.
  destination  Specifies the location and/or name of new files.
  /A           Copies only files with the archive attribute set,
               doesn't change the attribute.
  /M           Copies only files with the archive attribute set,
               turns off the archive attribute.
  /D:m-d-y     Copies files changed on or after the specified date.
               If no date is given, copies only those files whose
               source time is newer than the destination time.
  /EXCLUDE:file1[+file2][+file3]...
               Specifies a list of files containing strings.  Each string
               should be in a separate line in the files.  When any of the
               strings match any part of the absolute path of the file to be
               copied, that file will be excluded from being copied.  For
               example, specifying a string like \obj\ or .obj will exclude
               all files underneath the directory obj or all files with the
               .obj extension respectively.
  /P           Prompts you before creating each destination file.
  /S           Copies directories and subdirectories except empty ones.
  /E           Copies directories and subdirectories, including empty ones.
               Same as /S /E. May be used to modify /T.
  /U           Verifies each new file.
  /W           Prompts you to press a key before copying.
  /C           Continues copying even if errors occur.
  /I           If destination does not exist and copying more than one file,
               assumes that destination must be a directory.
  /Q           Does not display file names while copying.
  /F           Displays full source and destination file names while copying.
  /L           Displays files that would be copied.
  /G           Allows the copying of encrypted files to destination that does
               not support encryption.
  /H           Copies hidden and system files also.
  /R           Overwrites read-only files.
  /T           Creates directory structure, but does not copy files. Does not
               include empty directories or subdirectories. /T /E includes
               empty directories and subdirectories.
  /U           Copies only files that already exist in destination.
  /K           Copies attributes. Normal Xcopy will reset read-only attributes.
  /N           Copies using the generated short names.
  /O           Copies file ownership and ACL information.
  /X           Copies file audit settings (implies /O).
  /Y           Suppresses prompting to confirm you want to overwrite an
               existing destination file.
  /-Y          Causes prompting to confirm you want to overwrite an
               existing destination file.
  /Z           Copies networked files in restartable mode.

The switch /Y may be preset in the COPYCMD environment variable.
This may be overridden with /-Y on the command line.
```

Figure 8-1:
XCopy
syntax in
Windows
XP.

All .NET objects, including Web services, can now be deployed by using this method, which bypasses the need for registration in the Windows registry. Additionally, XCopy deployment has another advantage. XCopy enables different versions of your .NET applications or Web services to coexist side by side.

Web services are *self-describing,* so using a registry to tell the application about the objects or where they are located on the disk is not necessary.

Determining exactly which files are to be deployed — and where

You created a few main folders when you compiled your Web services application. The main folder is `<root>`. This folder is not actually named `<root>` but is the beginning point of your compiled Web application and is considered to be a Web application by IIS. This folder contains all .asmx files, as well as the web.config file. In addition, it contains

- ✔ \bin: This folder contains all compiled binary files and assemblies that the application uses.

- ✔ **Other folders:** Other folders (such as \inc or \common) may be necessary for your Web services applications, which may contain common routines used among Web services. These other folders are completely optional.

So, where do you deploy your Web services? When you develop your Web services, those Web services will reside completely within your development environment. Most likely, you also have testing, possibly staging, and certainly production environments. After you develop and compile your Web services, you must deploy them to these other environments.

For more information about compiling Web services applications, see Chapter 6.

Using XCopy to deploy a Web service locally

To deploy your Web services application, follow these steps:

1. **Choose Start➪Programs➪Accessories➪Command Prompt to open a command prompt.**

2. **XCopy your application.**

To use the XCopy command to copy your application in the folder location d:\inetpub\wwwroot\External\User to another server called PROD01 (using the same file structure), use this command:

```
XCopy d:\inetpub\wwwroot\External\User \\PROD01\D$\inet-
        pub\wwwroot\External\User /e /y /v
```

Notice the two switches at the end of the line. /e specifies that the entire folder structure from User and below will be created, even if the folders are empty. The /y switch indicates that files will be overwritten without prompting. The /v switch indicates that you want the files to be verified after they are copied. This is useful in a deployment scenario when you want to replace all files.

You must have write permissions on the folder to copy to the new server. If you don't have administrative privileges, you won't be able to use the administrative share to the D drive, called D$. Instead, you must have your administrator create a network share to the drive or folder and substitute the paths accordingly. For example, if the server PROD01 has a network share called External, which points to the \inetpub\wwwroot\External folder on the D drive, your XCopy command becomes

```
XCopy d:\inetpub\wwwroot\External\User
        \\PROD01\External\User /e /y /v
```

3. Close the Command Prompt window.

You see, deploying is just that simple!

Deploying Web Services on a Remote Network

A remote deployment is a deployment of a Web service that extends past the local network. In other words, people outside your immediate network will be able to use the Web service. For example, you might deploy the Web service on a server that is outside your company, meaning that the service is available to a wider network of users.

Suppose that you work for a consulting company, and you develop a Web services application for your client. After you go through your development and testing process off-site, you have to deploy the application into production on-site in the remote network. You have two ways in which you can deploy your Web services application remotely. These ways are outlined in the next two sections.

Knowing your copying options

When you copy files to a remote server, you can't do the old copy and paste thing. Visual Studio .NET has two methods for copying files to the new location:

✔ **File share:** This method allows you to copy files directly to a path somewhere on the network by using UNC notation (that is, `\\server\share\ folder`). You must have several pieces in place for this method to work:

  • **You need an administrative share.**

    This administrative share is automatically created when you install IIS and is called `wwwroot$`.

  • **You need to have administrative privileges.**

  • **You must be able to get to the administrative share over the network.**

    It is more likely that you will be able to access the administrative share if you are copying a project on a local network or have VPN access to the remote network.

The advantage of the file share method is that FrontPage server extensions don't have to be installed on the remote Web server.

✔ **FrontPage:** This method employs FrontPage server extensions to contact the remote Web server and perform specific authoring actions (just like the actions I need to perform when I'm tied to my desk all day).

When presented with the choice between using a file share and using FrontPage, I say, "Hello, FrontPage!" You will have better luck using the FrontPage option on a remote server. Period. *But,* FrontPage extensions must be installed on the remote Web server. For more information about installing FrontPage server extensions, visit the Microsoft Web site at `http://msdn.microsoft.com/library/default.asp?url=/library /en-us/dnservext/html/fpse02win.asp`.

Deciding what to copy

If you have decided what method you're going to use to copy files, the next step is to decide which files to copy. You have three options:

✔ **Only files needed to run this application:** Copies only the files that are necessary for this application to run, such as compiled DLL and executable files. Use this option if you are deploying to a production Web server and will not make changes on this remote server. If you need to make changes, you won't have the necessary source files.

✔ **All project files:** Copies every file that is contained within the project, even if it is not required when the project is run. This option includes files that are in any folder that is included in the project, regardless of hierarchy of those folders. Use this option if, at some point, you need to make changes to the source code files and recompile your project. If you are not sure which option to choose, this is the one for you!

✔ **All files in the source project folder:** Copies every file that is contained in the source folder and lower in the hierarchy. If files that are included in the project are outside this folder, they will not be copied. Use this option if you will need to make changes to the source code files but are sure that no folder references are outside the source project hierarchy.

Copying projects

One way to deploy your Web services project is to use the Copy Project Wizard. The Copy Project Wizard is a single-page wizard used to guide you through the process of copying your project to a remote (or even local) server.

To use the Copy Project Wizard, follow these steps:

1. **Open your Web services project in Visual Studio .NET.**

2. **Choose Project⇨Copy Project to invoke the Copy Project Wizard.**

   Doing so brings up the dialog box shown in Figure 8-2.

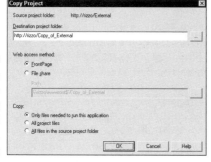

Figure 8-2:
The Copy
Project
Wizard
dialog box.

3. **Specify the New Project Folder: In the Destination Project Folder field, enter the folder name where you want your new project created.**

   The new folder will automatically be created. By default, Visual Studio.NET will try to copy to an HTTP folder with the name of `Copy_of_` followed by the name of your current project.

   You must use an HTTP URL location for either a local or remote server. For example, to create a new folder called `User` on one level down from the root of xyzcorp's Web server, type **http://www.xyzcorp.com/User**.

4. **Specify the Web Access Method.**

   You can use the file share method, or you can use FrontPage server extensions. See "Knowing your copying options," earlier in this chapter, for more information about each option.

5. **Specify the Copy options.**

   Next, you specify one of three options of what to copy. You can choose from these options (find out more about them in "Knowing what to copy," earlier in this chapter):

   • Only files needed to run this application

   • All project files

   • All files in the source project folder

6. **Click Finish.**

   Your new project will be created on the Web server and the specified files copied.

Deployment projects

A *deployment project* is a special type of project that you can create with Visual Studio .NET that will create an installation file that can be used to install your Web Services application. The advantage of using a deployment project over the Copy Project option is that you can send this installation file to someone (by e-mail or snail mail) where you don't have connectivity to the remote computer. You may not have connectivity because of firewall or permissions issues. In these cases, the deployment project is your best bet, but you'll likely have to put the deployment project on a CD and send it in the mail (although if it's small enough, you can e-mail it).

A couple types of deployment projects are available with Visual Studio .NET, but to deploy your Web services application, you use something called a Web Setup project. A Web Setup project will take your Web services project and create an MSI file that can be used by Windows XP or Windows 2000 natively.

Use these simple steps to create a Web Setup project:

1. **Open your Web Services Project in Visual Studio.NET.**

2. **Add a new Web Setup project to your current solution. To do so, right-click the solution in the Solution Explorer pane. Choose Add⇨New Project.**

   This invokes the New Project dialog box, which is shown in Figure 8-3. In the Project Types list, notice the Setup and Deployment Projects listing. This is the category that you will use for your new project.

Figure 8-3:
New Project
dialog box.

3. Select Web Setup Project.

You don't have to add the Web Setup project to your current solution. You can create a new Web Setup project in its own solution, but this setup is harder to configure. Therefore, adding a Web Setup project in the same solution as your Web services project is a good idea.

4. Give your project a name and choose a folder location.

For example, if you have a Web Services project named External, you may want to create a Web Setup project named External Setup.

5. When finished, click the OK button.

The new Web Setup project is created and added to the current solution, such as the one shown in Figure 8-4.

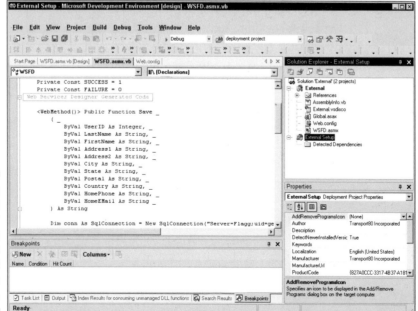

Figure 8-4:
Visual
Studio .NET
showing
Web Setup
Project
added into
the solution.

6. **Add project output. To do so, right-click the newly added Web Setup project (the one I named External Setup in Step 4) in the Solution Explorer pane and choose Add⇨Project Output.**

   This invokes the Add Project Output Group dialog box, as shown in Figure 8-5. Notice the name of your Web services project is already added and selected in the Project drop-down list.

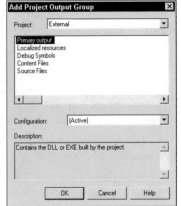

Figure 8-5:
The Add
Project
Output
Group
dialog box.

7. **In the Configuration drop-down list, choose the configuration that you want to use for the setup.**

   For example, if you want to deploy your Web services project into production, select the Release .NET configuration option. For more information about configurations and using the Configuration Manager, see Chapter 6.

8. **Click OK when you are finished making your project output choices.**

9. **Create your installation file. To do so, click your Web Setup project and choose Build⇨Build Solution.**

   Your Web Setup project is created in the subdirectory automatically associated and created with your configuration. For example, when you created your project, two folders (one called Debug and one called Release) were created automatically. Therefore, if you choose the Release configuration option, the output files are automatically placed in this folder. This folder is shown in Figure 8-6.

   Five files appear, as shown in Figure 8-6. These five files are

   `Project_Name.MSI`: Windows 2000 and Windows XP installer program. The Project_Name is the name of your Web Setup project when you added it to your solution.

   `InstMsiA.Exe`: Windows installer program for Windows 95 and Windows 98.

InstMsiW.Exe: Windows installer program for Windows NT

Setup.Exe: Generic setup program that launches the correct setup program for the operating system.

Setup.Ini: Contains setup configuration information.

10. **You must distribute the** MSI **file along with any additional files for the target operating systems.**

    If you are not sure which operating systems will be used, you must include all files in your distribution. When you distribute the required files, including the MSI file, you simply make sure that these files get to the remote server (by copying them, e-mail, snail mail, or other means). After the remote server has access to the files, the MSI file can be run to install the project.

Figure 8-6:
Output Files
for Release
Config-
uration of a
Web Setup
Project.

Registering Your Web Services with UDDI

Before your Web services can be consumed (as covered in Chapter 9), you must expose your Web services to the outside world. Exposing your Web services to the outside world is as easy as compiling your application and making sure that it exists in your production environment. So, what's all this business about registering?

Suppose you have a business telephone number. If there's no place to look up your phone number, nobody can find you, and your phone won't ring. Therefore, you list your phone number in the phone book, so people will be able to find you. Web services follow the same concept. You can expose your Web services to the outside world, but nobody will use them if they can't find them. That's where UDDI comes in. The following sections give you the skinny on what you need to know.

The term *publishing* can be quite confusing. For simplicity's sake, I am using the term *registering* to refer to the process of placing your Web service applications into one of the three UDDI directories available.

You may notice in steps and screen shots that Microsoft uses the word *publishing*. The term *registering* is easier to understand and avoids confusion, so that's what I use here.

By the way, UDDI stands for Universal Description, Discovery, and Integration. *UDDI* is a standard for discovering the Web services that a company exposes to the outside world. It is basically a big database, like the *yellow pages* or *white pages*. Three main UDDI registries exist: one each from Microsoft, IBM, and SAP. Each has agreements with the others to replicate and share the data, so it doesn't matter which one you register with. Because it doesn't matter, I show you how to use the Microsoft UDDI registry.

Step 1: Signing up for Passport

Before you can register a Web service in UDDI, you must first register your company. You only have to register your company once, so make sure that your business isn't already registered.

Registering your company is relatively painless, and any future Web services that you create can be registered to your company universally.

To register your company with the Microsoft UDDI, follow these steps:

1. **Choose Start➪Programs➪Internet Explorer to start the Microsoft Internet Explorer browser.**

2. **Navigate to the Microsoft UDDI Web site. To do so, use this URL:** `http://uddi.microsoft.com`.

3. **Click Register.**

   Clicking Register brings up the Web page shown in Figure 8-7.

4. **Sign into Microsoft Passport. (You must sign into Microsoft Passport to register your company with UDDI.) If you need a Passport account, go to** `www.passport.com` **to get one. To sign into Passport, simply click the Sign In icon.**

   (Microsoft calls this icon a *scarab.*)

   After you do this, the screen looks like it does in Figure 8-8.

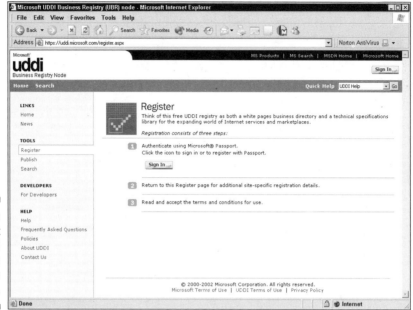

Figure 8-7:
Microsoft
UDDI
Registration
screen
before login.

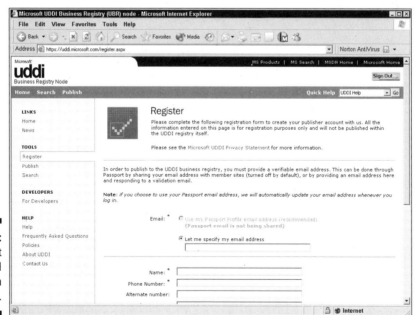

Figure 8-8:
Microsoft
UDDI
Registration
after login.

If you click the Sign In icon and the screen seems to just refresh, you can try two different things. The first is signing out of MSN Instant Messenger, if you are signed in. The second is going to the Passport Web site at `www.passport.com` and signing out. Then return to the Microsoft UDDI page and login again.

5. **Fill-in the fields for your company.**

   Remember when you fill in these fields, someone could be searching on one of these fields to find your company, so make sure to be as accurate as possible.

6. **Click Save.**

7. **Read and accept the Terms of Use.**

8. **Respond to the e-mail message that you will receive.**

   The Microsoft UDDI registration process will send you an e-mail message to verify the e-mail address that you entered into the registration page. Click the link in the e-mail message to finish the registration process. If this is successful, you will see a Congratulations page.

Step 2: Registering your company as a provider

After you register your company by using your Passport ID, you must then register your company as a provider. A *provider* is a hierarchical entity that offers one or more Web services. A provider belongs to a registered company, such as the one you set up in the preceding section.

Here's how to register your company as a provider:

1. **Choose Start⇨Programs⇨Internet Explorer to start the Microsoft Internet Explorer browser.**

2. **Navigate to the Microsoft UDDI Web site at** `http://uddi.microsoft.com`.

3. **Click the <u>Publish</u> link (which is used for registering your company as a provider).**

   If you are not already signed in to Passport, you will not be able to click this link. If you are prompted with the Sign In icon, click the icon and sign in with your Passport credentials that you created earlier. Otherwise, clicking Publish brings up the Web page shown in Figure 8-9.

   The UDDI Publish screen is divided into two panes, as most Microsoft hierarchical views are. The left pane allows you to drill down in the hierarchy, while the right pane shows more detail about the selected item in the left pane.

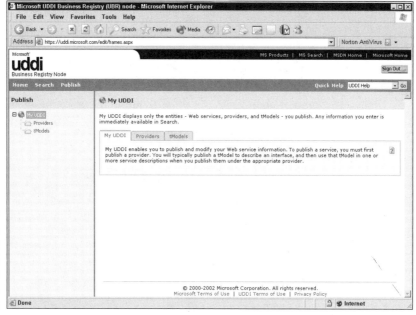

Figure 8-9:
Microsoft
UDDI
Publish
screen.

4. **Click the <u>Providers</u> link.**

   You can click either the item in the left pane or the tab in the right pane. They both bring you to the same place. Notice that no providers are registered.

5. **Click the Add Provider button.**

   Clicking Add Provider brings up a whole bunch of tabs and options, which are shown in Figure 8-10.

   The following tabs are shown at the top of the right pane for a single provider:

   Details: Contains names and descriptions of the provider.

   Services: Contains information about the Web services that a provider makes available. Such information includes the names and descriptions of your Web services along with bindings and categories. A *binding* is the access point into the Web service. A *category* is the classification of a Web service.

   Contacts: Identifies one or more contacts for a provider, in case users have questions, problems, or comments.

   Identifiers: Enables you to group providers logically together. This may seem unnecessary because you have already logged into a Passport account where you can add multiple providers. However, signing into Passport is just for administrative purposes. Logically, providers are not grouped without these identifiers.

Categories: Enables you to classify the services that are made available by the provider. Notice that this may be more general than the categories that are specified for a Web service (noted earlier on the Services tab).

Discovery URLs: Lists HTTP resources that someone can go to for more information about you as a provider.

Relationships: Enables you to publicly define the relationships (parent/child or peer/peer) to trading partners/providers that offer complimentary services.

Notice a couple of things on this screen. First of all, each of the tabs shown at the top of the screen can have multiple options available under it. The tab that is displayed by default is the Details tab. This tab contains one or more provider names. However, each of the provider names can be represented once in any language. It also contains one or more descriptions for the provider. Again, the same rule applies for multiple languages. You cannot add more than one name for a single provider in a given language.

6. **Change the name of your provider. By default, the name of the new provider is New Provider Name, which must be changed. To change this name, simply click Edit in the Name section and type the new name.**

You are prompted to change the name. You want to make this name the name of your organization. As an example, I enter Transport:80 Incorporated.

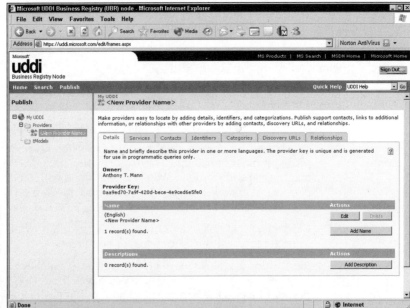

Figure 8-10: Microsoft UDDI Providers screen.

7. **Click the Update button when you are finished.**

   If you want to add additional names in other languages, click Add Name and follow the same procedure.

8. **Add a description for the provider. By default, no descriptions explain what you (as a provider) do. That's what the descriptions are for. To create a new description, click Add Description.**

   You are prompted to enter a description (up to 255 characters) that adequately describes what the provider offers.

9. **Click the Update button when you are finished.**

   If you want to add additional descriptions in other languages, click Add Description and follow the same procedure.

Step 3: Adding additional provider information

Now that you have added a provider and have given it a name and description, you are ready to alter the data that is represented in some of the other tabs (refer to Figure 8-10) that relate to a provider's offerings.

Contacts

To add contact-related data, just follow these simple steps:

1. **Click the Contacts tab.**

   You see a list of contacts that have been entered for the provider. If this is the first time you are entering the screen, no contact list appears.

2. **Click the Add Contact button.**

   For each contact, you can enter one or more e-mail addresses, phone numbers, and addresses. Additionally, you can add as many contacts as you wish. To add subsequent contacts, in the left pane, right-click the name of the desired provider under which you will add a contact and select Add Contact.

3. **Change the name of your contact.**

   By default, the name of the new provider is called New Contact Name, which must be changed. To change this name, simply click the Edit button in the Contact section.

   You are prompted to change the name. You want to make this name the name of your contact within the organization. As an example, I enter my name, Anthony T. Mann. Also, you can optionally add a Use Type. A *Use Type* is information about how the contact should be used, such as for technical support or administrative functions. This addition is optional.

4. **Click the Update button when you are finished.**

5. **Add a description for the contact. Descriptions for contacts are purely optional. However, if you wanted to describe the contact, simply click the Add Description button at the bottom of the screen.**

   This prompts you to add a single description in any language (English by default). A description may be something like this: Use this contact for all technical issues.

6. **Click Update when you are finished.**

7. **Enter e-mail, phone, and address data for the contact.**

   Following the same procedures that have been shown in the earlier steps, add e-mail, phone, and address data for the contact by clicking the tabs and adding the desired data. None of this is required.

Identifiers

An *identifier* is a way to group providers together logically by providing additional search criteria. A common way to do this is by selecting some business-related data that is common across all providers that you are entering. An example would be to use a Dunn & Bradstreet number (also known as a DUNS *number*). Add identifiers by doing this:

1. **Click the Identifiers tab.**

   You see a list of identifiers that have been entered for the provider. Most likely, none will be entered.

2. **Click the Add Identifier button.**

   An identifier needs three pieces of data, which are presented on the screen:

   > **tModel:** The identification scheme that you will use for your identifier. Notice that a lot of bogus tModels are in the database, so you'll have to ignore those. Most likely, you will choose Keyword.

   > **Key Name:** The name that you will use to associate the providers, such as DUNS or FederalID. However, you can choose any identifier that you wish to use that ties providers together logically.

   > **Key Value:** The value associated with the Key Name. Again, the value will link providers together logically.

3. **Fill in the data.**

   Fill in each field needed for the identifier.

4. **When you are finished, click Update.**

   You can proceed to add as many identifiers as you wish.

Categories

A *category* is a way to group the services or products that the provider belongs to. In other words, if you sell Web services that provide financial calculations, your categories may be Financial and Mortgage. You may wonder how a category gets defined. Each category is defined in a *categorization scheme*. At the time of this writing, there are nine categorization schemes that you can choose from:

- ✔ **uddi-org:types:** Categories used specifically for tModels, not for defining provider categories.

- ✔ **uddi-org:relationships:** Categories used specifically for relationships, not for defining provider categories.

- ✔ **ntis-gov:sic:1987:** Contains broad categories, such as Manufacturing and Retail Trade.

- ✔ **unspsc-org:unspsc:3-1:** Contains more detailed categories, such as Drugs and Pharmaceutical Products. Additionally, you can drill down further to such levels as Cardiovascular drugs.

- ✔ **unspsc-org:unspsc:** Contains detailed categories, like the unspsc-org: unspsc:3-1 category.

- ✔ **uddi-org:iso-ch:3166:1999:** Contains geographic categories, such as countries, cities, and states.

- ✔ **microsoft-com:geoweb:2000:** Also contains geographic categories.

- ✔ **ntis-gov:naics:1997:** Contains additional detailed categories.

- ✔ **VS Web Service Search Categorization:** Contains categories that are more germane to Web services. Categories include Collaboration and Financial.

To choose one or more categories, follow these steps:

1. **Click the Categories tab.**

   You see a list of categories that have already been entered for the provider, if there are any.

2. **Click the Add Category button.**

3. **Drill down into the categorization scheme discussed earlier and, finally, into the desired category.**

   To understand what I'm talking about with categories, take a look at Figure 8-11. It contains a list of categories from the VS Web Service Search Categorization scheme. Notice the numbers 1 and 2 at the bottom of the figure. These are links to additional pages of categories at the current level. After you choose a category, there may be more levels under that from which you can choose.

4. **You must drill down until no more levels are available.**

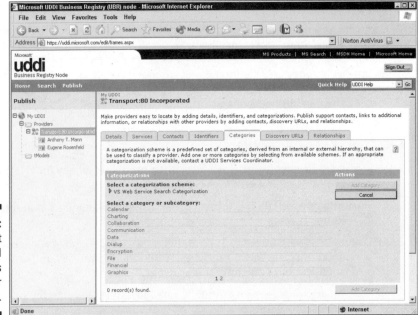

Figure 8-11:
Microsoft
UDDI
Categories
screen (for
a provider).

5. Click the Add Category button (again).

No Update button appears on this screen. The update is a button called
Add Category, even though the last button was also called Add Category.
After clicking this button, your category will be added. You can continue
to add as many categories as you wish.

This is the category that should represent the provider. You'll have a chance
later to enter one or more categories for each of the Web services that you
publish.

Discovery URLs

A discovery URL is not exactly what it seems. You may think of discovery
URL as *WSDL* (Web Services Description Language — covered in Chapter 9),
which is a URL to the discovery definition of a Web service. However, that is
not what is meant by *discovery URL* here. *Discovery URL* is simply a place
where a prospective customer can go to find out more information about the
services that you, as a provider, make available. This could be as simple as
your main home page. Add discovery URLs by following these steps:

1. Click the Discovery URLs tab.

You see a list of discovery URLs that have been entered for the provider.
At least one will be present. This is a business entity that was created
for you when you created the new provider.

2. **Click the Add URL button and type a URL and the Use Type.**

   A discover URL needs two pieces of data. The first thing it needs is the URL, such as `www.transport80.com`. The next piece of data is the Use Type. Just as you learned for Contacts, enter information instructing how this URL is to be used. For example, you may want to type **Corporate Web Site**.

3. **Click the Update button.**

   Your new discovery URL will be added to the list of discovery URLs.

Relationships

A *relationship* defines how two providers work together. A defined relationship is not necessary, but if you have a relationship with another provider, listing it here is a good idea. For example, if one provider of financial services has a relationship with another provider that authorizes credit cards, you would define the relationship under this tab. At present, three types of relationships (which come from the uddi-org:relationships categorization scheme shown in "Categories," earlier in this chapter) can be defined. These three types of relationships are the following:

- ✔ **Identity:** One provider is the same as another provider, but with a different name.

- ✔ **Parent/Child:** One provider is the parent, and one is the child. This is a good selection when one provider owns or operates the others.

- ✔ **Peer/Peer:** One provider is at the same level as the other. This is a typical scenario for a business-to-business relationship.

After you define the relationship, you also define the direction. In other words, does the currently selected provider have the relationship with the new provider or vice versa? Therefore, you must select the additional provider with which the relationship will be defined.

To add a relationship, follow these steps:

1. **Click the Relationships tab.**

   You see a list of all of the relationships that you have defined.

2. **Click the Add Relationship button.**

   A text box appears that enables you to search for the name of a provider with which you will create the relationship.

3. **Search for a provider. Enter the name (or partial name) of a provider; then click Search. Highlight the desired provider from the search results.**

   You see a list of relationship types and directions, and you'll select each of these in the following steps.

4. **Select the relationship type from the drop-down list provided.**

   Choose from one of the three relationship types in the drop-down list provided. Relationship types are discussed earlier in this section.

5. **Select the relationship direction.**

   The first option that is automatically presented is to indicate if your company has a relationship with the provider that you just searched for. The second option is the reverse, where the searched provider has a relationship with your company. Choose the appropriate option.

6. **Click the Add button.**

   Your new relationship is added, but it will have a status of Pending until the other provider approves the relationship. When the other provider goes to his/her relationships page, a status of Requested will be shown along with an Approve button. The other provider clicks this button to approve the relationship. After the relationship is approved, you see a status of Complete.

Publishing Your Web Services

After you register your company as a provider and configure its properties and other information, you can list the Web services that your company provides. Listing your Web services is known as *publishing*. You should publish any or all of the services that your company offers. Although the UDDI registry was designed to serve as a yellow pages or white pages directory for Web services, nothing forces you to enter the Web services that your company provides. In fact, you can just list the other services provided by your company, such as consulting or tax preparation. Although Microsoft doesn't (at this time) force the registration of Web services (over and above provider information) in the UDDI database, such registration was the original intent of UDDI.

A Web services listing is comprised of the following:

- **Details:** The name and description of your Web service.
- **Bindings:** The access point (URL) of your Web service and details about how to use the Web service. The information about a specific binding is called an *instance*.
- **Categories:** Classification for your Web service.

To keep your head from exploding, I have broken the process of publishing your Web services down into separate sections. I assume that you're reading along in order (and even performing the steps with your Web browser), so each section picks up where the last one left off.

Step 1: Setting up Web service details

Publishing your Web services is done on the Services tab in the UDDI registry under Publish. Here's how:

1. **Click the Services tab.**

   You'll see a list of all the Web services that you have published for your company.

2. **Click the Add Service button.**

   A new service is automatically created and associated with your company.

3. **Change the name of your service.**

   By default, the name of the new service is called **New Service Name**, which must be changed.

4. **To change this name, simply click the Edit button in the Name section.**

   You are prompted to change the name. You want to make this name the name of your Web service. As an example, I would type **Surv-A**, which is the name of my survey Web service for my company (and provider) Transport:80.

5. **Click the Update button when you are finished. If you want to add additional names in other languages, click Add Name and follow the same procedure.**

6. **To add a new description, click the Add Description button.**

   You are prompted to enter a description (up to 255 characters) that adequately describes what the Web service does.

7. **Click the Update button when you are finished.**

   If you want to add additional descriptions in other languages, click the Add Description button and follow the same procedure.

Step 2: Binding your Web service

After you have entered basic information about your Web service (name, description, and so forth), you have to start filling in the details of how to find your Web service. You do that by specifying binding information. Here's what you do:

1. **Click the Bindings tab.**

   You see a list of all the bindings associated with your Web service.

2. **Click the Add Binding button.**

   An empty binding is created for you. You have to change the values associated with the binding, which is covered in the following steps.

3. **Change the Access Point/URL Type of your binding.**

   By default, the name of the new service is shown as `http://`, which must be changed.

4. **To change this binding, simply click the Edit button in the Access Point section.**

   You are prompted to change the access point. For example, I typed **https://www.transport80.com/TP80/Surv-A**, which is the access point of my survey Web service.

5. **Then, change the URL Type, if needed.**

   Most likely the URL type will be `http` or `https`.

6. **Click the Update button when you are finished.**

7. **To create a new description for the binding, click the Add Description button.**

   You are prompted to enter a description (up to 255 characters) that adequately describes what the binding is for.

8. **Click the Update button when you are finished.**

   If you want to add additional descriptions in other languages, click the Add Description button and follow the same procedure.

Step 3: Entering instance info

Instance information is special discovery information that is related to your Web service. Instance information is used to add information about where Web services discovery information can be found. The most common way to do this is to provide a WSDL file (see Chapter 9). Each WSDL file needs its own Instance info. Follow these steps to add instance information:

1. **Click the Instance Info tab.**

   You see a URL and description that are used in conjunction with this Web service instance.

2. **Click the Add Instance Info button.**

   To continue with adding instance info, you must search for and select a tModel, so you are presented with a text box that enables you to search for tModels that describe your instance. If you don't find a tModel that suits your needs, you can add your own.

3. **Add a description for the instance. To create a new description for the instance, click the Add Description button.**

   By default, no descriptions explain the instance.

   You are prompted to enter a description (up to 255 characters) that adequately describes what the instance of your Web service is for.

4. **Click the Update button when you are finished.**

   If you want to add additional descriptions in other languages, click Add Description and follow the same procedure.

5. **Click the Instance Details tab.**

   You see a list of instance parameters and descriptions.

6. **Click the Edit button in the Instance Parameters section.**

   Clicking the Edit button enables you to enter a URL that contains the location of instance parameters. Instance parameters are the parameters that are used in conjunction with your Web service. For example, you may enter a URL of an HTML file that describes exactly how each of the parameters is used for your Web service. This field is completely optional.

7. **After you enter the URL, click the Update button to save your changes.**

8. **To create a new description for the instance parameters, click the Add Description button.**

   You are prompted to enter a description (up to 255 characters) that adequately describes what the instance parameters of your Web service do.

9. **Click the Update button when you are finished.**

   If you want to add additional descriptions in other languages, click the Add Description button and follow the same procedure.

Step 4: Specifying an overview document

An overview document is the WSDL file that is used to describe your Web service to another computer system. WSDL is covered in Chapter 9. *WSDL* (which stands for Web Services Description Language) is an XML file (which is covered in Chapter 3) that describes the parameters and datatypes for your Web service. This description is known as an *interface*. Here's how you specify an overview document (as if you couldn't guess by now):

1. **Click the Overview Document tab.**

   You see the URL and description that corresponds to the WSDL document. If this is the first time you are entering this screen, these fields will be blank, but you fill them in the following steps.

2. **Click the Edit button.**

   Clicking the Edit button enables you to edit or enter the URL that points to your WSDL file.

3. **After entering the URL, click the Update button to save your changes.**

4. **To create a new description for the instance overview document, click the Add Description button.**

   You are prompted to enter a description (up to 255 characters) that adequately describes the instance overview document for your Web Service.

5. **Click the Update button when you are finished.**

   If you want to add additional descriptions in other languages, click Add Description and follow the same procedure.

Step 5: Categorizing your Web service

The last step that you need to perform to enter your Web service in the UDDI registry is to categorize your Web service. Categorization is similar to how you categorized services for your company, but this categorization is for a specific Web service. For example, suppose you are a consulting company, but you have a Web service for the financial industry. You need to categorize your Web service in this manner:

1. **In the left pane, click the name of your Web service shown in the hierarchy.**

   The Details, Bindings, and Categories tabs appear in the right pane.

2. **Click the Categories tab.**

   You see a list of categories for your Web service. If this is the first time you have entered this screen, you see no categories, but you can add one quite easily.

3. **Add one or more categories.**

   To add a category to your Web Service, you follow the same procedure as that which is described earlier in this chapter for adding a provider category.

   However, know that this category is assigned to the Web service that you are offering instead of the provider, but the procedure is the same.

Chapter 9

Consuming Web Services

. . . .

. . . .

*I*f you've been reading from the beginning of the book, at this point you should know all about why you need Web services, how to construct them, and how to test them. However, you do not yet know how to use them. That's what this chapter is all about.

This chapter explores *using,* or *consuming,* Web services. These could be Web services that you wrote or Web services that exist within your corporate network or even on the Internet.

Sometimes I refer to *calling* a Web service. Calling is just another way of saying consuming.

Consuming a Web service is quite simple: It's a matter of instructing Visual Studio .NET where to find the Web service over the Internet. This instruction is known as creating a *Web reference*. In addition, Visual Studio .NET reads a special file (formatted as XML), called the *WSDL* (Web Services Description Language) file, in order to understand the details of the operations and arguments that a Web service exposes.

Web Services Clients

A Web services client can be any program or system that knows how to discover and use a Web service. Remember that a Web service is transmitted across a network by using standard HTTP through port 80. Therefore, Web services can be invoked without reconfiguring your firewall.

A Web service client may be any of the following (Web service clients are not limited to these, however):

- ✔ A Web browser, such as Internet Explorer
- ✔ A Visual Basic.NET application
- ✔ A Visual C# .NET application
- ✔ A Java application

Description and Discovery

To be useful, Web services must have programmatic capabilities. In other words, a Web service should be able to have values set and specific operations called from across the Internet or on your local network (intranet). For example, if you are calling (also known as *consuming*) a Web service that returns currency rate conversions (written by someone else), you would expect to be able to indicate the country for use in the currency rate conversion. The very fact that you can pass to the Web service the country for which you want the rate conversion means that the Web service is programmable.

Before Web services, when COM was the technology du jour, objects had to be listed in the Windows registry. Web services no longer need to be listed in the Windows registry, but the downside is that the definition of the services that are provided in the Web service must be self-describing. The self-describing nature of Web services is made possible through the industry standards called DISCO and WSDL, both of which are text files that use an XML format.

If you need a quick refresher on XML, see Chapter 3.

Discovery is the process of determining which operations, actions, and parameters a Web service supports. These operations, actions, and parameters are collectively referred to as its *interface*. Both DISCO and WSDL are described in the following sections.

Getting Funky with DISCO

DISCO is short for DISCOvery file. A DISCO file is a text file in XML format (surprise!, surprise!) and resides in the folder (with a `.DISCO` file extension) on the Web server where your Web service lives. However, if you search for it on your Web server's hard drive, you won't necessarily find it if you wrote your Web service by using Visual Studio .NET. That's because the DISCO file is not automatically generated by default.

In fact, the DISCO file doesn't have to actually exist for discovery to take place. Because of this fact, the information presented here is given only to increase your knowledge of how Web services work. I don't go into too much depth here because you are not likely to have to change anything in the DISCO file, but you should be aware of the process that takes place to enable discovery.

The DISCO file can be generated dynamically by specifying the ?DISCO argument in a URL that points to your Web service. For example, in Chapter 6, you learn how to create a couple of Web services. One is called Service1.asmx, and it resides on a Web server (my server is named rizzo) in a folder called VBWebService. To generate the DISCO file, you just enter the following into your browser:

```
http://rizzo/VBWebService/Service1.asmx?DISCO
```

The DISCO file that's generated and automatically named Service1.disco is shown here:

```
<?xml version="1.0" encoding="utf-8" ?>
<discovery xmlns:xsd="http://www.w3.org/2001/XMLSchema"
           xmlns:xsi="http://www.w3.org/2001/XMLSchema-
           instance"
           xmlns="http://schemas.xmlsoap.org/disco/">
    <contractRef
           ref="http://rizzo/vbwebservice/Service1.asmx?wsdl"
           docRef="http://rizzo/vbwebservice/Service1.asmx"
           xmlns="http://schemas.xmlsoap.org/disco/scl/" />
    <soap address="http://rizzo/vbwebservice/Service1.asmx"
           xmlns:q1="http://tempuri.org/"
           binding="q1:Service1Soap"
           xmlns="http://schemas.xmlsoap.org/disco/soap/" />
</discovery>
```

Notice that in the DISCO file, all the information is wrapped in <discovery> XML tags. Additionally, the DISCO file specifies standard namespaces where the discovery schema is located at www.w3.org. It also specifies a <contractRef> element, which is the location of the WSDL file that is dynamically and automatically generated. The WSDL file is used to describe the detailed interface of your Web service, as discussed in the following section.

WSDL

WSDL stands for *Web Services Description Language*. It is formatted as an XML text file and used by the DISCO file during the process of discovery to let the requesting program know about the specific interfaces that your Web service provides. Chapter 6 shows you how to create a Web service called WebService1. This Web service, hosted on a Web server named rizzo, has one method (also known as an *operation* or a *Web method*), called GetNameForUserID. This method accepts one argument (also known as a *parameter*), which is the UserID that will be looked up.

Based on this information, you could actually query the Web service and pass it a value like this:

```
http://rizzo/vbwebservice/Service1.asmx/GetNameForUserID?User
        ID=jjones
```

A problem occurs, however, if you don't know about the interfaces that a Web service supports. You don't know what methods it has, which arguments are expected for each method, and so forth. That's where WSDL comes in.

DISCO points to the WSDL file. If the WSDL file doesn't exist, you can generate it automatically by specifying the ?wsdl parameter on the URL, just like you did for the DISCO file. In other words, the following URL generates a dynamic WSDL file:

```
http://rizzo/VBWebService/Service1.asmx?wsdl
```

You probably won't need to alter the WSDL file if you use Visual Studio .NET to create your Web services. WSDL files are generated dynamically and automatically when they are needed, which is a good thing because if you had to generate the code yourself by typing out the necessary XML to make the discovery process happen, you'd have a tremendous headache by the time you were finished.

The XML needed for the WSDL file can be quite lengthy and complicated, so you'll be glad that it's generated for you. So, why am I about to show you what the WSDL file looks like if you don't need to worry about it? Simple — because in order to understand Web services, you really need to understand how they work, which also includes the discovery process.

The discovery process is made possible by DISCO and WSDL, both of which are text files written in XML.

Check out Listing 9-1, which shows the XML for a WSDL file needed for the discovery of the Service1 Web service (which contains a single method and a single argument).

Listing 9-1: WSDL auto-generated code for a simple Web service

```
<?xml version="1.0" encoding="utf-8" ?>
<definitions xmlns:http="http://schemas.xmlsoap.org/wsdl/http/"
             xmlns:soap="http://schemas.xmlsoap.org/wsdl/soap/"
             xmlns:s="http://www.w3.org/2001/XMLSchema"
             xmlns:s0="http://tempuri.org/"
             xmlns:soapenc="http://schemas.xmlsoap.org/soap/encoding/"
             xmlns:tm="http://microsoft.com/wsdl/mime/textMatching/"
             xmlns:mime="http://schemas.xmlsoap.org/wsdl/mime/"
             targetNamespace="http://tempuri.org/"
             xmlns="http://schemas.xmlsoap.org/wsdl/">
<types>
```

```
<s:schema elementFormDefault="qualified" targetNamespace="http://tempuri.org/">
<s:element name="GetNameForUserID">
<s:complexType>
<s:sequence>
  <s:element minOccurs="0" maxOccurs="1" name="UserID" type="s:string" />
  </s:sequence>
  </s:complexType>
  </s:element>
<s:element name="GetNameForUserIDResponse">
<s:complexType>
<s:sequence>
  <s:element minOccurs="0" maxOccurs="1" name="GetNameForUserIDResult"
             type="s:string" />
  </s:sequence>
  </s:complexType>
  </s:element>
  <s:element name="string" nillable="true" type="s:string" />
  </s:schema>
  </types>
<message name="GetNameForUserIDSoapIn">
  <part name="parameters" element="s0:GetNameForUserID" />
  </message>
<message name="GetNameForUserIDSoapOut">
  <part name="parameters" element="s0:GetNameForUserIDResponse" />
  </message>
<message name="GetNameForUserIDHttpGetIn">
  <part name="UserID" type="s:string" />
  </message>
<message name="GetNameForUserIDHttpGetOut">
  <part name="Body" element="s0:string" />
  </message>
<message name="GetNameForUserIDHttpPostIn">
  <part name="UserID" type="s:string" />
  </message>
<message name="GetNameForUserIDHttpPostOut">
  <part name="Body" element="s0:string" />
  </message>
<portType name="Service1Soap">
<operation name="GetNameForUserID">
  <input message="s0:GetNameForUserIDSoapIn" />
  <output message="s0:GetNameForUserIDSoapOut" />
  </operation>
  </portType>
<portType name="Service1HttpGet">
<operation name="GetNameForUserID">
  <input message="s0:GetNameForUserIDHttpGetIn" />
  <output message="s0:GetNameForUserIDHttpGetOut" />
  </operation>
  </portType>
<portType name="Service1HttpPost">
<operation name="GetNameForUserID">
  <input message="s0:GetNameForUserIDHttpPostIn" />
```

(continued)

Listing 9-1 *(continued)*

```xml
    <output message="s0:GetNameForUserIDHttpPostOut" />
  </operation>
</portType>
<binding name="Service1Soap" type="s0:Service1Soap">
  <soap:binding transport="http://schemas.xmlsoap.org/soap/http"
              style="document" />
<operation name="GetNameForUserID">
  <soap:operation soapAction="http://tempuri.org/GetNameForUserID"
              style="document" />
<input>
  <soap:body use="literal" />
  </input>
<output>
  <soap:body use="literal" />
  </output>
  </operation>
  </binding>
<binding name="Service1HttpGet" type="s0:Service1HttpGet">
  <http:binding verb="GET" />
<operation name="GetNameForUserID">
  <http:operation location="/GetNameForUserID" />
<input>
  <http:urlEncoded />
  </input>
<output>
  <mime:mimeXml part="Body" />
  </output>
  </operation>
  </binding>
<binding name="Service1HttpPost" type="s0:Service1HttpPost">
  <http:binding verb="POST" />
<operation name="GetNameForUserID">
  <http:operation location="/GetNameForUserID" />
<input>
  <mime:content type="application/x-www-form-urlencoded" />
  </input>
<output>
  <mime:mimeXml part="Body" />
  </output>
  </operation>
  </binding>
<service name="Service1">
<port name="Service1Soap" binding="s0:Service1Soap">
  <soap:address location="http://rizzo/VBWebService/Service1.asmx" />
  </port>
<port name="Service1HttpGet" binding="s0:Service1HttpGet">
  <http:address location="http://rizzo/VBWebService/Service1.asmx" />
  </port>
<port name="Service1HttpPost" binding="s0:Service1HttpPost">
```

```
   <http:address location="http://rizzo/VBWebService/Service1.asmx" />
   </port>
   </service>
</definitions>
```

Okay, so now you're frightened. You've just seen a bunch of XML markup, but try to relax. You don't need to understand it line for line. The point of showing you the enormous WSDL file generated from such a simple Web service is to illustrate the following:

✔ Because the WSDL file shown in Listing 9-1 contains so much XML code (even for a very simple Web service), you won't ever want to try to write a WSDL file yourself.

✔ Even though Listing 9-1 is just a basic description of a simple Web Service, it reinforces how important understanding basic XML concepts. Namespaces are particularly important. (Check out Chapter 3.)

In addition, if you are so inclined, you can look through this code in detail to understand the relationship between WSDL (using SOAP, which I discuss in Chapter 4) and your Web services. You see, all XML-related concepts build upon each other to form a complex system that enables Web services to function.

✔ The WSDL file shown in Listing 9-1 reinforces how an *alias* works with XML. Much of the first half of the WSDL file shown in Listing 9-1 contains a prefix, s:. After you read through Chapter 3 (to learn the basics of XML), you should understand that the alias is a way of shortening the amount of information that you would have to type into an XML file. Also, aliases allow for smaller files to be created. Can you imagine specifying the following namespace every time you use an s: prefix?

```
http://www.w3.org/2001/XMLSchema
```

That would be crazy! If this doesn't make sense to you, please take a few minutes to scan Chapter 3 again.

WS-Inspection

I promise that this is the last specification I mention in this chapter. I'm sure that you're getting burned out on this, so I'll be concise. WS-Inspection does for your Web server what WSDL does for a single Web service. In other words, WSDL is used to discover the interfaces exposed by a Web service. Similarly, WS-Inspection is used to discover all the Web services exposed by a Web server (because certainly, more than one may exist). The only disadvantage of WS-Inspection is that you have to know the URL location of the server.

Like most other things with Web services, WS-Inspection is a text file that is comprised of an XML document. Here's a sample of a WS-Inspection document in its most basic form:

```
<?xml version="1.0"?>
<inspection
          xmlns="http://schemas.xmlsoap.org/ws/2001/10/inspe
          ction/"
  <service>
    <description
          referencedNamespace="http://schemas.xmlsoap.org/ws
          dl/"

          location="http://www.transport80.com/survey/render
          .wsdl">
    </description>
    <description
          referencedNamespace="http://schemas.xmlsoap.org/ws
          dl/"

          location="http://www.transport80.com/survey/admin.
          wsdl">
    </description>
  </service>
</inspection>
```

The preceding WS-Inspection XML document contains `<inspection>` elements (and a corresponding namespace). Within the `<inspection>` elements is a `<service>` element that contains `<description>` elements — one for each Web service on your server. The WS-Inspection code presented in the preceding code is used to list two Web services in my company's Web farm, called `render` and `admin` for our `survey` Web service.

As with most technologies, multiple specifications become proposed and/or adopted to do specific things. Of course, too many specifications become quite difficult to understand and digest, unless you are intimately involved in the specification. WS-Inspection is just such an issue, but it seeks to perform simplification. You don't need to know too much about WS-Inspection; just be aware that the specification exists and know how it relates to XML.

Discovering UDDI

UDDI stands for *Universal Description, Discovery, and Integration.* UDDI is a centralized database that stores description and discovery information for Web services; it's a sort of "yellow pages" for Web services. UDDI is used to allow internal or external clients (see earlier discussion on clients) to "find" the Web services that you provide. In addition to a human-readable description of the services that a company provides, UDDI stores the URL location for the WSDL file, known as the *entry point* into the Web service.

Consider this example. Suppose that you wrote a Web service called `CalculateMortgage` that is sitting on your corporate server. A programmer is writing a program that displays mortgage information in a Web page, based on user input. However, the programmer doesn't know what parameters the `CalculateMortgage` Web service needs. So, how does the programmer find out? Does the programmer ask you? The programmer could do so, but that's not good use of your time. The programmer finds out how to use the `CalculateMortgage` Web service by using UDDI (through WSDL), assuming that you registered your Web service with a UDDI registry.

A UDDI registry enables you to go to one place to search for or discover what Web services and their interfaces (operations and parameters) are available from a given company or vendor, known as a *provider*.

Much like everything in Web services technology, the UDDI registry is not the brainstorm of Microsoft alone. A committee of companies came up with the specification and submitted it to the World Wide Web Consortium (W3C).

To get more detailed information about UDDI specifications, refer to `www.uddi.org`.

The following are the three prominent global UDDI registries, from which you can search for Web services to consume:

- Microsoft
- IBM
- SAP

If you want any more information about the IBM or SAP UDDI registries, point your browser to `www.uddi.org/find.html`. For the rest of this chapter, I focus on using the Microsoft UDDI registry (because this is a Microsoft-focused book). It may be interesting for you to know that each of the UDDI registries has agreements with the other ones so that data is replicated among them. In other words, if you register your company or Web services with the Microsoft registry, the data will be replicated once per day (or more frequently) with the other registries and vice versa.

Microsoft UDDI Registry

You can find the Microsoft UDDI Registry at `http://uddi.microsoft.com`. This, or any, registry provides three basic functions:

- **Search:** Enables you to find out what Web services are offered by vendors. This functionality is similar to the "yellow pages" or "white pages." Searching is covered in the next section in this chapter.

✔ **Register:** Enables you to register your company with the UDDI registry. UDDI register functionality is discussed in Chapter 8.

✔ **Publish:** Enables you to enter the specific Web services that your company offers. UDDI publish functionality is discussed in Chapter 8.

The Publish function of the Microsoft UDDI registry should not be confused with publishing your Web services into a production environment. Publishing, in the UDDI registry context, refers to the publishing of your services that you provide into the UDDI registry, much like the way you publish your business's phone number in the phone book.

Searching Microsoft UDDI registry

To search the Microsoft UDDI registry, point your browser to `http://uddi.microsoft.com/search`. Doing so brings up the Web page shown in Figure 9-1.

With the Microsoft UDDI registry, you have the ability to search in the following areas:

✔ **Category:** Enables the searching of categories of Web services. The categories of Web services are related to specific W3C specifications for categories. Categories are covered in Chapter 8.

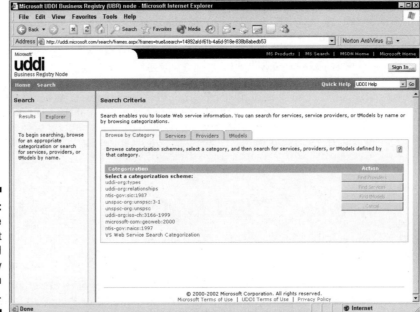

Figure 9-1: The Microsoft UDDI registry search page.

✔ **Service:** Enables searching of the specific services that a vendor provides, such as Mortgage.

✔ **Provider:** Enables searching for specific vendors, such as Transport:80 (my company).

✔ **tModel (also known as *Type Model*):** Enables you to search for the name of the XML document that describes services to the UDDI registry. tModels are not covered further in this book. You can find more information about tModels at `www.uddi.org`.

To search for a specific Web service, follow these steps:

1. **Choose Start⇨Programs⇨Internet Explorer to start the Microsoft Internet Explorer browser.**

2. **Use this URL —** `http://uddi.microsoft.com/search` **— to open the Microsoft UDDI registry search screen.**

3. **Click the Services tab.**

   You'll see a Web page that allows you to search for services.

4. **Enter the desired service name.**

   If you don't know the exact name of the service, you can use wildcard characters. A *wildcard character* enables you to put in a placeholder to do partial searches.

   For example, if you want to search for communications, you can simply type **Comm** or **Comm%**. Both bring up services, such as Communication, Commerce, and Commercial. However, if you type **%Comm,** your search will return services where the word ends in *Comm.* If you want to return all services where the word contains *Comm,* simply type **%Comm%.** Your search term is not case-sensitive.

5. **Further qualify your search.**

   You can also further qualify your search based on categories, which are covered in Chapter 8. Although tModels are not covered in this book, it's important to know that you can limit your searches further by specifying tModel information.

6. **Click the Search button.**

7. **Review the results.**

   In the left pane, you see the results of your search. If more than seven services match your description, you will have multiple pages of results. To view additional pages, simply click the desired page number at the bottom of the left pane where the results are shown. You may have to scroll down to see these page numbers.

   Click the desired service to view its details. Notice that both the left and right panes change. The left pane now shows the Explorer tab. The

Explorer tab allows you to navigate a tree relating to the service that you selected. The tree shows a hierarchy (as all trees do) where the company name (also known as the *provider*) is shown at the top. Then, the tree branches out into contact information and service information. Each is denoted by its own icon.

The right pane shows details about the selected item in the left pane. This is very similar to the way Windows Explorer works. The right pane also shows tabbed information, depending on the selection in the left pane. For example, if a contact is selected, Details, E-mail, Phone, and Address tabs are shown in the right pane. If a service is selected, the tabs are Details, Bindings, and Categories. However, if the provider is selected, the tabs shown in the right pane are Details, Services, Contacts, Identifiers, Categories, Discovery URLs, and Relationships.

Browse the results to find out if this is the service that you want to consume.

You must be careful if you want to search only for Web services that are available. Many companies place their services, such as consulting, into the registry for someone to find, even though the registry was meant to be primarily a Web services-only registry.

After you have found the Web services that you want to consume, or you want to consume Web services that you already know about (such as ones that you've created), you're ready to begin, so move on to the following section.

Using a Web Service for the First Time

Using (also known as *consuming*) Web services is easier than you may think. If you have programmed in any version of Visual Basic, from version 1 through 6, you programmed with COM (Component Object Model) objects by setting a reference to the DLL that contained the objects. After this reference was set, you could then make programmatic calls against the object(s) contained in the reference.

Using a Web reference follows exactly the same concept, except that the reference to the object(s) is not on a local machine using COM technology; instead, it is on a remote machine (passing through firewalls using SOAP) using Web services technology. Doesn't that make it easy? I'm going to show you just how easy it really is!

Suppose that you find a Web service that registers user names and addresses that you want to consume in a Visual Basic .NET application. (An example of how to write such a Web service is shown in Chapter 6.) First, the application must know where to find this Web service. You do this by creating a Web reference (again, similar to creating a reference to a COM object in earlier versions of Visual Basic). I have set up a Web service that you can try without needing to actually set up database access and the Web service itself. This sample Web service gives you the opportunity to try to consume a Web service without having to create one yourself. The sample Web service URL location is

```
http://wsfd.transport80.com/external/wsfd.asmx.
```

wsfd in the URL stands for *Web Services For Dummies.* You can also use the HTTPS protocol if you plan to enter real data, such as addresses and phone numbers, into the Web service. Remember that others who buy this book will be doing the same thing, so they will be able to see your data.

Three methods are available for this Web service:

- ✔ **Lookup:** Looks up, or searches contact data in the database, based on information provided in any/all fields. Lookup accepts these arguments (all of which are optional):

    - **UserID:** Unique identifier for each user record, if known.

    - **LastName:** Last name of the user.

    - **FirstName:** First name of the user.

    - **Address1:** First physical address line of the user.

    - **Address2:** Second physical address line of the user.

    - **City:** City of the user.

    - **State:** State (such as New Hampshire) or state code (such as NH) of the user.

    - **Postal:** Zip or postal code for the user.

    - **Country:** Country name or code for the user.

    - **HomePhone:** Home phone number, including area code of the user. This should not contain any punctuation (parentheses, dashes, or periods).

    - **HomeEMail:** Home or personal e-mail address for the user.

- ✔ **Save:** Inserts or updates data in the database. If the record doesn't exist, it will be inserted. If it does exist, it will be updated, based on UserID. Save accepts these arguments:

    - **UserID:** Can be 0 for a new record. If 0 is used, the next available ID will be generated and returned.

    - **LastName**

    - **FirstName**

    - **Address1**

- **Address2**
- **City**
- **State**
- **Postal**
- **Country**
- **HomePhone**
- **HomeEMail**

✔ **Delete:** Deletes a contact in the database, based on UserID. Delete accepts this argument:

- **UserID:** Must be a valid ID.

Consuming a Web Service in Visual Basic .NET

I want to take a moment to put the process of consuming a Web service into perspective. You have no doubt determined that you want to use a Web service. You know the URL location of the Web service because it is located either on your intranet or you have searched a UDDI registry (see the earlier section in this chapter) and found the location of the WSDL file. Perhaps you even wrote the Web service code using Chapter 6 as a guideline. In either case, a Web service is available to be called because it is hosted on a production Web server.

The first thing you must do to use the desired Web service is to either create a new Visual Studio .NET project or open an existing Visual Studio .NET project that will access, or consume, the Web service. To illustrate the point, I show you how to create a very simple project in Visual Basic .NET that will access a Web service.

Chapter 6 shows you how to create a Visual Studio project (both in Visual Basic .NET and Visual C# .NET), however, that chapter focuses on using these languages to create Web services. These Web services can then be consumed by a separate Visual Studio .NET project. In other words, Visual Studio .NET can be used to both write and consume Web services.

To create a new project (in Visual Basic .NET), just follow these steps:

1. **Choose Start⇨Programs⇨Microsoft Visual Studio .NET@⇨Microsoft Visual Studio .NET.**

   The Visual Studio .NET IDE starts.

2. **Click the New Project button.**

   Doing so brings up the New Project dialog box, as shown in Figure 9-2.

3. **Click ASP.NET Web Application and make sure that you have a valid location for the Web project and click the OK button.**

   My application is called `Consume`. It's in the `External` folder on a server named `rizzo`.

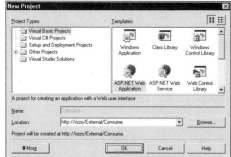

Figure 9-2:
New Project
dialog box.

4. **Open the code window for the** `WebForm1.aspx` **page. To open the code window, simply right-click the name of the form and choose the View Code menu.**

   The `WebForm1.aspx` page is added to the project automatically when you create a new project.

   The code window is shown within the Visual Studio .NET IDE.

5. **Declare namespaces used in the project. At the very top of the code page, add these three namespaces with the** `Imports` **keyword:**

```
Imports System
Imports System.Web.Services
Imports System.Web.Services.Protocols
```

6. **To add a Web reference to the Web service, right-click the name of your project in the Solution Explorer window and choose the Add Web Reference menu.**

   The Solution Explorer window is always shown in the Visual Studio .NET IDE.

   The Add Web Reference dialog box appears, as shown in Figure 9-3.

Figure 9-3:
The Add
Web
Reference
dialog box.

7. **At this point, you have two choices. Either you can enter the URL that points to the Web service, or you can search for it in a UDDI registry.**

Each of these options is shown in the next two sections, "Entering a Web service URL" and "Searching for a Web service URL." Regardless of which choice you make, you arrive at this step (Step 7). For this example, use a Web reference to my sample Web service

```
http://wsfd.transport80.com/external/wsfd.asmx.
```

8. **Click the Add Reference button.**

After you add the Web reference, the Solution Explorer now contains a reference to the Web service, as shown in Figure 9-4.

Figure 9-4:
Solution
Explorer
showing
new Web
reference.

9. **Rename the Folder if desired. To do this, simply right-click the folder and choose the Rename menu. Type in the new name and press the Enter key.**

   In Figure 9-4, notice that the folder that represents the Web service files is shown as `com.transport80.wsfd`. You can rename it if you want. This is important because you will refer to this name in your code, as you'll see shortly. Because this is my development server, I rename the folder as `Dev`.

10. **Create an instance of your Web Service object.**

    Now that a Web reference is declared, it's easy to create an instance of the Web Service object. Do this in the PageLoad event. Use this syntax: `DIM obj_var As New web_ref_folder.web_service_name`.

    Here, you can substitute the following:

    - `obj_var` is the name of the variable that you want to use to represent your new object. For example, an object that will be used to represent the WSFD Web service may be called `objWSFD`.

    - `web_ref_folder` is the name of the folder that you renamed in Step 9. Because Step 9 renamed the folder to `Dev`, you'll see this name appear automatically with Intellisense (which is the automatic helper that comes up when you type code in Visual Studio .NET) after typing the `New` keyword. This is shown in Figure 9-5.

    - `web_service_name` is the name of the Web service that is contained at the URL that you specified. My sample Web service name is called WSFD.

    Here's a sample of what the complete line of code looks like:

    ```
    Dim objWSFD As New Dev.WSFD()
    ```

11. **Manipulate your new object in code.**

    After you have created your object, you can call its methods and set its properties. When you set your Web reference, Visual Studio .NET reads the WSDL file. This is what allows Intellisense to work with your Web services.

    For example, you can call the `Save` method and pass its arguments. These arguments are listed earlier in this chapter in the section, "Using a Web Service for the First Time." Intellisense shows what arguments are expected, as shown in Figure 9-6.

Dev

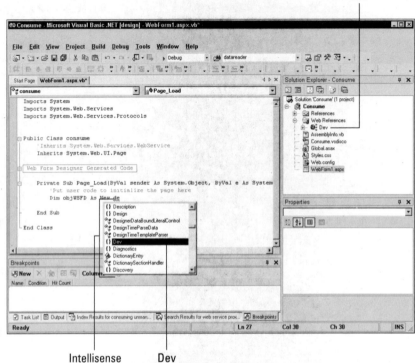

Figure 9-5:
Intellisense,
showing
Web
Reference
folder name.

Intellisense   Dev

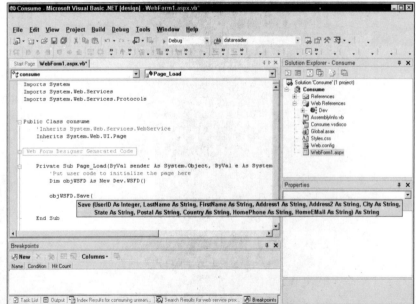

Figure 9-6:
Intellisense
showing
arguments
for Web
service
method.

You must assign values to arguments in code. Most likely, these values will come from form fields on the screen. However, for the sake of simplicity, here's an example of calling the Save method and passing arguments:

```
ret = objWSFD.Save(0, "Mann", "Anthony", "123 Main
        Street", vbNull, "Portsmouth", "NH", "03801",
        "USA", "(603) 111-1111", "tmann@transport80.com")
```

Notice that the object that you created in Step 10 is being used by calling the Save method and passing values for each of the arguments. The value that is returned from the Save method is assigned to the ret variable, which was declared as a string. It was declared as such because that's what the WSDL file indicates as the return type.

Because this is a Web page, this line of code presents the return value on the screen:

```
Response.Write("UserID is: " & ret)
```

ret is the new UserID for new users or the existing UserID for existing users.

Check out Listing 9-2 to see how the code will look when you put everything together.

Listing 9-2: The results of your test project

```
Imports System
Imports System.Web.Services
Imports System.Web.Services.Protocols


Public Class consume
    Inherits System.Web.UI.Page

    Private Sub Page_Load(ByVal sender As System.Object, ByVal e As
            System.EventArgs) Handles MyBase.Load
        'Put user code to initialize the page here
        Dim objWSFD As New Dev.WSFD()
        Dim ret As String

        ret = objWSFD.Save(0, "Mann", "Anthony", "123 Main Street", vbNull,
            "Portsmouth", "NH", "03801", "USA", "(603) 111-1111",
            "tmann@transport80.com")

        Response.Write("UserID is: " & ret)


    End Sub

End Class
```

Entering a Web service URL

The preceding section, "Consuming a Web Service in Visual Basic .NET," referred (in Step 7) to a choice in selecting a Web service. One way to do this is to simply enter the URL path of your desired Web service file (including the ASMX file extension). Chapter 6 shows you how to create a Web service to access a database of users. It was called `wsfd.asmx`. I have created and compiled this application for you to try out; it is located on one of my development servers. You can find it at

```
http://wsfd.transport80.com/external/wsfd.asmx
```

Therefore, when the Add Web Reference dialog box is shown (as in Figure 9-3, shown earlier in this chapter) you simply manually enter the URL in the Address field and press Enter — just like you would do in your browser. The address that you enter can be on your intranet or the Internet. After you enter a valid URL to your Web service's ASMX file, you see information presented about the operations (also known as *methods*) that your Web service exposes. This is shown in Figure 9-7.

You can click on any of the operations to get more information about them, but the Web reference does not get as specific as an operation or method. The reference is the entire Web service. You decide which operations you will use in your code.

After you have added the Web reference, you can continue creating your Visual Studio project, as outlined starting with Step 8, under the section, "Consuming a Web Service in Visual Basic .NET," earlier in this chapter.

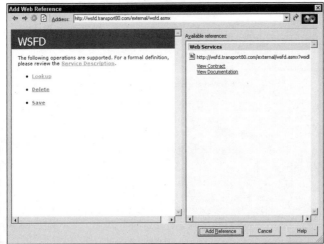

Figure 9-7:
Operations available for a Web service.

Searching for a Web service URL

If you don't know the URL of a Web service that you want to use, you can search for the URL within the Add Web Reference dialog box. To search a UDDI registry, simply click the desired registry in the left pane. Two UDDI registries are listed in this pane; they are the Microsoft UDDI Registry and the Microsoft Test UDDI Registry. The test registry is available for you to test registrations and usage of a UDDI registry. After you are finished testing, you can enter data into the live registry.

To use either of these registries, simply follow these steps:

1. **Click the link or the picture associated with the registry.**

   Clicking a UDDI registry brings up the dialog box shown in Figure 9-8.

2. **Perform a search by entering criteria.**

   The screen is divided into two sections, known as *panes*. The left pane allows you to search for a specific service or a provider. A *provider* is typically a company that offers a Web service. Click the Search button adjacent to the text box into which you enter data.

   For example, search for Web services that provide credit card services. Do this by typing **Credit** in the Service Name box. Click the Search button.

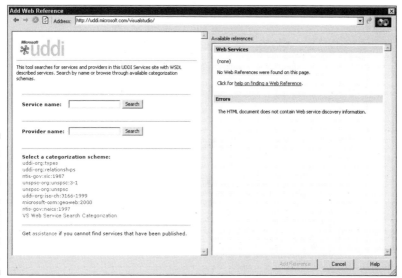

Figure 9-8:
Add Web Reference dialog box, showing UDDI search facility.

3. View Search Results.

After performing a search, the results will appear in the left pane. How can this happen in the left pane? Simple — the Search Criteria area goes away before the results are displayed! If results are returned, you must drill down into the results until you get to the URL associated with the WSDL file for the Web service. If you want to do another search, click the link labeled "Click here to search again." The left pane will switch back.

If you searched for credit in Step 2, you can drill down into a Web service, as shown in Figure 9-9.

The provider and service chosen are completely at random (no affiliation exists between the company shown and this book). I have not used or tested this Web service, so I am not endorsing it in any way. I just wanted to show you how the UDDI registry works.

4. Click the Interface Definitions URL.

At this point, the Add Reference button is not enabled. This is because you've only searched for a Web service and drilled down to find details. You haven't actually selected a Web service.

5. To select a Web service, click the URL in the Interface Definitions section.

This URL is the HTTP location of the WSDL file corresponding to the Web service. Clicking the URL changes the screen to show the WSDL file in the left pane and additional details in the right pane, as shown in Figure 9-10.

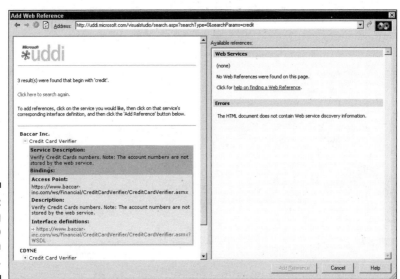

Figure 9-9:
Drilling
down into
search
results.

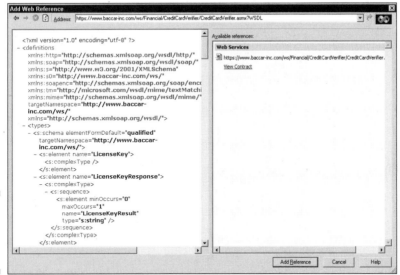

Figure 9-10:
Selecting
a Web
service.

Notice that the Add Reference button is now enabled.

5. **Click the Add Reference button.**

After you click the Add Reference button, the Web reference that you have selected is added into your Visual Studio. NET project. You can now continue with creating your project, as outlined starting with Step 8, under the section, "Consuming a Web Service in Visual Basic .NET," earlier in this chapter.

Chapter 10

Constructing Applications with Building Block Services

*O*ne of the great things about .NET is the capability to use someone else's software that was written as a Web service. This means that you don't have to reinvent the wheel every time you need to incorporate a needed piece of functionality. As you know, a *Web service* is a piece of reusable code that can be invoked over the Internet or on your local network. A *building block service* is a term that Microsoft came up with to describe the essential functionality, built with Web services, that is needed by most applications.

However, a building block service has a further classification — because the user, not some server, performs a function, the user has complete control over the data that is transmitted across the Internet. Talk about empowerment!

There are lots of authentication services, map services, Web surveys, messaging services, and other services available over the Internet. However, that doesn't mean that all these services are Web services — or that the services are offered as building block Web services. You can use one of many technologies to provide services similar to the ones described in this chapter. This chapter offers a list of the *kinds* of Web services that are available as building block services. See Chapter 1 for a refresher on the difference between a service that's provided over the Web and a Web service.

Although Microsoft coined the term *building block service,* I take the term one step further and discuss not only Microsoft building-block services, but also some third-party building-block services that I consider to be essential to most applications.

In this chapter, I point out some great building block services that you can use in your own applications to get them up and running in no time. These services are by no means a complete list of everything that is available. It is just a subset of what is available from Microsoft and other choice vendors of building block services.

Knowing Your Options

Any application that has the capability to consume a Web service can use a building block service. Consuming these building block services conceptually is quite simple. However, depending on the complexity of the specific desired Web service, the details of implementation and coding may be complex. Typically, most building block services are not free. In fact, they can be quite expensive. But, if you consider the cost of developing the functionality yourself, these services can be of exceptional value. So the question is really, why wouldn't you consider using a building block service?

You have lots of options when it comes to building block services. Although Microsoft coined the term, many other companies provide these services in a slew of categories in all shapes and sizes. I give you detailed information on implementing a few specific building block services later in this chapter to help speed up your implementation.

CRM services

CRM stands for Customer Relationship Management. CRM is a hot concept in Information Technology and business. So what the heck is it? CRM is a category of enterprise applications that promotes and enforces good customer service and sales force automation (for following up leads and helping to automate the entire sales cycle). In addition, a couple of building block services fall under this category because users can control the data that is being used in order to promote better customer service.

Here's a look at the types of applications that qualify as CRM services.

Online surveys

Every business, industry, and organization needs to survey its clients, users, members, or employees. Testing to find out how you stand with these groups of people is important for promoting good customer service and improving overall performance.

Because there are so many online survey options available over the Web (not all of which are actually Web services), this section tracks the online survey Web service provided by Transport:80, called Surv-A (www.surv-a.com).

However, in general, you should look for an online survey that is a bona fide Web service because this option lets you control functionality by calling the Web service from your own applications.

Bottom line? Services like Surv-A keep you from having to create the complex code for configurable and secure surveys all on your own. That allows you to concentrate on more important stuff.

With a service like this, the power of data is in the user's hands because the user can opt to take the survey or not. Also, the user can decide which questions to answer. For example, if a question of a sensitive nature is asked, the person taking the survey can simply avoid it.

Utilizing surveys on Surv-A follows this process:

1. **Configure the questions and answers of the survey.**

   This configuration includes formatting options, such as whether the questions are required and if the survey should automatically remove leading and trailing spaces from text answers.

2. **Copy the unique link to your survey given to you by Surv-A and e-mail that link to your target audience.**

3. **When your target audience clicks on the link in your e-mail, the survey is displayed.**

   The display of your survey is known as *rendering*.

4. **Retrieve and analyze your data at any time after your survey goes live.**

Any of the above processes can be performed by using the Surv-A Web site or by consuming the Web services interface programmatically in your own applications. Consuming Web services is shown in Chapter 9.

Survey benefits

To retain customers (which is one of the core reasons to use CRM software), you should survey your customers to find out how well you are doing in your business, to find out how happy your customers are, or even just to get some feedback or ideas for future products and services. Most businesses that provide survey services (including Surv-A) allow you to include this needed functionality in your applications without having to write it yourself.

Depending on which company you go with, you can gain the following benefits of using a building block online survey that utilizes Web services technology, such as Surv-A:

 ✔ **No Hardware Investment:** For example, all data is stored within the Surv-A system on redundant and fault-tolerant servers so that you don't have to worry about using your own hardware.

- ✔ **Security:** Generally you can count on high security. All data is stored securely and transmitted securely over the Internet by using 128-bit SSL encryption.

- ✔ **Multiple Formats:** Data can be retrieved by HTML, XML, e-mail, and MSMQ (Microsoft Message Queue). Multiple formats give you ultimate flexibility in using results in your own organization.

- ✔ **Many Usages:** Surv-A cannot only be used for conducting surveys of your users, but also can provide for online registration forms, custom quotations, online tests, rating systems, questionnaires, and more.

Costs

To use the Surv-A building block Web service, the license fee per processor and per server costs $500. Instead, if you are writing your application to span multiple Web servers or have lots of processors, you may want to take advantage of the $2,500 enterprise license, which incorporates all servers, regardless of the number of processors in each server. Both the per-processor license fee and enterprise license fee are annual fees. In addition to the license fee, you are charged, based on a graduating scale, for the responses received from surveys and for some other ancillary services, such as advanced reporting. The graduating price scale can be found at www.surv-a.com/TP80/pricing.aspx.

I show you how to do some basic coding with this Web service, you can check out the usage of Surv-A, which is covered later in this chapter in the "Surv-A for Online Surveys" section.

Mapping

Building mapping applications by scratch is exceedingly complex. They aren't the kinds of applications that even your best IT guy can whip up with some code and some duct tape. But with that complexity comes a ton of features that can give you important data that you wouldn't find any other way.

The reason mapping programs are so complicated is because they deal with *spatial data*. Programs that deal with spatial data can be used to pinpoint any specific location on earth. In other words, if you search for a specific address, a mapping program must ultimately determine the latitude and longitude of the location before it can give you a street address.

Maps can be used in a variety of scenarios, such as

- ✔ Viewing sales territories
- ✔ Assigning technical service calls
- ✔ Mailing list regions
- ✔ Viewing statistics
- ✔ Finding patterns in sales

The benefits of mapping

Many applications today can benefit from mapping applications. A mapping application enables you to map your data visually. Wouldn't seeing the locations of all of your service calls be nice? How about taking that thought one step further and seeing, in real time, where all of your service people are physically located at any time by using GPS (Global Positioning System) technology? The latter is a very complex example, but it opens the door to your imagination.

In fact, your mapping needs might be quite simple. You may just want to provide directions to your office. The bottom line is that visually representing data on the screen in the form of maps can be quite beneficial.

An additional benefit of mapping falls under the category of business intelligence. *Business intelligence* is a technology that helps you make better business decisions by uncovering patterns in your data.

Sometimes, you don't even know what you're looking for because you just have raw data within your organization. For example, suppose you have some raw data that indicates sales figures, dates, and addresses. Without mapping, you might just see the total value of all sales, and you might conclude that you hit your sales goal. However, if you map the data, you might be able to see that 90 percent of your sales are on the east coast. This might be important to know so that you can adjust your marketing strategy to increase sales in the rest of the country.

An outstanding building block service for mapping is MapPoint .NET from Microsoft. You may have heard of, or even used, the prior version, called Microsoft MapPoint, or the scaled-down version, called Streets and Trips.

These services are great because they provide a worldwide searchable database of physical addresses and locations, and they also show a very accurate graphical map of where those locations are. In addition, you can get driving directions from MapPoint, complete with updated, real-time road construction information. This construction information allows the system to compute the most accurate routes to avoid congestion.

The new Web service version, called MapPoint .NET, has all of these capabilities, plus, it extends the product one step further by making it a building block service that you can use in your own applications, but it is quite pricey. (See the following section, "Costs.")

MapPoint .NET takes mapping technology further than it has ever been taken before. It represents the very apex of mapping technology. Here's what it can do:

✔ **Conduct proximity searches:** A *proximity search* allows you to search a specified range of spatial data. For example, you can search for the national park in the southwestern United States that is closest to Mexico City. You could also search for any other possible proximity data that you can conceive of.

✔ **Make distance calculations:** You can use *distance calculations* if your central office needs to determine which field service calls are physically possible within a single day, based on distance and routing.

✔ **Add customized data for your business:** MapPoint .NET enables you to upload your own specific data (such as the locations of all of your customers, all of your stores, and so on) to include in your proximity searches. When your own data is uploaded, you can perform customized spatial proximity queries that can provide a list of names and addresses of customers who last responded to your direct mail campaign.

When viewing the spatial, or mapped, data, you may be able to discern patterns in responses, whereas looking at cold hard facts may not show such patterns.

Costs

As you may imagine, you don't get all this functionality for free. If you think that MapPoint .NET sounds great, well . . . you must be prepared to pay for it. Microsoft provides two licensing models (all in U.S. dollars) that businesses are charged on a yearly basis:

✔ **Per user:** This is a good pricing model when you know how many users you will have, such as in a call-center application or some other internal application. The cost is a flat $15,000 plus a per-user fee. The larger the number of users, the higher the per-user fee.

✔ **Per transaction:** This is a good pricing model when you have no idea how many users will be accessing your application, such as an Internet application. Microsoft defines a *transaction* as a request-response to/from the MapPoint .NET service. Based on the number of transactions in a year, you will be charged a fee, which starts at $15,000 for two million transactions.

If you don't want to incur these costs just to find out if you want to use the MapPoint .NET Web service, you can sign up for a 45-day evaluation account to try it out. To sign up for the evaluation account, visit the Web site at `www.microsoft.com/mappoint/net/evaluation/`.

Getting started

To get started with MapPoint .NET, you should download the Software Development Kit (SDK) at `http://msdn.microsoft.com/mappoint/net`.

The MapPoint .NET SDK has a complete set of documentation that includes examples for every object, property, method, and enumeration in the MapPoint .NET Application Programming Interface (or API). The *API* is a set of programmatic objects that let you manipulate MapPoint .NET programmatically, allowing for complete customization.

Depending on what you want to do with your mapping application, it could be quite simple to code or exceptionally complex. However, no matter what, remember that the complex spatial calculations are done for you, and that you won't be able to hire and write the complex mapping functionality that Microsoft makes available for $15,000.

Instant Messaging (1M) services

You have no doubt used MSN Messenger (or some other messenger service) to communicate and send instant messages to your friends and family. However, did you realize that your employees can benefit from this service as well? (Not just for fun, mind you — for increased productivity.) In fact, when you streamline, simplify, and reduce the cost of communication, the improvement of your staff's productivity can result in dollar signs when it comes to your business' bottom line.

Benefits

I would be remiss to suggest that you should implement IM services simply because you *can*. However, if you do implement your own instant messaging service by using MSN Messenger, you are afforded these distinct benefits and advantages:

- You don't have to open additional ports in your firewall.
- You can control who is sending and receiving instant messages.
- You can include "live help" functionality for real-time customer service without incurring huge telephone costs.
- You can log IM conversations to record the text of each conversation (just as you can with e-mail).

Considerations

Microsoft calls its IM building block service MSN Messenger Connect for Enterprises, and makes the service available through two authorized IM partners, Facetime Communications and IMLogic. The Web services offered by each of these companies incorporate separate pricing and programming models.

Visit Facetime Communications at `www.facetime.com` and IMLogic at `www.imlogic.com`. Visit each of these Web sites to determine if it makes sense for you to include IM functionality within your organization.

Because these companies offer a variety of a la carte services, I cannot list exact pricing here. However, you can visit the Web sites to find contact information and to get pricing if you are interested.

Authentication services

Authentication is the process of validating a user's credentials (user name and password) to gain access to a system. If your applications are developed and deployed solely within your organization, you can authenticate a user with a directory service, such as Active Directory (which is built into Windows 2000). However, authentication can be quite tricky with distributed applications. Suppose that you have a remote Web service that you call from within your organization, and that service requires authentication from your users. Without a centralized authentication scheme, you'd have to require your users to log into your internal system and then log in again to the remote Web services system. This logging-in process can be quite cumbersome. Imagine what would happen if your application included ten Web services, each having its own authentication scheme!

There is a difference between authentication and authorization. *Authentication* controls who has access to a system. In other words, authentication proves that you are who you say you are. *Authorization* controls what resources (files, folders, printers, and the like) a user has access to after he/she is authenticated.

Enter Microsoft Passport! Microsoft Passport is a building block service that solves the problem of authentication in a distributed environment. In fact, the user has to be authenticated with Microsoft Passport only once. This authentication scheme is referred to as Single Sign-In (or SSI).

Benefits

Implementing Single Sign-In, or SSI, has quite a few benefits for your company. Benefits include:

- ✔ **Industry standard:** Microsoft Passport is fast becoming the standard for centralized authentication and SSI. Because Microsoft maintains it, you can be assured that your data is kept securely and is encrypted over the Internet. In fact, most users will already be accustomed to Passport and will already have accounts. Many high-end Web sites and vendors have licensed Passport, including Microsoft-owned businesses such as MSN, bCentral, HotMail, and the like.

✔ **Free for end users:** Although the price tag for implementing Passport within your organization is high, end users can set up a free Passport account from which to be authenticated.

✔ **Works on mobile devices:** PocketPC-enabled devices, such as cell phones and PDAs (Personal Digital Assistants), can use any Passport-enabled Web site.

✔ **Built-in upgrades:** Many technologies that will be incorporated and supported by Passport in the future will be automatically enabled without recoding your Web site. Such technologies include smart cards and digital certificates.

Costs

Implementing Microsoft Passport is not free. Microsoft charges a license fee for your company to use Passport authentication. It does not, as mentioned earlier, charge an end user of your site to be authenticated with Passport. So do you want to implement Passport? If so, get ready to spend a whopping annual fee of $10,000 (in U.S. funds) to license the technology for use in your entire organization, plus this product has an additional periodic compliance fee of $1,500.

These fees are for your company to license the technology, not for each URL or each Web server that needs Passport authentication. Even so, it's a pretty hefty price tag, especially for small- and medium-sized businesses. On the other hand, if you can afford it, it does provide a nice, centralized authentication scheme.

Much like with the MapPoint .NET service, you can create an evaluation account to see how Passport will work for you in your organization before you sign a contract. To sign-up for the evaluation account, visit this Web site: www.netservicesmanager.com.

Getting started

To get started with Microsoft Passport, you need to do two things:

✔ Each user requesting authentication needs to have a Passport account. Create these accounts easily by pointing your browser to www.passport. net/Consumer/.

✔ You must implement Passport in your site (which is the expensive part). To help with implementing Passport authentication in your site, Microsoft has created the Microsoft Passport SDK (or Software Development Kit). The SDK can be downloaded for free at www.microsoft.com/netservices/.

Downloading the SDK is free, so that you can plan the implementation of your site; but if you are going to use the SDK in a live environment, that's when you have to pay the piper.

Pros and Cons of Using a Prefab Web Service

You have lots of options when it comes to building block services. Although Microsoft coined the term, many other companies provide these types of services in a slew of categories in all shapes and sizes. I give you detailed information on implementing a few specific building block services later in this chapter. Even though determining which of the Web services you will consume in your own applications may be difficult, you should know that, normally, Web services (and those classified as building block services) offer these benefits (or pros):

- **High ROI:** ROI stands for return on investment. In other words, if someone could show you that you would save money by purchasing a specific software package, wouldn't it be a no-brainer to purchase it? Well, this is what defines ROI. In fact ROI means that the investment made yields a very high return. This is not unlike when you buy a stock low and sell it high (although in 2001 and 2002, many people were doing the opposite).

    ROI is a relative term. The return might take years to quantify or realize. On the other hand, you may have an immediate cost savings. Most likely, with building block services, you'll see ROI quite soon. For example, you know that Microsoft charges an annual license fee of $10,000, plus a periodic compliance fee of $1,500, to implement Passport. This sounds like a lot of money, especially if your company is small. However, you are not only getting to use the functionality with only a few hours of coding, but you get the reputation carried by Microsoft. This all yields an incredibly high ROI.

    CRM building block services such as online surveys can yield a high ROI, as well. Say you want to implement surveys within your CRM package or even on their own over the Internet. Well, for even basic configurable functionality, you would have to employ several developers for at least a year. With many ready-made ROI services (such as the Surv-A Web service), you have no upfront charges and can begin implementing surveys right away.

    Both Passport and Surv-A coding examples are shown later in this chapter in the section called "A Smattering of Services."

- **Scalability:** Most building block services are scalable so that they can grow and shrink as your business changes. Because Web services to be hosted in a Microsoft environment are built by using the .NET Framework, scalability is already built in. In fact, it is one of the core design requirements of .NET. Therefore, make sure that you check with your building block services vendor to see if the vendor's product is scaleable (but most likely, it is).

✔ **Reality:** In reality, some Web applications are so unbelievably complex that nobody in your IT department could possibly create them from scratch. And paying another business to create such a service is just not worth it. No matter how much the services cost, they are worth it if they are offered as a building block service. An example of this is the MapPoint .NET building block service. If you need to incorporate mapping functionality into your applications, you have no other way to go. I would not be surprised if Microsoft has invested hundreds of thousands of hours (if not more) in developing this product.

✔ **Flexibility:** Most building block services allow you to try before you buy. You can normally test the service, and if you decide you like it, then you can invest the money to purchase or license it. You may even determine, after evaluation, that you, in fact, want to develop similar functionality yourself from scratch.

In most comparisons, you must have cons along with the pros. Building block services are no exception. However, most likely you'll find that licensing building block services is the best route to get up and running quickly and effectively. Here's the downside (or cons) of using building block services:

✔ **Cost:** Even if you want to use a building block service, such as Passport or MapPoint .NET, you may find the licensing cost too prohibitive to incorporate it no matter what! You may even agree with my earlier statement about high ROI, but you just don't have the cash! Going broke in order to access a service is not the wisest business decision!

✔ **Functionality:** Even though it may make sense for you not to do development work in-house, you may not get exactly the functionality that you require. Hopefully, the building block service is configurable enough to allow you to code the missing pieces. Even better, perhaps the building block service vendor is willing to make your requested changes so you don't have to do it internally. You should fully check out the functionality available through these services to see if it meets your needs.

✔ **Lost productivity:** Some of the building block services are so cool that your employees may just play with them all day long. Two services that fall into this category are MapPoint .NET and IM. Users may actually lose productivity if they are playing with the mapping functionality all day long, which is, after all, very neat! Also, if your employees are suddenly flaming each other with IMs and productivity goes down, you won't lose as much money as you would have if you built your own IM service from scratch — but you will lose money. These may not be issues — as long as you are aware that productivity may actually go down and put measures in place to prevent your staff from having *too* much fun. (I mean, come on. It's still work, right?)

To nip the productivity issue in the bud, think about offering these services only to employees who have to use it, or set up rules for when the services are to be used — and when they should be set aside. (No using IM when e-mail, the phone, or a face-to-face conversation is possible!)

✔ **Speed:** From a purely theoretical point of view, the speed of implementing code that runs over the Internet is slower than code running on your own servers internally. The reality is that the Internet and broadband connections are getting better all the time. If the Web service is designed correctly, speed shouldn't be too much of a factor.

A Smattering of Services

In this section, I show you some specifics of how you can implement some building block services in your own code. There is not enough room here to show every building block service mentioned in this chapter, so a couple of choice services are listed herein that contain coding samples in Visual Basic .NET. If you need more information about how to write a basic .NET application using Visual Studio .NET (which includes Visual Basic .NET and any other installed language), see Chapter 6.

Implementing Microsoft Passport

As mentioned earlier in this chapter, Microsoft Passport is a building block service that provides Single Sign-In (SSI) functionality by using a centralized authentication scheme. A Web site that is Passport enabled is immediately apparent by the use of standard icons placed on the site, as shown in Figure 10-1.

Notice, in Figure 10-1, the Sign In icon, which Microsoft calls *scarab* (but nobody can tell me why it is so named). This icon indicates two things. First, the site authenticates you with Passport. The second thing is that you are currently not logged into Passport. If you were, the icon would show Sign Out instead of Sign In.

SSI works by logging you into Microsoft Passport upon successfully logging into your network. This can only be made possible when cookies are enabled on a client's workstation. A *cookie* is a small file that contains profile or personal information and is stored on the workstation's hard drive. It's possible to have cookies stored in memory and not on the hard drive, so when the computer is turned off, no trace of personal information appears. However, in-memory cookies must be programmed by the software developer.

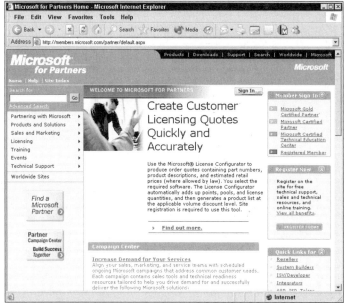

Figure 10-1:
Sample
Web site
using
Microsoft
Passport
functionality.

Passport has four types of cookies:

- ✔ **Ticket:** Contains positive authorization known as a *ticket.* These cookies are generally written to the main domain, such as `xyz.com` because these cookies contain properties that are germane to all sites in a domain.

- ✔ **Profile:** Contains profile information used along with the ticket cookie and is also written to the main domain, such as `xyz.com`.

- ✔ **Consent:** Contains secondary information when different sites in a domain use different properties. An example is when `a.xyz.com` uses different properties than `b.xyz.com` in the same domain.

- ✔ **Secure:** Cookie that contains SSL information, if secure authentication is requested.

Passport administration

Like most Microsoft products, if you are going to use Passport authentication, a configuration tool is available to make things easy for you. The administration tool is installed after you install the Passport SDK. To access the administration tool, simply choose Start⇨Programs⇨Microsoft Passport SDK⇨Passport Administration Utility. The utility is a one-page tool whereby you set many options. Figure 10-2 shows what this utility looks like.

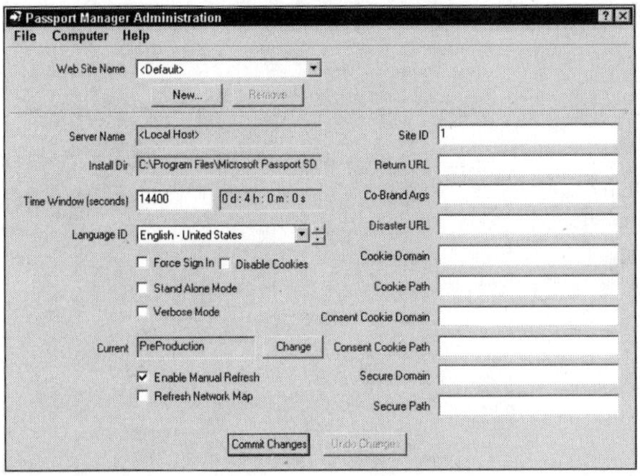

Figure 10-2:
The
Passport
Administra-
tion Utility.

To find out about the configuration options for the Passport Administration Utility, see Table 10-1.

Table 10-1	Passport Administration Utility Options
Field	**Description**
Web Site Name	Name of the Web site that you will be configuring Passport for. By default, the default Web site on the local machine will be shown. Select the desired Web site from the drop-down list or create a new one by clicking the New button.
Server Name	Name of the server on which the Web Site Name will be selected. To select a different server, choose the Computer⇨Select Server menu and select the desired server.
Install Dir	The name of the folder (directory) where the Passport SDK is installed. This cannot be changed from this utility.
Time Window	The amount of time you can be signed in, given in seconds. The default value is 14,400, or four hours.
Language ID	Select from the drop-down list of languages. This will be used as the selected language to send information from the client to the Passport service.
Force Sign In	If checked, this will force the user to sign in to the Passport service.

Field	Description
Disable Cookies	If checked, this will disallow client-side cookies to store profile information. If this happens, information must be passed on the query string.
Stand Alone Mode	If checked, will treat all cookie information as being valid, thereby not sending information to an authentication server because the authentication server is expected to be down.
Verbose Mode	If checked, gives more detailed information for troubleshooting.
Current	Through the Change button, enables you to change the environment. You can select from Production, PreProduction (the default), Beta PreProduction, and Other.
Enable Manual Refresh	Flags that partner information (stored in the `partner.xml` file) can be downloaded to the test passport site.
Refresh Network Map	Downloads the `partner.xml` file to the test server if Enable Manual Refresh is checked and you click the Commit Changes button.
Site ID	Unique identifier for your company's Passport site.
Return URL	The URL that the system returns to after sign-in completes successfully.
Co-Brand Args	Arguments used to specify that the Passport login page will use your own branding (logos, images, and the like).
Disaster URL	URL used for redirection when site is in Stand Alone mode and the user does not have a valid cookie with profile information stored.
Cookie Domain	Domain where cookies should be written.
Cookie Path	Path in the domain where cookies should be written.
Consent Cookie Domain	Domain where consent cookies should be written.
Consent Cookie Path	Path in the domain where consent cookies should be written.
Secure Domain	Domain where secure cookies should be written.
Secure Path	Path in the domain where secure cookies should be written.

After you set your desired options for the Web site, click Commit Changes.

Passport process

The process of implementing Passport in your site is not exactly straightforward, but it is not exceedingly complex either. Implementing Passport consists of very simple steps:

1. **Sign an agreement with Microsoft Corporation.**

2. **Install the Passport SDK on the Web server.**

3. **Write your application code in any language that can consume a Web service, such as Visual Basic .NET or Visual C# .NET, to test whether users are already authenticated.**

   This code should be configured and written in such a way that it runs every time a user enters the portion of your Web site that requires authentication.

4. **Write code to redirect users who aren't logged into the Passport site to log in.**

5. **After a user logs in, you can access profile information for the logged-in user on the Passport Web site.**

   The user entered this profile information when he or she configured the Passport account with Microsoft.

Listing 10-1 shows how you might implement Passport in Visual Basic .NET code.

The code shown here is not intended to be complete. It is intended to give you an idea of how easy it is to use the Passport building block services. The Passport objects that you can use in your code, such as the PassportIdentity object (shown in Listing 10-1), are located within the System.Web.Security namespace. Namespaces are discussed in Chapter 3.

Listing 10-1:   Implementing Passport

```
'declare namespace for Passport objects
Imports System.Web.Security

'declare passport object
Dim objPassport As New PassportIdentity()

'declare other variables
Dim bAuth As Boolean
Dim nRes As Integer

'test to see if user is already authenticated
bAuth = objPassport.IsAuthenticated()
```

```
If bAuth = False Then
    'attempt to login and use all defaults
    nRes = objPassport.LoginUser(Nothing, -1, -1, Nothing, -1, Nothing, -1, -1,
            Nothing)

    'test to see if authenticated
    bAuth = objPassport.IsAuthenticated()

End If
```

TIP

In Listing 10-1, notice that the main line of code calls the `LoginUser` method. It passes a bunch of arguments, some of which are integers and some of which are strings. However, notice in Listing 10-1 that there are only values -1 and `Nothing`. This is because substituting the value -1 for any place an integer must be specified and `Nothing` where a string must be indicated instructs the `LoginUser` call to use all default values.

The arguments expected by the `LoginUser` method are:

✔ `szReturnURL`: Returns the URL that the user will be redirected to upon successful login into the Passport service. If this value is `null` (or `Nothing` in Visual Basic), the value specified in the Passport Administration Utility will be used.

✔ `iTimeWindow`: Sets the amount of idle time, in seconds, where the user's session will be valid without forcing the signing into Passport for further Web activity. If this value is -1, the Passport Administration Utility value will be used.

✔ `fForceLogin`: If this value is `true` (or -1 in Visual Basic), it will compute idle time by subtracting the current time from the time the user logged into Passport. If the value is `false` (or 0 in Visual Basic), it will compute idle time by subtracting current time from the time that the ticket was refreshed.

✔ `szCOBrandArgs`: These are special URL parameters that are used when Passport is participating in co-branding (where two parties advertise their own companies for a common purpose). If this value is `null` (or `Nothing` in Visual Basic), the value specified in the Passport Administration Utility will be used.

✔ `iLangID`: This is code, or an ID, that represents the language to be used for the sign-in page. If you pass a value of -1, the values specified in the Passport Administration Utility will be used.

✔ `strNamespace`: Domain namespace is used if the user that logs in does not have a Passport account. I cover namespaces in Chapter 3. Pass a `null` or `Nothing` value to use the default value specified in the Passport Administration Utility.

✔ iKPP: This indicates special policies used for collecting data for children's Web sites. A value of -1 indicates to use the default Passport Administration Utility value.

✔ fUseSecureAuth: If this value is true (or -1 in Visual Basic), it will use secure authentication. If the value is false (or 0 in Visual Basic), it will not use secure authentication.

✔ oExtraParams: This is used to specify extra text in the dialog boxes that are presented during the authentication process. A null or Nothing value indicates that the value specified in the Passport Administration Utility is to be used during the login process.

Where do these default values come from? They come from the values that you entered using the Passport Administration Utility. Therefore, your coding becomes quite simple. If you have any changes to make, simply make them in the Administration Utility. There is one downside, however: If you have lots of Web servers, this may be more difficult to administer. You may find that it is easier to manage the arguments specified in code.

For more information about how to code, administer, and implement Passport, you can view the documentation in the Passport SDK or visit this Web site: www.microsoft.com/netservices/passport/.

Surv-A for Online Surveys

All companies have the need for implementing online surveys in their organizations. Surveys provide companies with the ability to do the following:

✔ **Generate new leads:** You can survey a group of prospective customers and target them with specific questions. The results of these surveys can be used to determine the seriousness of a prospective customer, which may result in a sales lead.

✔ **Qualify leads:** You can further refine your surveys to qualify the leads and group them into categories. For example, you have a question that asks "What is your timeframe for purchase?" and provides the following answers:

1. Less Than 2 Weeks

2. 2 Weeks–4 Weeks

3. 1 Month–3 Months

4. 3 Months–6 Months

5. Greater Than 6 Months

The leads that have answered the question with "Less Than 2 Weeks" may be considered to be a qualified lead, and you would want to follow up on those first.

✔ **Test customer satisfaction:** Find out how you're doing with your customers by asking them in a survey. In fact, you can entice your customers to answer the survey by indicating that by answering the survey, they become eligible to win a prize. (Of course, you have to actually give out the prize.)

✔ **Integrate into CRM packages:** Customer Relationship Manager (CRM) packages, such as Microsoft CRM from Microsoft Business Solutions (formerly known as Microsoft Great Plains), enable you to focus on your existing customers as well as track new leads and opportunities. With Surv-A, you can survey your existing database of customers to ask them things like "Please tell us what we can be doing better" or "Rate our service on a scale from 1 to 10."

The writing of configurable online surveys and collection of data is a complicated business. The Surv-A building block Web service enables you to configure and incorporate online surveys within your own application. It does this by providing three separate Web services:

✔ **User Administration:** This enables you to add and remove users and administrators for a client. After you indicate who will be allowed to administer surveys, you can begin creating those surveys. The Web service for user administration is located at

```
www.surv-a.com/tp80/Surv-
        A/Services/UserAdministration/User.asmx
```

✔ **Survey Administration:** Enables you to configure and administer online surveys. This includes adding and removing surveys, questions within those surveys, and answers within questions. After you configure surveys, they are available for targeted users to respond to them. Users responding to a survey is also known as *taking a survey*. The survey administration Web service is located at

```
www.surv-a.com/TP80/Surv-
        A/Services/SurveyService/SurveyAuthoring.asmx
```

✔ **Rendering:** After your surveys are configured by using the Administration Web Service, when a user wishes to participate in the survey, the Surv-A rendering engine takes all configuration information into account and renders a survey in HTML. Then it sends the survey to the target client. This client can be a browser, an e-mail message, a portal, or any other target that accepts HTML. There are three separate Web services that deal with rendering a Surv-A. The URLs are

```
www.surv-a.com/TP80/Surv-
        A/Services/SurveyRendering/RenderHTML.asmx
www.surv-a.com/TP80/Surv-
        A/Services/SurveyService/SurveyRetrieval.asmx
www.surv-a.com/TP80/Surv-
        A/Services/SurveyService/SurveyAnswers.asmx
```

The `SurveyRetrieval` Web service is used to retrieve a survey that you will perform an action against (add or delete questions and so forth). The `SurveyAnswers` Web service is used to retrieve answers for questions on a survey as well as save them to the database. The `RenderHTML` Web service takes answers from the survey database and formats them as HTML. This HTML is sent as a string of text through the `RenderHTML` Web service.

✔ **Reporting:** When each user finishes an online survey, the raw data is stored off-site in a secure format. What good is collecting the data if you can't analyze it? Therefore, the reporting Web service enables you to retrieve the data collected by the Surv-A engine. The reporting Web service URL is located at:

```
http://www.surv-a.com/TP80/Surv-
          A/Services/SurveyReporting/Report.asmx
```

Online survey concepts to know and love

Most calls to the Surv-A Web service take one or more of the following arguments. They are key to understanding how to manipulate surveys in code:

✔ `ClientID`: A 16-byte unique identifier, known as a GUID (or Globally Unique IDentifier) that represents a unique Surv-A client for billing purposes. A client can have one or more users. A client can also have one or more surveys. A `ClientID` can be thought of as a numeric representation of a company that wishes to conduct surveys.

✔ `UserID`: A GUID that represents a unique identifier for a user. A user can be someone that takes a survey (if anonymous surveys are not allowed) or someone who administers a survey on behalf of a client. A `UserID` can be thought of as a numeric representation of a person that wishes to use the Surv-A system.

✔ `SurveyID`: A GUID that represents a unique ID for a survey. Normally, the `SurveyID` is not enough to program a survey. You also need a `ClientID` and a `UserID`. This eliminates the possibility of another client "guessing" a `SurveyID` and altering it maliciously.

✔ `SectionID`: A GUID that represents a section within a survey that will be used as a container for questions and answers. A single survey can have one or more `SectionIDs`, but most surveys have only a single `SectionID`.

✔ `QuestionID`: A GUID that represents a question within a section, within a survey.

✔ `AnswerID`: A GUID that represents an answer within a question that is within a section and, of course, a survey. (This is starting to sound like "The Twelve Days of Christmas," huh?)

✔ LanguageID: An integer that represents the language used when rendering a survey. A LanguageID of 1 indicates English. Additional languages will be added at a later date. It is possible to have a single survey rendered in multiple languages for different users, based on their preference.

Because I don't want to spend the entire chapter talking about surveys, I'll just show you a couple of the basic things that you can do with the Surv-A Web services. In the Visual Studio .NET code, you must set a Web reference to the Web service that you will be accessing. Setting Web references in Visual Basic .NET (a language in Visual Studio .NET) is shown in Chapter 9. In this example, you access both the SurveyAnswers and RenderHTML Web services. See the section "Surv-A for Online Surveys," earlier in this chapter, to find out what functionality these Web services provide.

After you set a Web reference to the URLs noted earlier in this chapter for the SurveyAnswers and RenderHTML Web services, rename them to SurveyAnswers and SurveyRender respectively. You should rename the Web services because when you set a Web reference (which I discuss in Chapter 9), the automatic name is not easily used in code. After you rename the Web service, you can refer to that name in code quite easily. Listing 10-2 shows how you might implement a survey using the Surv-A Web service in Visual Basic .NET. This listing shows you how to retrieve a survey with a known SurveyID, display it in a special Visual Basic .NET control, called a literal, and then save the survey taken by the user.

The line numbers in Listing 10-2 are shown for informational purposes only. They are not part of the code.

Listing 10-2: Implementing a Surv-A

```
 1:  Private Sub Page_Load(ByVal sender As System.Object, ByVal e As
              System.EventArgs) Handles MyBase.Load
 2:      'create GUID representing SurveyID
 3:      Dim gudSurveyID As New Guid("{F1E9C072-E378-4713-A09B-2219B5A153B6}")
 4:
 5:      'instantiate a new RenderHTML object
 6:      Dim objRenderHTML As New SurveyRender.RenderHTML()
 7:
 8:      'place the HTML in the literal control
 9:      Me.Literal1.Text =
              objRenderHTML.RenderSurveySectionAsString(gudSurveyID,
              SurveyRender.RenderOption.RenderQuestionsAndAnswers)
10: End Sub
11:
12: Private Sub cmdSave_Click(ByVal sender As System.Object, ByVal e As
              System.EventArgs) Handles cmdSave.Click
13:      'Set a reference to Web service
14:      'This web service is responsible for saving the data
```

(continued)

Listing 10-2 *(continued)*

```
15:    Dim objRendering As New SurveyRender.RenderHTML()
16:
17:    'two arrays used for some type conversions
18:    Dim arrValues(Request.Form.Count) As String
19:    Dim arrKeys(Request.Form.AllKeys.GetLength(0)) As String
20:
21:    Dim objAnswers() As Object    'holds the answers collection
22:    Dim intResult As Integer     'return code for saving
23:
24:    'The form post can not be transmitted as a web services parameter,
25:    ' so convert the key value information into string arrays
26:    Request.Form.CopyTo(arrValues, 0)
27:    Request.Form.AllKeys.CopyTo(arrKeys, 0)
28:
29:    ' convert the simple array information into a structured answers array
30:    objAnswers = objRendering.FormPostToAnswer(arrKeys, arrValues)
31:
32:    'use the web service to save the answers to the remote database
33:    intResult = objRendering.SaveAnswers(objAnswers, True)
34:
35:    'check the result to see if it worked
36:    If intResult <> 0 Then
37:       MsgBox("Save Failed")
38:    End If
39:
40:    End Sub
```

Listing 10-2 is broken into two subroutines: `Page_Load` and `cmdSave_Click`. Visual Studio .NET creates `Page_Load` automatically for you and is shown between lines 1 and 10. `cmdSave_Click`, a completely arbitrary name that I chose, calls the subroutine when a Save button is clicked on the Web form. `cmdSave_Click` is shown between lines 12 and 40.

The `Page_Load` subroutine contains three simple lines of code and is used to retrieve a survey in HTML format from the Surv-A database. The first line of code, line 3 in Listing 10-2, declares a variable to hold the funny-looking SurveyID (with all the dashes and alpha-numeric characters). The SurveyID is a unique identifier that is assigned to one specific survey. The second line of code, line 6, simply declares a `RenderHTML` object that is contained within the `SurveyRender` Web service. The last line of code, line 9, calls the `RenderSurveySectionAsString` method of the `SurveyRender` Web service and passes it two arguments. The first argument declares the SurveyID in the first line of code. The second argument, shown in Listing 10-2 as `RenderQuestionsAndAnswers`, can be one of the following:

- ✔ `RenderAnswers`: Renders only the answers for a survey

- ✔ `RenderQuestions`: Renders only the questions for a survey

- ✔ `RenderQuestionsAndAnswers`: Renders the questions and the answers for each question for a survey

- ✔ `Unspecified`: Reserved for other possibilities in the future

The code in the `cmdSave_Click` subroutine is a little more involved because there is a technical hurdle that it overcomes. The technical hurdle is encountered when an object returned from one Web service needs to be used by another Web service. You can't exactly pass objects from one Web service to another, so the data in that object is converted into a string, which is a process known as *serialization*.

Line 15 sets a reference to the `RenderHTML` Web service. Line 18 holds an array of values due to the technical issues. The number of items in the array is the number of items on the form, which is, after all, questions on the survey. Line 19 is used to hold an array of keys, or IDs, of the HTML elements on the form. Lines 21 and 22 simply declare variables that are used later in the procedure. Line 26 copies all values on the form to the array, which was declared in line 18, while line 27 copies the keys to the array declared in line 19. Line 30 assigns a reference to an object by calling the `FormPostToAnswer` method of the `RenderHTML` Web service and passing the two arrays as arguments. Line 33 is used to actually save the survey values. The second argument, shown as `True`, indicates that data should be saved to the database. `False` would be used to test code without saving data. Finally, the return value from the saving of the survey is tested in code between lines 36 and 38. If the save fails, an error message is displayed. This return value can be one of the following:

- ✔ 0: Save is successful

- ✔ 1: Error in connecting to Surv-A database

- ✔ 2: Error saving Surv-A

So what did the Surv-A code show you? Simple! It showed you how to use a building block service to create survey functionality in your own applications without having to know or spend the time coding the intricacies of survey-processing technology. You also didn't have to store any data, as that is stored within the Surv-A Web site. Sample code for the other Surv-A Web services (for reporting and administration) is not shown in this chapter due to space constraints. Check out the Surv-A Web site (detailed previously in the chapter) for more information on using these Web services.

Part IV
Advanced Topics

The 5th Wave   By Rich Tennant

"We're not sure what it is. Rob cobbled it together from paper clips and stuff in the mail room, but MAN, wait till you see how scalable it is."

In this part . . .

Now that you have mastered the basics of creating Web services on the .NET platform, you're ready to investigate more-advanced topics that are likely to arise in your enterprise. Chapter 11 shows how to secure your Web services. Chapter 12 tells you how to plan for your Web services projects, such as software and hardware configurations. Chapter 13 discusses how to migrate from other technologies, such as COM and DCOM, to Web services.

Chapter 11

Securing Your Web Services

In This Chapter

▶ Diving into security basics

▶ Setting up SSL on a Web server

▶ Configuring the .NET framework

Security is one of the hottest topics in Information Technology (IT) today. Consumers and businesses all want to make sure that data is secured against hackers (also known as people with too much time on their hands). Oddly enough, data needs not only to be protected against hackers, but also protected from co-workers, prying eyes, and every other person that does not need to have access to data. It does not have be secured only against a malicious person.

Security is quite an involved topic; it's so involved, in fact, that this chapter can only whet your appetite for this crucial subject. This chapter explores some of the concepts behind security and what that means to your Web services projects. Remember that a Web services project is hosted on a Web server. This translates to the fact that anything you would do to secure your Web pages are typically the same precautions that you must take for your Web services projects.

Security Primer

Before diving headfirst into securing your Web services, explore some of the key topics and terminology surrounding security in general. Have a look at the following items:

✔ **Secure Sockets Layer (SSL):** A level of security that encrypts data across the Internet by using digital certificates from a trusted authority. This trusted authority does due diligence to determine that you are who you say you are when you apply for the certificate. For more information, see the section "SSL certificates" later in this chapter.

✔ **Firewall:** A security device, either hardware- or software-based, that prevents hackers from getting in to your servers.

✔ **Demilitarized Zone (DMZ):** A network configuration whereby multiple firewalls are configured before and after a bank of computers to allow some level of protection to external computers but significant protection to internal computers.

✔ **Active Directory:** Microsoft's implementation of directory services whereby a central database of users, computers, printers, and other resources and servers exists. Active Directory is easy to manage and will enforce authentication and authorization of resources.

✔ **Virtual Private Network (VPN):** A method of configuring a point-to-point tunnel where a dedicated connection is created between a client and a server over the Internet.

SSL

SSL is one of the most common technologies used to secure your Web services projects. However, SSL only affects what someone can *sniff* over the Internet. To "sniff" traffic means to use hardware or software to inspect the traffic going across an unsecured network. SSL does not limit who has access to which resources. Using SSL only means that you are ensured that your data will be encrypted from your browser to the server somewhere on the Internet. For more information about controlling authentication, see the "Active Directory" section later in this chapter.

SSL basically works by requiring one or more parties involved in a security transaction to *prove* who they are to see if they can be trusted. Before seeing how this works, take a look at Figure 11-1. It shows my company's Web site, which uses SSL. SSL is initiated by indicating `https` (instead of `http`) in the URL of a Web browser. The Web server must also be configured to accept SSL connections, which I discuss later in this chapter.

Notice three things in Figure 11-1:

✔ **The `https` protocol in the URL.** This indicates that SSL is to use the secure form of the `http` protocol. If you were to just type a URL into the browser, such as `www.transport80.com`, your connection would not be secure. You must either type the `https` protocol or have your code automatically redirect the page whereby the `https` protocol is specified in code. Because this is just a home page that doesn't include any sensitive data, it doesn't make sense that SSL be required by typing `https`. SSL transactions are slower than non-secure transactions, so use them only when you need them.

✔ **The lock icon in the bottom-right part of the browser.** This lock icon indicates that the page is secured with an SSL certificate from a trusted authority. If a certificate is installed on the Web server but is not from a trusted authority or is not valid for your specific domain, you receive the warning shown in Figure 11-2.

On the other hand, if the certificate installed on the Web server is valid, from a trusted authority, and for the correct domain, you receive no warnings when the Web page loads. If you want to view information for the certificate, you simply double-click the lock icon. Doing so brings up a dialog box similar to that shown in Figure 11-3.

✔ **The level of encryption.** If you hold the mouse pointer over the lock icon, you can see the level of encryption. Figure 11-1 shows 128-bit encryption, which is the highest level available for Web browsers and is suitable for high-end transactions, such as banking. However, you do experience a trade-off between encryption level and speed. For example, you can have a 56-bit certificate that will be faster than a 128-bit encryption certificate, but it won't be as secure. 128-bit encrypted certificates are virtually impossible to hack.

Https indicates a secure connection.

Figure 11-1:
Transport:80
Web pages
secured
with SSL.

Security lock icon shows the Web site is secure.

Figure 11-2:
SSL
certificate
warning
dialog box.

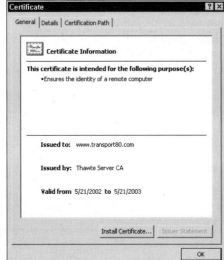

Figure 11-3:
Viewing
a valid
certificate.

You should also know that it is possible to have a hardware-based SSL accelerator card installed in a Web server. An accelerator card will handle SSL encryption, thereby freeing up resources on the Web server. As stated previously in this chapter, SSL transactions are slower than non-SSL transactions. Therefore, if you have many browser sessions that all create SSL transactions, it may make sense to free the Web server from having to encrypt the Web traffic and have the accelerator card do it. Accelerator cards can get quite pricey, but they do offload some of the time that it takes to perform encryption from the processor on the motherboard to the SSL card. You can find details about this card on the Compaq Web site at

```
http://www.compaq.com/products/servers/security/
```

You can also find other manufacturers of SSL accelerator cards by searching the Internet for *SSL accelerator card.*

To see how you can configure SSL on your Web server (if you are not using an accelerator card), see the "SSL certificates" section later in this chapter.

Firewall

A *firewall* is a physical hardware device or software on a computer that explicitly blocks certain types of traffic through a network. In addition, it can be configured to explicitly allow only certain types of traffic and block all others. The types of traffic that firewalls can block or allow are

✔ Specific TCP/IP addresses or ranges of addresses

✔ Specific ports used to transmit data

✔ Specific users

This may not sound like a firewall can block very much, but think about it. You can specify that only a specific TCP/IP address be allowed access to your network. Likewise, only a specific group of users, or only traffic through port 80 (which is the typical port used for Web traffic) can be configured. In other words, firewall configuration can be quite secure. However, the tool is only as good as its configuration. Just placing a firewall in your network doesn't cut it. You have to configure the firewall properly. To help you understand how you can configure a firewall to permit or block traffic by using TCP/IP ports, Table 11-1 shows common ports used for Internet traffic.

Table 11-1	Common TCP/IP Ports
Port	**Description**
21	FTP (File Transfer Protocol): Used for transferring files over the Internet.
23	Telnet: Terminal emulation, command-based window for executing TCP/IP commands.
25	SMTP (Simple Mail Transport Protocol): Used for sending e-mail.
53	DNS (Domain Name System): Used for translating user-friendly names to TCP/IP addresses.
68	DHCP (Dynamic Host Communication Protocol): Used by a server for dynamically configuring workstation TCP/IP addresses and other network information.
69	TFTP (Trivial File Transmission Protocol): Used for the remote installation of software.

(continued)

Table 11-1 *(continued)*

Port	Description
79	Finger: Used to find out information about a particular user on a particular server.
80	HTTP (HyperText Transfer Protocol): Used for general Web traffic, including Web services, but not securing with SSL encryption.
88	Kerberos: Special security authentication built into Windows 2000 and later.
110	POP3 (Post Office Protocol, Version 3): Used for retrieving e-mail, but not encrypted with SSL.
119	NNTP (Network News Transfer Protocol): Used to retrieve news group information without using SSL encryption.
123	NTP (Network Time Protocol): Used for setting all computers to the time specified by a time server.
143	IMAP (Internet Message Access Protocol): Used for getting e-mail and transmitting messages, but not using SSL.
161	SNMP (Simple Network Management Protocol): Used for monitoring and managing a Windows-based network.
220	IMAP3 (Internet Message Access Protocol, Version 3): Used for getting e-mail and transmitting messages.
389	LDAP (Lightweight Directory Access Protocol): Used in requesting data from Active Directory, but not being secured with SSL.
443	HTTPS (HyperText Transfer Protocol — Secure): Used for general Web traffic, including Web services, while also securing with SSL encryption.
520	RIP (Routing Information Protocol): Used for routing between different networks.
563	NNTP (Network News Transfer Protocol): Used to retrieve newsgroup information while also using SSL encryption.
636	LDAP (Lightweight Directory Access Protocol): Used in requesting data from Active Directory, but being secured with SSL.
993	IMAP (Internet Message Access Protocol): Used for getting e-mail and transmitting messages using SSL.
995	POP3 (Post Office Protocol, Version 3): Used for retrieving e-mail, but encrypted with SSL.

Port	Description
1433	Microsoft SQL Server: Used for Microsoft SQL Server administrative database communications.
1434	Microsoft SQL Server Monitor: Used for Microsoft SQL Server monitoring database communications.
1521	Oracle: Used for Oracle database communications.
1701	L2TP (Layer 2 Tunneling Protocol): Used for VPN connections.
1755	Windows Streaming Media: Used for audio/video media that is streamed in real time across the Internet.
3389	RDP (Remote Data Protocol): Used for Microsoft Terminal Server.
4000	ICQ chat sessions: Used for real-time chat sessions with the ICQ product.
5010	Yahoo! Messenger: Used for real-time chat sessions with the Yahoo! Messenger product.
5631	Symantec pcAnywhere: Used for communicating with remote computers.
5632	Symantec pcAnywhere: Used for communicating with remote computers.
8080	HTTP (HyperText Transfer Protocol): Alternate port sometimes used for testing purposes, but not secured with SSL encryption.

TCP/IP works by *listening* on a certain port number for network traffic. When a request comes in on a certain port, the listening program will respond in the manner that is applicable to the program. TCP/IP ports are defined in the range of 0 to 65535, with the most common ones listed earlier in Table 11-1. Programs send data across the Internet (and on your internal network) by sending packets of data. A *packet* is a certain predetermined amount of data packaged into a small, manageable size; all the packets together constitute the entire data. This method of breaking up data into packets makes transmission more manageable and reliable to send across the wire. If a single packet failed to reach its destination because of busy network traffic or some other glitch, the TCP protocol resends the packet until it reaches the destination. Therefore, the data being broken up into packets makes it easier to resend compared to the alternative — resending all the data in its entirety — which can be quite lengthy.

Another factor involved in transmitting Internet traffic is the use of a *proxy server*. A proxy server is used as a central gateway through which Internet traffic is gauged, metered, and restricted. Not all companies use proxy servers, but if one is installed, it doesn't necessarily take the place of a firewall. A proxy server can be used, for example, to prevent users from accessing an inappropriate site. In fact, a proxy server can block a specific URL, while a firewall only blocks ports.

UDP, which stands for *User Datagram Protocol,* is similar to TCP in that it *listens* on a specific port, but one major difference exists between UDP and TCP. Although TCP verifies that the packets of data actually reach their destination and reassembles packets into the correct order (if they are not received in order), UDP does not. UDP just simply sends the packets, and the receiving program may *catch* them — or it may not. The reason why this may be advantageous is that TCP carries some overhead with it in the form of additional resources and information contained in the packet. Furthermore, TCP must take the time to verify the packets. UDP does neither of these things and therefore, it is faster. UDP is most useful in streaming media applications where a lost packet is not the end of the world — it's just annoying. Additionally, for very high-speed networks where reliability and speed can be guaranteed, it may make sense to use UDP.

A hardware or software firewall is configured to allow specific access by TCP/IP address, user, and/or by port number. For example, if a firewall is configured to listen only on ports 80 and 443, then only SSL and standard HTTP Web traffic, and no other traffic, will be permitted through the firewall. In this configuration (where only ports 80 and 443 are opened), you won't be able to send and receive e-mail because ports 110 and 25 also were not opened. Therefore, you must consider carefully which ports *must* be opened and close all others by configuring your firewall.

Hardware products made by Cisco, SonicWall, and others can be quite expensive. If you wanted to go the software route, Microsoft has a great product called *Internet Security and Acceleration Server,* or ISA for short. To use this product, you have to make the investment in a server and the software, but they can be less costly than a hardware firewall solution. However, most high-end network configurations still use hardware-based firewall solutions. If you want more information about ISA, visit the Microsoft Web site at www. microsoft.com/isa.

DMZ

A DMZ (or demilitarized zone) is used to create levels of protection between your computers that face the Internet (known as the *external* network) and those that are used only inside your company (known as the *internal* network). You are probably very curious as to why you would do this. Because a picture is worth 1,000 words (or 10,000 words with inflation), take a look at Figure 11-4; it features a block diagram that shows a DMZ.

In the diagram, notice the bank of servers in the middle area known as the DMZ. These computers are said to be *in the DMZ.* These computers are typically Web servers and e-mail server relays (that simply pass on the e-mail to a *real* e-mail server) that must interface with the outside world. An e-mail server relay is not always necessary, but does provide a level of protection, as the external network has no direct access to your e-mail server. On the other hand, servers, such as a database server, do not need to directly access the outside world, so they can be on the internal network. The Web server may have to access the database server, but the outside world does not (and probably should not). Therefore, the point of the DMZ is to protect your computers from the outside world, while not protecting them so much that nobody can access them.

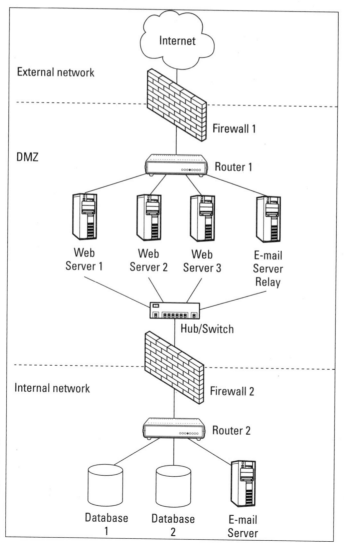

Figure 11-4:
A typical
DMZ
configu-
ration.

Active Directory

Microsoft Active Directory is the centralized account management database that provides access to resources within your corporate network. Active Directory came with Windows 2000 servers and is carried forward in the new .NET servers as well. The use of Active Directory has proven to be a very secure and robust way to authenticate users. Prior to Windows 2000 was Windows NT server, which also had a user-based authentication scheme but was not as robust as Active Directory.

At the core of Active Directory is a security concept called Kerberos. Microsoft named this concept after the three-headed guard dog in Greek mythology because Kerberos is composed of three main modules:

- **Client:** User or computer that wishes to gain access to a resource (such as a folder, file, or printer).

- **Server:** Computer that contains the requested resource.

- **Key Distribution Center (KDC):** Authentication mechanism that provides resource grant access tokens, known as a *ticket*. If, along with the request, a service ticket is presented to the server, access will be granted.

With Active Directory, a client requests access to a resource. To do so, he or she (or even another computer system) requests access to that resource by using a login ID and password. If the login is granted (also known as *authenticated*) and the user has privileges to access the resource, then a ticket is issued and passed to the requested resource. The operating system then enables access to the resource.

Access is granted by comparing permissions at the user and group levels. A user can be assigned privileges individually, or those privileges can be assigned to a group to which the user belongs. Users and groups are also known as *containers*. Privileges can even be assigned to containers. If assigned to both, rules have to be applied to determine the effective privileges (also known as *permissions*). Here's the basic rule: The higher of the permissions levels is granted unless one of the container's permissions is *No Access*. In the latter case, the user will not be able to access the resource.

For example, suppose that a user named John is a member of the Sales group. Alison is also a member of the Sales group. The Sales group has read-only access to a folder named SalesLeads. John has read/write access to the SalesLeads folder, while Alison has no access to the SalesLeads folder. Additionally, Adam is a member of the Executive group, which has read/write access to the SalesLeads folder. As a user, he also has read/write access to the SalesLeads folder.

Can you guess which effective permissions both John and Alison will have? Table 11-2 shows the effective permissions for this example, following the rules I just outlined.

Table 11-2	Active Directory Effective Permissions Example		
User	*User Permission*	*Container Permission*	*Effective Permission*
Adam	Read/Write	Read/Write	Read/Write
Alison	No Access	Read-Only	No Access
John	Read/Write	Read-Only	Read/Write

Active Directory is an outstanding technology that is used to grant or deny access to the resources on your network. Just as with every Microsoft program, it has a nice, easy-to-use graphical interface. Forgive me if I don't show a screen shot! I don't want to cause a security breach by showing you the specifics of my network.

VPN

Using a VPN (or virtual private network) is a great way to protect your environment, while allowing people or other resources to have access to your network. If you have set up a firewall and/or a DMZ configuration (see earlier discussions in this chapter), you may have blocked access that legitimate users need. For example, suppose you have set up your network according to the diagram in Figure 11-4. Additionally, you have opened only ports 25, 80, 110, and 443 to allow only Web and e-mail traffic through your firewall.

A VPN typically allows a client to "tunnel" through one or more firewalls to gain access to server resources directly. After a VPN connection is established, a client communicates with the internal network from the external network as if the firewalls were not present at all. In a Microsoft environment, VPN does this by using Kerberos authentication when the client requests that the point-to-point tunnel be created using the L2TP protocol through port 1701. Therefore, for a VPN connection, port 1701 will have to be opened as well as ports 25, 80, 110, and 443. When a VPN connection is attempted, if the user supplies the appropriate credentials, the user will be granted access. After access is granted, the user will gain access to the same resources that are available when the user is physically located inside the internal network. Furthermore, the VPN can be set up to allow only secure connections.

Like firewalls, VPNs come in hardware and software varieties. A hardware-based VPN can be quite costly. In most circumstances, a software-based VPN works just fine. Also, if you use a Windows 2000 Server or any of the Windows .NET servers, the ability to set up a VPN connection comes built-in. All you have to do is configure it. I won't take up valuable pages by showing how this is done, but consult the online help for either of these products and search for *VPN.*

Web Server Configuration

Because Web services are hosted on a Web server, the configuration of the Web server becomes a very important security matter. Internet Information Services (IIS) is the type of Web server used within Microsoft's operating systems. These areas allow configuration in IIS:

- ✔ TCP/IP address restrictions
- ✔ User authentication methods
- ✔ SSL certificates

Each of these is covered on the next few pages.

TCP/IP address restrictions

You can assign two types of TCP/IP address restrictions on an IIS Web server. The first is the TCP/IP address that IIS listens on. Multiple TCP/IP addresses can be assigned to a single server. This situation typically occurs because multiple network cards (also known as NICs) are installed on the server. If this is the case, you can restrict which TCP/IP addresses are handled by the Web server. I refer to these TCP/IP addresses as *Web site listening addresses* because the Web server will only listen on these addresses, as specified by the internal NIC cards.

The second TCP/IP address restriction limits traffic based on the external TCP/IP address of the computer requesting access. This access restriction allows only specific TCP/IP addresses to access the Web site. I refer to this type of restriction as *access restrictions* because the Web server will only allow network traffic on the addresses specified as external addresses.

Web site listening restrictions

If you have more than one TCP/IP address assigned to the server, you can restrict those addresses served by a Web site by following this procedure:

1. **Choose Start⇨Programs⇨Administrative Tools⇨Internet Information Services to open the IIS Manager.**

2. **Drill down until you get to the Web site you want to restrict.**

3. **Right-click the desired Web site.**

4. **Select Properties from the menu provided to bring up the Properties dialog box.**

   Selecting Properties brings up a tabbed dialog box that can be used to control properties for the selected Web site. The Web Site tab is shown automatically and is represented in Figure 11-5.

5. **Select the desired IP address from the drop-down list provided.**

   If you do not configure anything, all IP addresses that are assigned to the current computer will be used to communicate and respond with this Web site. This option appears as (All Unassigned). On the other hand, if you want to use a specific IP address, simply choose it from the drop-down list. Additionally, you can click the Advanced button and assign more than one IP address manually.

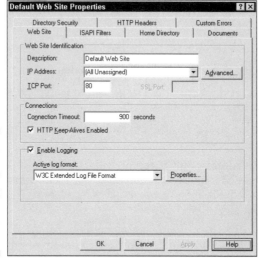

Figure 11-5:
The Web Site tab of the Default Web Site Properties dialog box.

6. **Select the desired listening ports.**

   By default, non-SSL Web sites listen on port 80. If you want to change this port, do so in the TCP Port text box or by configuring it after clicking the Advanced button. If you want to change the default SSL port from 443, do so in the assigned text box or, again, by clicking the Advanced button.

   If, after clicking the Advanced button, the SSL text box is disabled, you do not have an SSL certificate installed on the computer. Therefore, you have no need to configure an SSL port because the Web server could not respond to the SSL request. To request or install an SSL certificate, see the "SSL certificates" section later in this chapter.

7. **Click OK to save your changes and close the dialog box.**

Access restrictions

If you want to limit which TCP/IP addresses are allowed to send requests to a Web server, you can do that quite easily. This limitation is useful when you want to ensure that only one department or set of users accesses your Web site. Follow these easy steps to restrict access to the Web site:

1. **Choose Start⇨Programs⇨Administrative Tools⇨Internet Information Services to open the IIS Manager.**

2. **Drill down until you get to the Web site you want to restrict.**

3. **Right-click the desired Web site.**

4. **Select Properties from the menu provided to bring up the Properties dialog box.**

   The Properties dialog box for your selected Web site appears.

5. **Select the Directory Security tab on the Properties dialog box.**

   Selecting the Directory Security tab brings up the Web Site Properties dialog box, as shown in Figure 11-6.

6. **Click the Edit button in the IP address and domain name restrictions area.**

   This button will be enabled only if you are running IIS on a Windows 2000 Server or higher. It will be disabled on any workstation operating system, such as Windows 2000 Professional or Windows XP (either Home or Professional).

   Clicking Edit brings up the IP Address Restrictions dialog box, as shown in Figure 11-7, which enables you to enter restriction information.

7. **Enter your default restriction information.**

   Depending on what you are trying to do, you need to choose a default restriction method, either

- **Granted access:** Default restriction whereby every computer is allowed access to the Web site, except for the Web site IP addresses that you explicitly list. This is useful when you have a large number of computers that can access the Web site but only a few that should be restricted. This is the default option.

- **Denied access:** Default restriction whereby every computer is denied access to the Web site except for the ones that you explicitly list. This is useful when you have a small number of computers that can access the Web site but many that should be restricted.

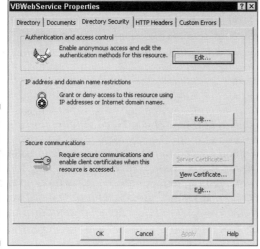

Figure 11-6:
The Directory Security tab of your Web Site Properties dialog box.

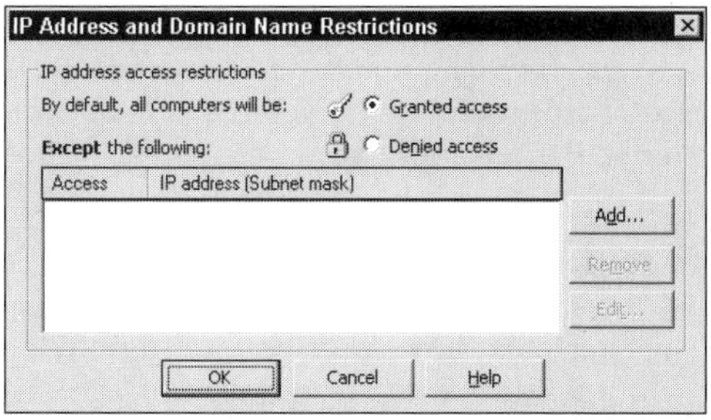

Figure 11-7:
IP Address and Domain Name Restrictions dialog box.

8. **Enter specific IP exclusion information.**

   To add an IP addresses, click the Add button. Doing so gives you three options:

   - **Single computer:** Enables you to exclude a single computer's IP address from the default restriction method (specified in Step 7).

 • **Group of computers:** Enables you to exclude a range of computers' IP addresses from the default restriction method. To do this,
 you must include the network ID and subnet mask of the range.
 For example, you might enter **192.168.0.0** with a subnet mask of
 255.255.255.0 for every computer that begins with **192.168.0** and
 ends with the last number being anything between **0** and **255** on
 the **255.255.255.0** subnet. These numbers are commonly used for
 internal networks.

 • **Domain name:** Enables you to specify a specific domain name to
 except from the default restriction method. You should use caution
 when selecting this option because it can be resource-intensive.

 9. **Click OK to save your restriction information and close the Address
 Restrictions dialog box.**

 10. **Click OK to save your information and close the Web Site Properties
 dialog box.**

User authentication methods

A *user authentication method* is used to determine how a user will be authenticated and granted access to the requested resource after all of the TCP/IP
address restrictions have been passed. For more information on the types of
TCP/IP address restrictions are available in IIS, refer to "TCP/IP address
restrictions," earlier in this chapter.

A user can be authenticated in one of the following ways:

✔ **Anonymous access:** Enables anyone to access resources on a Web site.
 However, because all resources require a specific security context
 (meaning a user ID and password), an anonymous user that will have
 access to the requested resource must be selected. This is typically the
 option you would choose if your application, rather than the Web server,
 will check security.

✔ **Integrated Windows authentication:** A Windows NT challenge/response
 mechanism whereby the user's browser prompts for a user ID, password,
 and domain name. The user must have an account on the Windows NT
 domain. Integrated Windows authentication does not work through a
 proxy server or a firewall.

✔ **Digest authentication:** Similar to integrated Windows authentication but
 requires a Windows 2000 server (or higher) Active Directory installation.
 The main advantage in digest authentication is that it does work through
 a proxy server or a firewall.

✔ **Basic authentication:** A *last-resort* method where Active Directory is not
 installed, but you must authenticate users that exist in a Windows NT
 domain. The main problem with this method is that all passwords are

sent in clear text across the network. If people were listening for packets by using a network device known as a *packet sniffer,* they would be able to see the passwords being transmitted. If you are going to use this type of authentication, use SSL at least to encrypt the passwords.

✔ **.NET Passport authentication:** Enables the Microsoft .NET Passport Web service to authenticate a user for single sign-in (SSI) applications. For more information about Passport, see Chapter 10. This option is available only in Windows XP or Windows .NET Server.

To specify the authentication method(s) that you will use for your Web site, follow this procedure:

1. **Choose Start⇨Programs⇨Administrative Tools⇨Internet Information Services to open the IIS Manager.**

2. **Drill down until you get to the Web site you want to set the authentication method for.**

3. **Right-click the desired Web site.**

4. **Select Properties from the menu provided to bring up the Properties dialog box.**

   The Properties dialog box for your selected Web site appears.

5. **Select the Directory Security tab from the Properties dialog box.**

   Selecting the Directory Security tab brings up the Directory Security tab of the Web Site Properties dialog box, as shown in Figure 11-6, earlier in this chapter.

6. **Click the Edit button in the Authentication and Access Control area.**

   Clicking the Edit button brings up the Authentication Methods dialog box, as shown in Figure 11-8, which enables you to select your authentication method(s).

7. **Select one or more desired authentication methods.**

   Use the discussion at the beginning of this section, select one or more of the desired authentication methods.

   If you choose Enable Anonymous Access, you must select or enter a user name and password that will impersonate the Web user for the purpose of accessing resources. By default, the user name is *IUSR_machinename,* where *machinename* is the name of your server. This user account is created automatically when IIS is installed.

   In Windows .NET server or Windows XP only, if you choose Integrated Windows Authentication, Digest Authentication, or Basic Authentication, you can enter the domain that the user is likely to belong to into the Realm text box. This prevents the user from having to enter a domain when a challenge dialog box appears in the browser.

If you choose the Enable Passport Authentication option (which is not available on Windows 2000), you cannot choose any other option besides Enable Anonymous Access. Additionally, you'll have to select or enter the default domain used in conjunction with Passport.

8. Click OK to save your changes and close the dialog box.

Figure 11-8:
Authentication Methods dialog box as shown in Windows XP or Windows .NET Server.

SSL certificates

SSL certificates are used to encrypt data across the Internet and your internal network. SSL certificates are *not* used to control authentication to your Web site; SSL certificates guarantee only that the data to and from the site is encrypted.

SSL certificates are all about trust. Suppose that you want to do banking transactions over the Internet with your favorite banking Web site, such as XYZ BankCorp (a made-up name). You go to www.xyzbank.com and start conducting business. However, how do you really know that www.xyzbank.com is a reputable organization and not some guy in his basement. You really don't! Well, there is one way.

If the bank's Web site transfers data by using SSL encryption, it must have an SSL certificate installed on all of its Web servers. If it has no certificate, it is impossible to create the SSL connection. So where does this certificate come from? It comes from a trusted source. This trusted source does some level of due diligence to ensure that your company is legitimate. For external Web sites, you need to get your SSL certificates from a source that has been deemed reliable and is in business to research a company's validity before the certificate is issued. To find out which companies are trusted authorities, follow this procedure:

1. **Choose Start⇨Run and type MMC at the prompt to open the Microsoft Management Console (or MMC).**

2. **Within the MMC, choose File⇨Add/Remove Snap-In. to add the Certificates snap-in.**

   The Add/Remove Snap-In dialog box appears.

3. **Click the Add button in the Add/Remove Snap-In dialog box.**

   The Add Standalone Snap-In dialog box appears.

4. **Select Certificates.**

5. **Click the Add button in the Add Standalone Snap-In dialog box.**

6. **Click Service account when prompted for the type of certificates that will be managed.**

7. **Click Next.**

8. **Click Finish.**

9. **Close the Add Standalone Snap-In dialog box.**

10. **Click OK in the Add/Remove Snap-In dialog box.**

11. **Expand the certificates shown in the MMC to reveal Trusted Root Certification Authorities.**

12. **Click the Certificates folder under the Trusted Root Certification Authorities.**

    Clicking this folder brings up the Trusted Root Certification Authorities screen, as shown in Figure 11-9.

    The list of companies that is shown in Figure 11-9 is a list of trusted authorities that can issue SSL certificates. Personally, I have used Thawte as my certificate provider. It's reasonably priced and have good service. It's Web site is available at www.thawte.com.

If you do not use a certificate that is issued by a trusted authority, your clients receive a warning stating that when they try to establish an SSL connection with your server.

Requesting a certificate

Before you install an SSL certificate, you must request a certificate from a certificate server. This certificate server should be from a trusted authority in a production environment but can be generated within Windows 2000 server or Windows .NET server.

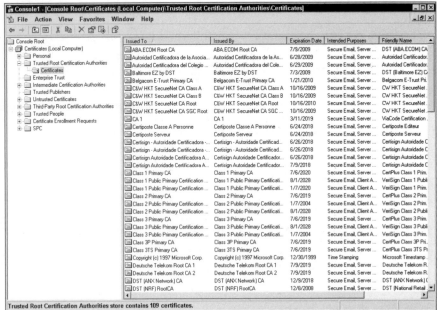

Figure 11-9:
Trusted Root
Certification
Authorities.

To request a certificate, use the IIS Manager from the folder representing the root of a Web site. If you only have one Web site on a Web server, this will likely be listed as "Default Web Site." Requesting a certificate cannot be done at a folder location within the Web site.

Trusted authority certificates

To request a certificate from a trusted authority, follow these steps:

1. **Choose Start⇨Programs⇨Administrative Tools⇨Internet Information Services to open the IIS Manager.**

2. **In the IIS Manager, drill down until you get to the Web site you want to request a certificate for.**

3. **Right-click the desired Web site.**

   It is likely that this Web site is a folder labeled "Default Web Site."

4. **Select Properties from the menu provided to bring up the Properties dialog box.**

5. **Select the Directory Security tab in the Properties dialog box.**

6. **Click the Server Certificate button.**

   Clicking this button invokes a Certificate Wizard, showing the opening screen.

7. **Click Next to display the Server Certificate step.**

   By default, the Create a New Certificate option is checked, which is the one that you need.

8. **Click Next to display the Delayed or Immediate Request step.**

   You have a choice to prepare a request, but send it later or to send the request immediately. The request can only be sent immediately if you have a Windows 2000 or higher server with Certificate Services installed. If not, the option to send the request immediately will be disabled. If you are requesting a certificate by a third-party trusted authority, the option to prepare the request but send it later is needed. Ensure that the prepare option is selected.

9. **Click Next to display the Name and Security Settings step, enter the name of your certificate, and choose the desired bit length.**

   By default, the name presented is the same name as your Web server. If you want to change this, make sure that the name adequately depicts the purpose of the certificate.

   Also choose the desired bit length. 1024 is selected by default, which is 128-bit security. This is fine for most applications.

10. **Click Next to display the Organization Information step and enter the name of your organization and the department that is requesting the certificate.**

    These are used by the certification authority to verify your organization. You will likely use the full legal name for your organization. If you are not using this for a specific department, your organizational unit might be something like Corporate or Root Certificate.

11. **Click Next to display the Your Site's Common Name step and enter the URL or name of that site.**

    The common name is how you will tie your certificate to a Web site address. If the certificate will be used on a Web server that will be accessed over the Internet, you need to enter the URL of that site. For example, I use `www.transport80.com`. If the Web server is used internally, it can use a NETBIOS name of the server. For example, one of my Web servers is named `rizzo`, so I could enter that. However, if I do this, I'll only be able to achieve SSL connections internally, not externally.

12. **Click Next to display the Geographical Information step and enter the country, state/province, city/locality information that indicates where your business is located.**

    This will also be used by the certification authority to verify your corporate information.

13. **Click Next to display the Certificate Request File Name step and choose the location and filename for your request file.**

    The information gathered by using this wizard will be encoded and must be written to a file. This file needs to be sent to a certification authority, who responds with a corresponding file, which must be imported. In this step, you simply choose a location and filename for your request file. Typically, the default filename and location are fine.

14. **Click Next to display the Summary step. Review all information in the summary screen. Click Back and correct any information necessary.**

15. **Click Next to display the Final step.**

16. **Click Finish to generate the certificate request file.**

    If you were to look at the certificate request file in Notepad, you would see a standard, uniform file that contains encrypted information about all data collected by using the wizard. This is shown in Figure 11-10.

Figure 11-10:
Certificate
request file.

You must send this certificate request file to your desired trusted certification authority for processing. The trusted certification authority company normally allows you to e-mail or upload the file for automatic processing.

Self-issued certificates

Self-issuing a certificate is basically the same as requesting a certificate from a third-party certification authority, except that the request is handled by a Windows 2000 server or Windows .NET server that is running certificate services. Certificate services must be installed and configured as a root CA(Certification Authority). If a server is not configured to run certificate services, you will not be able to automatically send your request for a certificate online.

To self-issue a certificate, follow the same procedures listed under the "Trusted authority certificates" section, earlier in this chapter, up until step 8. At Step 8, select the Send the Request Immediately to an Online Certification Authority option. If no servers are running Certificate Services on your local network, this option will not be enabled.

Steps 9 through 12 are exactly the same. You must enter the information that is pertinent to your organization and certification configuration. However, because you are not going to send a certification file to a certification authority, Step 13 enables you to choose from a list of available certification servers that are on your network.

Continue with the rest of the steps. After you click Finish, the certificate is generated and automatically installed. To view the certificate, see the "Viewing the certificate" section later in this chapter.

Installing the certificate

Before you can install the SSL certificate, you must have requested it from a third-party trusted source. If you issued your own certificate, it is automatically installed, so you don't have to follow this procedure.

To continue with this procedure to install the certificate, you must have received a *.CER file from your certificate authority. Most likely, this file will be e-mailed to you by the certification authority. If you have received this file, continue with the installation procedure, as follows:

1. **Choose Start⇨Programs⇨Administrative Tools⇨Internet Information Services to open the IIS Manager.**

2. **Drill down until you get to the Web site you want to request a certificate for.**

3. **Right-click the desired Web site, such as the Default Web Site, to present a list of menu options.**

4. **Select Properties from the menu provided to bring up the Properties dialog box.**

5. **Select the Directory Security tab in the Properties dialog box.**

6. **Click the Server Certificate button.**

   Once again, you are presented with a welcome screen.

7. **Click Next to display the Pending Certificate Request step and process the pending request or delete the pending request.**

If you have never requested a certificate by creating a certificate request file, you will not see this step. If you don't see the Pending Certificate Request step, close the wizard now and refer to the "Trusted authority certificates" section earlier in this chapter to find out how to request a certificate.

You have two choices at this step. You can process the pending request, or you can delete the pending request. You would delete the pending request if you created it in error. Otherwise, you must process the pending request after you receive a response file from the certificate authority. Select the Process the Pending Request and Install the Certificate option.

8. **Click Next to display the Process a Pending Request step.**

   Enter the path and filename of the *.CER file that you received from the certificate authority.

9. **Click Next to display the Certificate Summary step.**

   This summary screen contains certificate information from the certificate authority.

10. **Click Next to display the Final step.**

11. **Click Finish to install the SSL certificate and close the wizard.**

Viewing the certificate

After you have installed the server certificate, you can view it to see its attributes, including the expiration date. To view the certificate, follow these steps:

1. **Choose Start⇨Programs⇨Administrative Tools⇨Internet Information Services to open the IIS Manager.**

2. **Drill down until you get to the Web site you want to request a certificate for.**

3. **Right-click the desired Web site, such as the Default Web Site.**

4. **Select Properties from the menu provided to bring up the Properties dialog box.**

5. **Select the Directory Security tab in the Properties dialog box.**

6. **Click the View Certificate button.**

   The certificate appears. It should look similar to the one shown in Figure 11-11.

Notice at the top of Figure 11-11 that the certificate cannot be verified. This is because it was issued by an internal certificate services server, not by a trusted authority.

Figure 11-11:
Viewing the
installed
certificate.

Web Services Configuration

To enable the security of your Web services, the .NET framework allows for a couple of configuration options. You can adjust for security at the framework level. Security settings for the .NET framework are set in the .NET framework configuration console.

To open the .NET framework configuration console, you must have the .NET framework installed on your Web server. Then, to open the console, choose Start⇨Settings⇨Control Panel⇨Administrative Tools⇨Microsoft .NET Framework Configuration. Choosing this series of menus brings up the configuration console, as shown in Figure 11-12. In the list of folders in the left pane, notice a folder named Runtime Security Policy. This is the parent container under which you configure your security options. Each of these security options writes data to .NET security files that are located in the .NET framework directory. This directory is, by default, located in the C:\WINDOWS\ Microsoft.NET\Framework\v1.0.3705\CONFIG folder. This folder contains a bunch of configuration files in an XML format. Instead of learning the ins and outs of these files, simply use the configuration console.

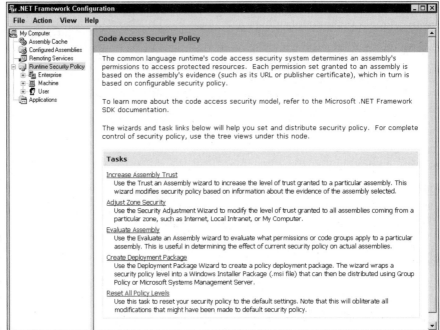

Figure 11-12:
The Runtime
Security
Policy
Console.

You use the configuration console to adjust the security settings for assemblies that will be handled by the Web server on which the configuration console is running. There are three levels for which you can create assembly policies:

✔ **Enterprise:** Configures assembly security for the entire enterprise, including all machines.

✔ **Machine:** Configures assembly security for a specific machine only.

✔ **User:** Configures assembly security for a specific user only.

It is possible to configure security policies at all three levels, but the most restrictive policy will actually be applied at runtime. This is in contrast to the way Active Directory works. See the "Active Directory" section, earlier in this chapter.

Within *each* of the three policy levels (Enterprise, Machine, and User), you can configure three types of policies:

✔ **Code Groups:** Defines a classification of code (or assemblies). By default, only one code group is defined, which is called All Code. You can create additional code groups if necessary. Code groups are assigned permissions by using permission sets. You may, for example, create a code group named Financial, which is a specific set of libraries designed to handle financial transactions. The Financial code group might require different permissions levels than all other code, hence the need for a separate code group. The fact that your code itself can have security assigned to it is referred to as *evidence-based security*.

✔ **Permission Sets:** Defines the permissions available to a code group. Because multiple permissions can be assigned to a code group, permissions are grouped together into a set. A permission set can contain any number of these predefined permissions:

- Directory Services
- DNS
- Event Log
- Environment Variables
- File Dialog
- File IO
- Isolated Storage File
- Message Queue
- OLE DB
- Performance Counter
- Printing
- Registry
- Reflection
- Security
- Service Controller
- Socket Access
- SQL Client
- User Interface
- Web Access

Each of these permissions contains different configuration options, which cannot be covered in this chapter. For more information on these options, consult the documentation that comes with the .NET framework. However, if your permission sets include any of the aforementioned permissions, you are prompted for specific configuration information when you select the permission.

✓ **Policy Assemblies:** A list of compiled assemblies that are subject to the defined policy.

To alter any of the security policy information presented here, you simply click the desired level in the tree and choose from the links presented. For example, suppose that you want to add a new permission set for the enterprise policy; simply click the Permission Sets folder under the Enterprise folder. Doing so presents a link, named Create New Permission Set, on the right part of the screen. Clicking this option enables you to name the new permission set and choose from the list of all standard permissions. This example is shown in Figure 11-13.

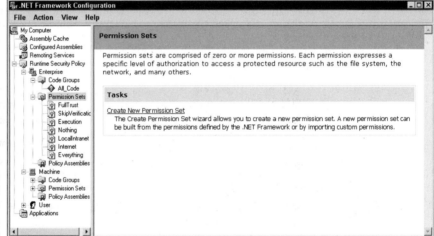

Figure 11-13:
Creating
a new
permission
set.

Likewise, code groups can be configured in the like-named folder. A code group is actually considered to be a child of the code group, All_Code. To create this child code group, simply click the All_Code group in the left pane. In the pane on the right side of the screen, you see the Add a Child Code Group option, as shown in Figure 11-14.

You create a policy assembly a little differently because there are no child folders. To create a policy assembly, right-click the Policy Assemblies menu and select the Add menu. Finally, choose the assembly to be included in the policy.

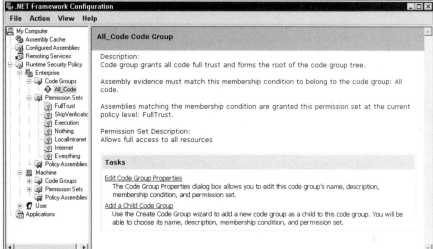

Figure 11-14:
Creating a
new child
code group.

Chapter 12

Planning for Web Services

· ·

· ·

*I*f you want to be successful in doing anything in life, you must plan. With real estate, you hear the often-quoted phrase, "location, location, location." Well, similarly, with any software project (Web services included), an appropriate phrase to use is "planning, planning, planning."

For example, you must consider hardware, software, and personnel resources. You also have many design considerations, such as session state and assembly versioning, to review. Additionally, you must plan for some organizational policy considerations, such as disaster recovery. This chapter explores all of these topics to give you a good idea of how to get the planning process started. Remember, if you plan ahead, you'll be grateful in the long run.

Getting Started

Chances are good that if you bought this book, you already know that you want to implement Web services in your business organization. However, you may still be wondering just where to begin. Every organization is different, but big or small, complicated or simple, your business needs to find a Web solution that returns the biggest bang for the buck. That's right, I'm talking about those three important letters: ROI.

To determine your return on investment (ROI), you should follow these general guidelines:

1. **Identify the problem.**

   This is probably the easiest step of all.

   For example, your sales force might be ready to mutiny because they can't find an easy way to access client information while they're on the road. This is a clear problem that your solution must solve. What luck! This would be a great candidate for a Web services project!

2. **Consider all possible solutions.**

   Solutions can range from ridiculous (having your sales staff print out the contents of the entire database before going on the road) to pie in the sky (creating an interface that enables sales staff to access a variety of different kinds of data using wireless PDAs). When you weigh all the solutions, you'll probably find yourself deciding on a Web service somewhere in the middle, such as a Web-based program that enables users to get information with an Internet connection.

   Nothing's worse than spending time on a solution that will be obsolete in a year. Find a reasonable middle ground to start, especially if you're new to Web services and want to hedge your bets. If you work out your plan well, you will come up with a Web service solution that is completely scalable. Keep reading for more information about scalability.

3. **Make a decision, set a deadline, and decide on a budget.**

   This stuff is pretty self explanatory, right? But don't forget that if no one in your company is really up on the ins and outs of Web services, talking to a consultant may be worth the extra money and time. To find a consultant that can help with your Web services projects, especially on the Microsoft platform, you should choose a company that is listed as a Microsoft Certified Partner, such as my company, Transport:80 Incorporated. To find a partner, point your browser to the Microsoft Web site:

   ```
   http://directory.microsoft.com/resourcedirectory/Solution
          s.aspx
   ```

   For information about Transport:80, you can visit our Web site at www.transport80.com.

Of course, the next step is to get your plan underway. Here is a list of areas to plan for:

- ✓ **Resources:** You know, people and stuff. Namely, the people who are going to build the Web service, the people who will be using it, and of course, the machines and software the people will be using.

- ✓ **Configuration:** Remember *Field of Dreams*? If you build it, they will come, right? Yeah. But that means that you have to build it, which means configuring not just hardware but also software.

✔ **Security:** I can't emphasize enough how nonnegotiable this part of the puzzle is, so don't overlook it or plan to work out security "later."

✔ **Disaster recovery:** Like security, disaster recovery is something to plan for now, not later. Even if you have never had a system crash before and have excellent disaster recovery plans in place now, you need to integrate the new service into those plans.

✔ **Scalability:** Maybe you have plans to add more Web services or more servers over a five-year time frame. Maybe you have plans to double your workforce in the next three years. Or both. You get my drift — don't waste a lot of money and time creating an inflexible service that you can't expand upon.

✔ **Session state:** You'll have to decide how to handle the transfer of data from page-to-page as you move through a Web site.

Although I have divided these planning considerations into neat little categories, none of this information is cut and dried. You can't think about scalability without thinking of hardware, and you can't think about hardware without thinking about software and configuration. Also, all these things are woven together in a particular fabric that makes *your* business unique; don't forget this fact! No matter how tidy the information I provide in this chapter may be, you have to customize your plan so that it fits your business like a glove.

Gathering Resources

Gathering resources is exactly what it sounds like: You need to determine how many and what kind of resources your organization will need when implementing a system. Resources include things such as personnel, hardware, software, and more.

Evaluating personnel resources

Determining personnel requirements for implementing or building Web services projects is a very difficult thing to quantify because your personnel needs are affected by the following:

✔ **Skill level:** Do the people that will be building your Web services have enough experience to easily grasp the concepts of Web services, or are they straight out of college. On one hand, there is no substitute for experience, and experience may help speed development time. On the other hand, a fresh mind, straight out of college, may be able to learn the concepts behind Web services faster than an experienced person because, after all, you might not be able to teach an old dog new tricks very easily.

- **Training:** If your IT department folks are not familiar with Web services at all, they may need to go to training. Training can be a good thing, but it can also affect time and budget. Be aware of this when evaluating your personnel resources. Likewise, if you implement Web services on a Linux platform instead of a Microsoft platform, it may seem like the cost of implementation is cheaper; but in fact, you'll have to train your personnel to support Linux. Microsoft has actually done studies to prove that, because of training (and also implementation), the cost of a Web services project is less expensive on the Microsoft platform.

- **Web services knowledge:** If every person on your IT staff has read this book or kept up to date with some of Web services technologies, these people might be a very good resource to place on a Web services project, as opposed to someone who needs to learn the concepts. Just as with training (listed in the last point), the lack of knowledge of Web services on a Linux platform tends to increase the cost and time-to-market with your Web services project over the Microsoft alternative platform.

- **Business knowledge:** For your new Web services projects, you must consider the business knowledge of your IT personnel. In other words, do they understand exactly what the business problem is, what needs to be done, and why it needs to be done? Furthermore, do they understand the business timelines and reason for those timelines? If the IT personnel understand all of the these things, this knowledge will go a long way to shortening the learning curve and timelines for the project. Having IT personnel understand the real business behind the solution is invaluable.

Because Web services technology is very new, you may find it difficult to locate someone with enough experience to implement your Web services in a fairly quick manner. Additionally, it may be tough to find someone who can manage such a project, especially a complex one.

Also, as with all software projects, it takes a whole host of skilled and responsible people to pull off a Web services project, including the following:

- **Executive sponsor:** Responsible for promoting and approving the project.

- **Project manager:** Manages the entire project to make sure that it stays on track, on schedule, and on budget. Sometimes the project manager will also assign resources.

- **Resource manager:** In larger IT shops, sometimes a resource manager is employed to manage the resources and skills necessary for projects. This person can effectively place the same resource on multiple projects simultaneously, which curbs overall costs.

- **Designer/Architect:** Designs the Web services solution, considering enterprise issues, security, disparate data, disaster recovery, and so forth. The designer/architect may also be responsible for planning the hardware and software environment.

✔ **Network engineer:** In some organizations, manages and designs the internal infrastructure, including the configuration of hardware. Not all organizations have the network engineer plan for hardware; sometimes the designer/architect does it.

✔ **Developer:** Develops the software.

✔ **Tester:** Tests the software.

Before embarking on a Web services project, make sure that each member of the team understands the goals of the project, what Web services are and what they aren't, and why you are implementing the solution. Perhaps you should even buy them a copy of this book.

Evaluating hardware resources

A Web services project doesn't necessarily need any additional hardware. Remember that a Web services project is hosted on a Web server, such as IIS. Therefore, if you have a Web server already in your organization, this may be fine to also host your Web services project.

You may need additional hardware if your solution is an intensive one. For example, if you are going to have your Web services perform a massive database query, you may need to buy a beefy database server in addition to utilizing your new or existing Web server.

Just know that you don't *have to* beef up the hardware just because you're developing a Web services project. There are many hardware parts that you must consider when beefing up your hardware, such as the following:

✔ **CPU type:** For any production system, you shouldn't use anything less than an Intel Pentium IV. Some people use AMD processors to save costs, but Microsoft works very well with Intel processors. (That's why there is an IT joke that calls this combination *WINTEL* — for Windows and Intel.)

✔ **CPU speed:** The speed of the processor is increasing all the time, with speeds over 2GHz (gigahertz — or 2 million hertz — or 2 million instructions per second). I wouldn't recommend using anything less than 1.5GHz for a production system.

✔ **Memory:** The amount of memory in your server is critical. Memory is also cheap, so don't skimp in this area. For a production Web server, I wouldn't recommend anything less than 1GB (gigabyte) at an absolute minimum, but normally 2GB is better. If your Web server is also a database server, then you probably don't want less than 4GB memory.

✔ **Disk space:** Disk space is also cheap. Most programs are disk hogs, so you'll need a large disk drive. At a bare-bones minimum, you'll want at least a 40GB hard drive, but it's hard to get less than that these days. Of course, if you are using the same server for database and Web functions, then the size of your hard drive may need to be increased substantially. See "Handling hard drive configuration issues," later in this chapter, for additional disk drive configurations.

Evaluating software resources

Okay, this may be a little obvious, but a Web services software project is hosted on a Web server, so you must plan for the installation of at least some new software. You may not need all the software shown in Table 12-1, but I guarantee that you will need at least some of it.

Table 12-1	Software Planning	
Server	*Software*	*Description*
Web	IIS	Internet information services (Web server)
Web	.NET Framework	Web services environment
Web	FrontPage Extensions	For publishing Web services projects to a Web server
Database	SQL Server	Needed when accessing a database
Dev	Visual Studio.NET	Development environment for creating Web services applications

Making Configuration Plans

After you have planned for the hardware and software that you will install for use with your Web services projects and determined who will do all the work, you need to get those technogeeks to work. Normally, someone will be assigned as the project manager who controls all aspects of the project, making sure it is on track, on time, and on budget. Either the project manager or a resource manager will assign someone, such as an architect or designer, to plan the configuration.

Basically, the architect/designer or network engineer has to plan the *configuration* of the software and hardware so that everything in your Web service works according to plan. Configuration can be very simple or very complex, depending on your environment and the complexity of the project.

Dealing with Server Configuration Issues

To give you an example of the complexities of configuration (and the necessity for planning ahead), here's a scenario that involves only one hardware type — servers. Say you have three Web servers and two database servers.

You use the three Web servers for *load balancing*. Load balancing is a pretty basic concept. Three servers are better than one when it comes to handling the load of users accessing the Web service.

Okay. That was simple. But how do you want to use your database servers? You have more than one option, and your decision is really going to depend on the type of Web service you're creating, how much data you're dealing, with, and how much backup you need. Here are some options:

- ✔ **Use one server for fault tolerance:** One database server faithfully performs its database duties just as it always did, while you use the other one for fault tolerance. *Fault tolerance* is the capability of a backup system to take over if one server fails or if the software stops responding.

  When you use a backup system for fault tolerance purposes, the backup system is in a configuration known as *failover*. All computers that are grouped together for failover are referred to as a *failover cluster*. There are two failover designs: Active/Active and Active/Passive. In an Active/Active failover cluster, the multiple servers that make up the cluster are completely operational all the time. If one machine fails, the remaining servers take up the load. In an Active/Passive failover cluster, only one server in the cluster is active at any one time, while all other servers are inactive, or passive. In an Active/Passive configuration, the passive server only becomes active when the first active server fails. An Active/Passive cluster is cheaper and easier to implement than an Active/Active cluster. The reason that an Active/Passive cluster is cheaper is that normally you don't have to pay for the software licenses on the passive computers because only one server actually functions at any one point in time. Check with your software vendor for licensing requirements in cluster configurations to be sure.

- ✔ **Partition data on both database servers:** *Data partitioning* is placing some data on one computer and other data on another computer. If you are using Microsoft SQL Server 2000, data partitioning (also sometimes known as *horizontal partitioning*) is a built-in feature. If you are using any other database server, check with the manufacturer of the software to see if it allows horizontal partitioning.

  Data partioning helps to distribute the load of data across the two servers (just the way three Web servers work together to balance the load on the front end of the Web service). For example, records with the last name beginning with the letter *A* through *M* are on one server, and last names beginning with *N* through *Z* reside on the other server.

> Data partitioning can be great if you have a large volume of data, but it doesn't provide for fault tolerance.
>
> ✔ **Buy two more database servers:** If you want to have true fault tolerance with partitioning, you can place each of the partitioned computers in a failover cluster. However, to do so, you need twice the number of servers for your database environment. (For you math whizzes, that's four database servers instead of two.)

This scenario is ridiculously simple, actually. The designer/architect who is in charge of coming up with a configuration plan needs to know vital information about your existing servers, the data being dealt with, the number of people using the Web service, and so on.

Handling Hard Drive Configuration Issues

You must consider your hard drives in any and every configuration plan. Slow or poorly performing hard drives can significantly and adversely affect performance of even the most well-designed Web service.

I actually already touched on this factor earlier in the chapter, but I can't emphasize enough the fact that the choice you make in *how* to configure server hard drives plays a role in how your Web service will eventually function.

For example, it is better and faster to have two physical hard drives in a server than one. In this configuration, you typically have the operating system installed on one drive (drive C) and your application installed on a new drive (drive D).

The purpose of this configuration is to free up the operating system to do whatever is necessary for operations (such as virtual memory swapping and so forth) without taking up resources required to access data on the hard drive for your application. The net effect of this configuration is faster performance.

Additionally, you can configure your disk drives into sets for speed enhancement and fault tolerance. These sets are known as RAID (Redundant Array of Inexpensive Disks). *RAID* is a standardized hardware and/or software specification that enhances speed, performance, and fault tolerance; the most common configurations of RAID are described in Table 12-2.

Table 12-2	RAID Configurations	
RAID Level	*Purpose*	*Name*
0	Performance	Striping
1	Fault tolerance	Mirroring
5	Performance and fault tolerance	Striping with parity
10	Performance and fault tolerance	Mirroring with striping

You can implement any of the following RAID configurations by either the hardware or by the software operating system. (Windows 2000 or higher is recommended.) However, hardware RAID controllers perform better but cost more than the software solution.

✔ **RAID 0 is known as *striping*.** It works by dividing the data into blocks, and instead of writing the data to a single disk, it stripes the data in blocks across all disks at the same time. Disks configured for striping are part of what is known as a *striped set*. This means that data is written to the disk very quickly. However, if one of the drives fails in the striped set, you lose all of your data. A way around this is to use RAID 5 or RAID 10.

✔ **RAID 1 is known as *mirroring*.** The main purpose of RAID 1 is to achieve fault tolerance. Every byte of data is written to all drives in the mirror set at the same time. This way, if one disk drive fails, the others contain the data.

✔ **RAID 5 is known as *striping with parity*.** RAID 5 works essentially the same as RAID 1 in that data is divided into blocks and striped across all disks in the striped set. However, RAID 5 has one major difference: You need an extra disk for a RAID 5 configuration (over a RAID 1 configuration). This extra disk is used to calculate a checksum known as *parity*. Because of this parity, it becomes possible to recreate the data if one disk fails. This way, you get the performance boost of RAID 1 with the fault tolerance benefits achieved if a hard drive fails. RAID 5 does have one problem, though: If more than one disk fails, the parity can't recreate the data. Note that the additional drive is not the "parity" drive. The parity information is written for different blocks on different drives. The reason for the extra drive is to achieve the same level of capacity as the RAID 1 solution while providing fault tolerance.

✔ **RAID 10 (also called RAID 1 + 0) is known as *mirroring with striping*.** First, data is striped across all disks in the striped set, just as RAID 0 does. It also mirrors the data for each disk in the striped set, just like RAID 1. RAID 10 offers the best performance and fault tolerance, but is also twice as expensive because it needs twice as many disks.

Creating Software Configuration Plans

Your plans for software configuration may turn out not to be all that complex, really. You may need to do a little tinkering, or you may have to do a lot. It just depends on what you want your Web service to do as well as how much new equipment you're using. (Buying three new servers? You can guarantee that you'll be tinkering with the software on them!)

Whatever you do, don't put the cart before the horse! Don't even consider planning software configuration before you have a solid configuration plan in place for your hardware.

Operating system

You don't have too much to configure within the operating system itself. However, you can do a couple of things to ensure better performance and to keep it as simple as possible.

- ✔ **Only install the services required by the server.** For example, don't install MSMQ (Microsoft Message Queue) if you aren't going to use it. Remember that every application consumes resources, especially programs that run in the background. You may even consider, if your budget allows, having servers dedicated to a specific purpose (Web servers, database servers, integration servers, and so forth).

  Don't install SQL Server on the server that handles Web requests if you have a separate database server with SQL Server installed.

- ✔ **Install on a separate drive or volume.** Installing the operating system on a separate disk drive or volume can yield dramatic increases in performance.

- ✔ **Increase virtual memory.** Computers have to do all computations in memory. Virtual memory is an area on your hard disk that is used to temporarily move areas of physical memory to disk, thereby freeing up physical memory for calculations. Increasing the virtual memory can help increase performance, especially if you don't have enough memory (RAM).

- ✔ **Uninstall services that are automatically installed or automatically enabled.** For instance, the Run As service in Windows 2000 is automatically installed and automatically starts up. However, it is probably not going to be used on a server.

.NET Framework

The .NET Framework allows for only a couple of possible configuration options. You can configure it in the following ways:

- ✔ **Assembly configurations:** Configures the global assembly cache (or GAC) and configured assemblies. For more information about GAC, see Chapter 6.

- ✔ **Remoting services properties:** Configures communication properties for .NET remoting, which is not covered in this book. For Web services, you don't need to configure these properties. If you want to read up on .NET remoting, you can check out this long URL:

  ```
  http://mdsn.microsoft.com/library/default.asp?url=/
          library/en-us/dndotnet/html/introremoting.asp
  ```

- ✔ **Security policies:** Configures the enterprise, machine, and user security policies. These configurations are discussed in Chapter 11.

- ✔ **Applications:** Enables you to indicate which applications use the .NET Framework. One such application is Microsoft Visual Studio .NET. After you add an application to the list, you can configure the assemblies associated with that application. In general, you won't need to do anything with this configuration.

Internet Information Services (IIS)

IIS is Microsoft's Web server; it is built into Windows 2000 and the Windows .NET servers. Prior to Visual Studio .NET, you had to manually change IIS configuration parameters for Web sites that you created. Currently, you really don't have to configure anything when you use Visual Studio .NET to either create or deploy your Web services applications. It's all done for you, with few exceptions. The remaining IIS configurations center around security and SSL. These issues are covered in Chapter 11.

FrontPage Server Extensions

FrontPage Server Extensions are applications that run on the Web server and enable your development tools to connect with your Web servers. Applications like this are known as *ISAPI filters*. (ISAPI stands for *Internet Server Application Programming Interface*.) ISAPI filters consume resources on the Web server, so unless you need them, you should uninstall them.

To see whether you have FrontPage Server Extensions installed on IIS Version 5 and higher, follow these steps:

1. **Open IIS Manager.**

   Choose Start➪Programs➪Administrative Tools➪Internet Information Services to open the IIS Manager.

2. **Expand your server.**

   Click the plus sign (+) to the left of your server name to reveal the Web Sites folder.

3. **Open Web Sites properties.**

   Right-click the Web Sites folder and select Properties. This action brings up the properties for the Web Sites folder, as shown in Figure 12-1.

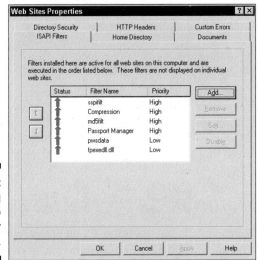

Figure 12-1:
Configuring the Web Sites folder properties.

4. **Look for FrontPage Server Extensions.**

   If the FrontPage Server Extensions are installed on your Web server, you'll see a filter with the name `fpexedll.dll`. Notice two things about this entry: First, the priority is set to `low`. FrontPage Server Extensions are used only for authoring tools to connect to the server and not for everyday operational usage, so it makes sense that the priority is low. Second, the arrow facing upwards in the status column means that the FrontPage Server Extension is currently loaded.

   If you find that your Web server doesn't have the FrontPage Server Extensions installed, you can download and install the file from the following URL:

   `www.microsoft.com/frontpage/downloads/default.htm`

If you determine that you need to make property changes to the FrontPage Server Extensions configuration, perform the steps in the following sections. Keep in mind that, because the process is somewhat involved, I broke the steps into multiple sections.

Step 1: Configuring FrontPage Server Extensions properties

After you have the FrontPage Server Extensions installed, you can configure a few properties relating to these extensions. Here's how:

1. **Open IIS Manager.**

   Choose Start⇨Programs⇨Administrative Tools⇨Internet Information Services to open the IIS Manager.

2. **Drill down through the list until you get to the desired Web site.**

3. **Open the Web site's properties.**

   To do so, right-click the desired Web site and select Properties.

4. **Click the Server Extensions tab.**

   The Server Extensions tab is shown in Figure 12-2.

5. **Configure the screen properties.**

   You have a couple of options, which I cover in the next section.

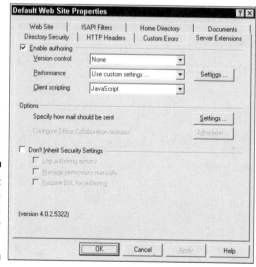

Figure 12-2:
Configuring
FrontPage
Server
Extensions.

Step 2: Deciding on the right screen property changes

If you're starting where you left off in the previous section, The Default Web Site Properties dialog box is on-screen right this moment.

If you haven't already done so, click the Server Extensions tab. Then follow these steps.

1. **Make sure that the Enable Authoring option is selected.**

   The main purpose of FrontPage Server Extensions is to enable authoring tools to access a Web server. However, after your server is in production, you may want to disallow this option and skip to the Step 3, which follows, or to the following section, "Step 3: Tightening security and server extension settings."

   This option is only available on the root Web (which is most likely called Default Web Site) and enables you to version your source code control program, customize performance settings, and modify client-side scripting options.

2. **Tinker, as needed, with the following options:**

   • **Version control:** Enables you to version your source code in a source code control program, which can either be a built-in program or Visual SourceSafe (if installed).

   • **Performance:** Enables you to tune the Web site for a specific number of pages that are in the Web site. By default, you have the choice of using custom settings, which you can view or change by clicking the Settings button. Otherwise, you can select from the drop-down list of specific ranges.

   • **Client scripting:** Enables you to choose the language (either VBScript or JavaScript) that will be used if the FrontPage Server Extensions automatically generate code. Using JavaScript for client scripting is a good practice because it will work with most browsers.

3. **To specify how e-mail is handled, click Settings.**

   From here, you can specify the e-mail server name and e-mail address.

   If they're installed, you can also configure Office collaboration features. In English, that means you can configure the Office Web Server (OWS) collaboration features. You really don't need to know about this, but if you're curious, any good book on Microsoft Office 2000 or later should contain information on OWS.

4. **To change the Don't Inherit Security Settings, click to select this option.**

By default, the Don't Inherit Security Settings option isn't selected. That is, by default, the current Web site will inherit the security settings from its parent. (If you're tinkering with the default Web site, the settings are inherited from the server itself.)

If you don't want to change the default security setting, skip to Step 8 within this list.

5. **To activate the Log Authoring Actions setting, click to select it.**

   If checked, all authoring actions will be logged through the FrontPage Server Extensions.

6. **Although it is ill advised, you can manually manage permissions by clicking the Manage Permissions Manually option.**

   If checked, you must configure all aspects of security yourself.

7. **To adjust the SSL for Authoring setting, click to select it.**

   If checked, the client will be forced to communicate over HTTPS for secure transmission of data. SSL is covered in Chapter 11.

8. **Click OK to save your changes and close the screen.**

   Follow the instructions in the following section to continue the configuration process.

Step 3: Tightening security and server extension settings

Because you can change permissions on a Web server, it may be necessary to tighten the security on your Web server. I recommend this practice because you don't want unauthorized people to change code on your Web server or perhaps even steal (or creatively acquire) it. The process that tightens security also checks for any errors in the configuration of your Web sites. This process is known as *checking* server extensions. To check server extensions, follow this procedure:

1. **Open IIS Manager.**

   Choose Start➪Programs➪Administrative Tools➪Internet Information Services to open the IIS Manager.

2. **Drill down in the list until you get to the desired Web site.**

3. **Check Server Extensions.**

   Right-click the desired Web site and choose All Tasks➪Check Server Extensions.

4. **Tighten security if desired.**

   After you initiate the check, you'll be prompted with a dialog box like the one shown in Figure 12-3.

Figure 12-3:
Tightening
Server
Extension
security.

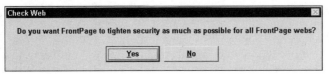

If you rerun this utility, you'll be asked every time if you want to tighten security. Just because you ran it one time and tightened security doesn't mean that this utility checks the security status before asking you the question.

If you want to tighten FrontPage security, select Yes. Regardless of your choice, the utility will check for errors anyway. If any errors exist, you'll be notified to see if they were automatically corrected, as shown in Figure 12-4.

5. **Click Close.**

If any errors exist that could not be automatically corrected, you must determine what the error is and correct it manually.

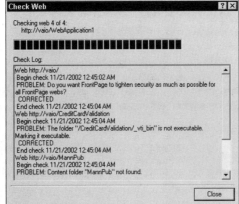

Figure 12-4:
Checking
FrontPage
Server
Extensions.

Creating a Security Plan

Security is one of the biggest topics in information technology — it's a huge hot button. Of course, you must plan for security. To help you, many things related to security are built into the .NET Framework, SOAP, IIS, and even the operating system itself. However, just because you have some built-in security features doesn't mean that you don't have to make additional plans for your security.

To adequately plan for your security, you must consider the following questions:

✔ **How will users be authenticated?** Your application may dictate that users don't have to be authenticated; they can be anonymous. On the other hand, you may need to authenticate users in order to gain access to the system.

✔ **What privileges will users have after they are authenticated?** Users may be able to perform all tasks within your system, or you may have different levels of access or privileges. In other words, perhaps anonymous users can browse the system, but only specific users that are deemed to be administrators can administrate specific tasks.

✔ **How will you prevent hackers?** You will most likely need to set up security from a networking infrastructure perspective in such a way that your organization is not vulnerable to security attacks. This is typically done by setting up network segments and firewalls. (See Chapter 11, where I discuss firewall configurations in detail. In fact, Figure 11-4 shows you a firewall configuration that provides a DMZ, or demilitarized zone, to protect your network.) Additionally, you can minimize security risk if you use a VPN solution to transmit data to and from two specific points.

✔ **Will you encrypt your data?** For sensitive data, such as personal and financial information, you should consider encryption. Not only should data be encrypted (with SSL) when it is sent out over the Internet, but you should consider encrypting sensitive data when it is stored in the database as well. This way, when someone has access to the database, they can't just "read" passwords and financial information.

✔ **How will you back up and restore data?** See the following section, "Creating a Disaster Recovery Plan," for more information.

Keep these questions in mind as you or your designers/architects plan for your Web services projects and your other software projects.

Creating a Disaster Recovery Plan

Disaster recovery is the action of recovering data after a software or hardware failure. A disaster may be a hard drive failure, nonresponsive hardware, network failures, or any other natural (or unnatural) event that makes the IT manager at your company well up with tears of sadness and pain.

Consider this example: Suppose that all you have three Web servers to balance the Web server load capacity. (See "Dealing with server configuration issues," earlier in this chapter.) Your database server is part of an active/passive cluster. All of your hard drives are mirrored in a RAID 10 configuration. However, your site goes down after your load balancer fails.

Now what? Well, if you had planned for this scenario, you could have added redundant load balancers.

Or not. Load balancers are typically hardware devices. Pricey ones, at that. Because these devices rarely fail, it may not be worth the added expense to have an extra one in place.

Still, if you don't get one, your disaster recovery plan isn't really complete. The idea is to make sure that *all* your IT systems are completely protected in the case of a disaster. You have to weigh the costs against the potential consequences. You see, fault-tolerance (like everything else in life) is a tradeoff. It shows a perfect-world scenario of how your network would be completely fault tolerant.

Because time is money, you *must* make a specific plan for how you will handle a disaster; this is called a *disaster recovery plan*.

If you're lucky (and smart), disaster recovery planning won't break you financially because you have been updating your disaster recovery plan gradually as your systems and needs have evolved.

If you're still saying "Disaster *what?*" your disaster recovery environment probably doesn't look like this figure. In fact, you probably don't have any plan at all. So you'd better hustle. Not to scare you or anything, but every second you don't have a plan in place is another second of vulnerability. Repeat: "I need to have a disaster recovery plan." Again. Louder. With emphasis. I want to hear some real emotion here . . . otherwise you will be very emotional later when all your data is gone.

A disaster recovery plan is a document that you write that should include at least these elements:

- ✔ Overview or purpose
- ✔ Backup plan and schedule
- ✔ Restoration plan to restore backups of data, if necessary
- ✔ Network diagram
- ✔ Block diagrams of major functional areas to help troubleshooting
- ✔ Departments that need to be involved and tasks associated with those departments

✔ Approximate timeframes needed to bring systems and subsystems back online

✔ Procedures for every eventuality, as in hard drive failures, and so forth

✔ Dependencies of one procedure on another (In other words, a specific order in which procedures must be performed.)

A disaster recovery plan will get you up and running fast in the case of a failure. Again, planning is key!

Factoring Scalability into Your Plan

Scalability refers to the capability to expand your system as load increases. If you don't plan for scalability, you'll have a very hard time expanding your system. Scalability is divided into the following two categories:

✔ **Scale up:** This refers to the capability to add resources to your existing servers to handle more processing power. You can add more disk space, memory, CPUs, and so forth. Although scaling up doesn't require much planning, your existing hardware and software must be able to handle scale up.

For example, if your motherboard only accepts one CPU, you can't scale up your CPUs. Likewise, if your motherboard only accepts 2GB RAM and you want to scale-up to 4GB, you'll have to replace your motherboard.

Likewise, you need to consider whether your operating system will handle scale up. Even though memory management and configuration is handled mostly automatically in Windows 2000, you have to make sure that you selected the appropriate edition of the operating system.

For example, Windows 2000 Server allows for a maximum of 4GB RAM, but Windows 2000 Advanced Server allows for a maximum of 8GB RAM. Therefore, if you are using Windows 2000 Server and you currently have 4GB RAM, you can't scale up without upgrading the operating system. For more information about the limitations of each operating system from Microsoft, visit their Web site at www.microsoft.com/windows.

✔ **Scale out:** This refers to the capability to add additional servers to handle additional processing load. For example, suppose that you have two Web servers in your production environment. The holiday shopping season is coming up, and you want to add another two servers. Does your application allow for this? You must make sure that your applications can handle "switching" among Web servers.

How will traffic be routed between the servers? This topic is covered in the following section.

Planning for Session State Issues

The Web is essentially *stateless*. This means that one request coming into a Web server knows nothing about previous or subsequent requests into the same Web server.

In other words, suppose that a client makes a request to a Web server to provide some financial account details. The first request that comes into the Web server would be to log in. The next request would be to return financial details about your account. The second request knows nothing about your first request. It doesn't inherently know that you successfully logged in, so you must account for that in your applications. This is known as *session state*. Session state is the ability to pass information, or state, about the Web session to another request in the same session. That's an important issue.

The issue with session state becomes even *more* of an issue when you have a load balancer between the Internet and your Web servers that is managing the load and sending Web requests to the next available Web server. Having this configuration in place means that the first request that logged you in may be executed on a different server than the one that handles the return of your account information. As you can see, you must tackle many difficult issues with managing session state.

User authentication is not the only reason that you need session state. You may simply need to know which page the user was last on so that you can take some action based on this knowledge. In other words, session state is affected by the context of the user's session.

To give you an idea as to why things are handled the way they are in .NET, and also to point out some backward compatibility issues, here's some information about the days before the .NET Framework. Prior to the .NET Framework, you had the following options for maintaining session state, each of which may not be a perfect solution:

- ✓ **Client-Side Cookies:** You can maintain session state in cookies, but the browser has to support them. Most browsers will allow cookies to be turned off, so you may not be able to use this solution.

- ✓ **Posting form data in hidden fields:** Although this book isn't about HTML, it is possible to send data in an HTML field that is hidden from everyday view on the Web page to another Web page. This data can contain programmer-defined session state information. However, this wouldn't work very well if the next request goes to a different server. Additionally, there is a potential security risk in using hidden fields, as anyone can view these fields by using the View⇨Source menu from within Internet Explorer.

✔ **URL encoding:** Session state data can be passed along from form to form in the URL; it is passed as *parameters.* This is probably the most common way to handle session state. The following URL is an example of this: `www.transport80.com?ID=343kkdi335ko22p44nj21098`.

The ID parameter has special meaning that is valid for only the session but can span multiple Web servers. However, your designers/architects must make sure that your applications aren't designed in such a way that usernames, passwords, and other security-related information are passed in the URL.

✔ **Database:** Session state data is maintained in a database. The Web server generates a unique ID, called a *session ID,* which can be used as the basis for looking up session state data. A lot of overhead is required for this solution because you must manage the database. Also, this adds to the cost of your solution.

With the advent of the .NET Framework, you can have your Web pages handle session state automatically. Automatic session state is maintained through something called *View State.* More overhead is involved with using View State because more data is transmitted between server and client, but you don't have to code as much yourself. Make sure to plan how your Web services application will handle session state, whether you plan to use automatic session state management within .NET or come up with your own scheme. You may need to use your own scheme if you are upgrading your code to .NET because you are handling session state currently. On the other hand, you may want to use automatic session state if you are building a new application from scratch.

Assembly Versioning

Since the inception of Windows, it has relied on DLL files for extensibility and sharing of libraries. These DLL files contained an internal, embedded versioning scheme, but no process or system existed to enforce versioning policies.

The .NET Framework supports *real* versioning. When you compile your assemblies into DLLs, you can assign a version number. It's a good idea to plan your version numbers, and if you are going to take advantage of versioning in assemblies, your assemblies must be strong-named. Strong-named assemblies are discussed in Chapter 6.

Because the .NET Framework allows for multiple versions of an assembly to coexist, at runtime, the system must know which version to actually use. The coexistence of assembly versions is also known as *side-by-side assemblies.*

To indicate how to handle versioning in the .NET Framework, you must specify a *publisher assembly policy*. These policy files, written in XML (of course), indicate the following:

- ✔ Policy level (either machine or application)
- ✔ Specific assembly version
- ✔ Newest assembly version

A publisher policy file doesn't have to exist; in fact, it should exist only if you plan to make your assemblies backwards compatible. If not, only the newest version of your assemblies will be used.

You should determine whether you'll need to support multiple versions of your assemblies on the same machine at the same time. You may find it helpful to review the discussion of assemblies in Chapter 6 and throughout the .NET Framework SDK documentation.

Chapter 13

Migrating from Other Technologies

In This Chapter

▶ Historical object technologies

▶ Migration considerations

▶ Interoperability

*Y*ou've read through this entire book. You like what you see. You want to implement Web services on the .NET platform. However, you have many existing systems already in your organization that do not use Web services. You cannot just flip the switch and be up and running with this new technology. There are many considerations to ponder when thinking about migrating from prior technologies to .NET Web services. Migration is not easy. Therefore, it takes quite a bit of manpower to migrate. Microsoft provides special assemblies in .NET for the express purpose of interoperating with COM objects so that you aren't forced to migrate. If you do decide to migrate to .NET Web services, you can take advantage of all the wonderful new features, performance enhancements, and productivity enhancements that .NET offers. This chapter helps you to understand the issues relating to migration from other technologies to .NET Web services.

The Latest and (Not So) Greatest

A tremendous amount of work has been done in the computer industry and in Information Technology to get to the point where we are today with distributed computing. Each of the technologies has met with some level of success. However, if they were perfect technologies, we wouldn't need Web services. Likewise, Web services won't be the last technology around. It also has its pros and cons. Read on to discover more.

To help you understand the text throughout this chapter, refer to Figure 13-1, which illustrates distributed technologies.

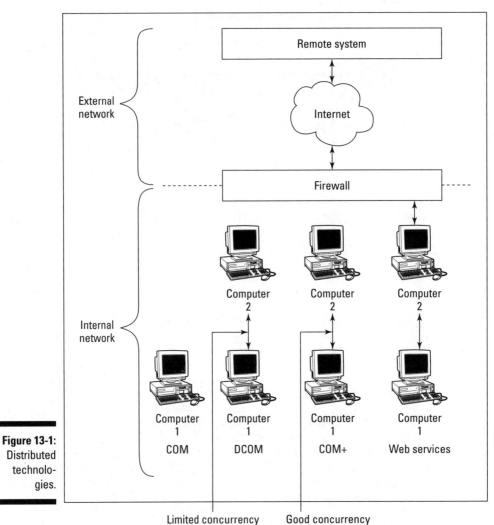

Figure 13-1:
Distributed
technolo-
gies.

To comprehend why Web services are needed and the problems they solve, it helps to understand the problems and issues with earlier technologies. Each of these is discussed on the next few pages.

COM

COM is a Microsoft technology for architecting software into objects. *COM* stands for Component Object Model. COM components could be written in many languages, such as C++ or Visual Basic. COM components provided a rich model that allowed for reusable components to be created, installed, and deployed. However, these activities were not necessarily easy to do.

The creation of objects was fairly straightforward, except that if the objects were created in Visual Basic, they could not take advantage of inheritance, which is a traditional component of OOP (object-oriented programming). If the objects were created in C++, programmers had to potentially learn a completely new programming language just to take advantage of inheritance.

Furthermore, COM only worked on a local computer. In other words, the object that you wished to invoke could not reside on a server or other workstation. It had to exist on your local workstation. Therefore, components could only interact with each other if they all resided on your local workstation.

In Figure 13-1, earlier in this chapter, notice that COM is really only used on a single computer. If you want COM objects to be installed on another computer, you had to install them on the other computers. The installation of COM objects registered a unique ID, known as a Class ID, that was associated with the COM component. Class IDs caused problems when one version was installed on a computer but a different version was on another computer. There was no warning that the old version was even being upgraded during installation.

DCOM

DCOM (or Distributed COM) was a technology that allowed for COM objects to be located on other computers. In other words, objects could be distributed. It was a logical progression in the COM world. In fact, DCOM was based on open standards.

DCOM was difficult to get working correctly. It included a utility, called `DCOM-CNFG`, which allowed you to configure how the COM objects would be distributed. DCOM also had a feature called dynamic port allocation, which enabled easy configuration and programming (or invoking) of COM objects. DCOM, too, had its own set of problems. Because of the dynamic nature of the port allocation, DCOM was difficult to get working through a firewall. Even though the dynamic port allocation only worked in a specific range of ports, you would never want to open all of those ports in your firewall.

Additionally, DCOM (and COM) made writing multithreaded applications for use on servers difficult or impossible. Because of this, concurrency usage was a real performance issue, because components were not very reusable in a distributed environment.

Figure 13-1 (earlier in this chapter) shows that DCOM was an advance over COM, but still only communicated (with few exceptions) on the internal network. It was difficult to configure to go through a firewall. It also included limited support for *concurrency,* wherein multiple users can access the objects at the same time.

COM+

COM+ was introduced in the Windows 2000 operating system and was a great improvement over DCOM. Not only did it eliminate the `DCOMCONFG` utility, but it also included some major enhancements. First of all, COM+ allowed for all existing COM components to work without rewriting them. Next, it handled the complexity of threading and concurrency. *Threading* is the term given to basic unit that an operating system uses to execute a process by allocating processor time. Multiple threads can be invoked, or spawned, to run a process. If this isn't enough, COM+ added support for transactions.

Transactions are a concept by which code must execute completely or not at all. An example of a transaction is that of a banking transaction. Suppose you wanted to transfer funds from your checking account to your savings account. This task is actually broken up into two distinct parts. First, the money must be deducted from your checking account (if there are enough funds). Second, the funds must be added to your savings account. Both of these parts of the transaction must be completed in their entirety or not at all. You can't afford the first part of the transaction to work, but not the second. This is also true of some COM operations. Therefore, COM+ supports this.

COM+ allows for components to be written in any technology, just like .NET components today. This proves to be great for productivity. Developers can use the language that they know without needing to learn something new.

Figure 13-1 (earlier in this chapter) shows that COM+ allowed for interoperability among computers; but like DCOM, it had issues with configuring for use through a firewall. Therefore, COM+ also was typically used on internal networks only. However, COM+ was greatly improved over DCOM because it was good with threading and concurrency management.

Web services

You've undoubtedly found out a lot about Web services in this book. Web services provide a great way to allow platform independence while connecting systems together. The reason that this is possible is because Web services operate on an agreed-upon standard. Web services standards are adopted by the W3C (World Wide Web Consortium). Once adopted, each of the companies that wish to implement the standard goes to work on how it can comply with the standards. Sometimes, these companies offer additional functionality as well.

Web services are said to be *loosely coupled.* This means that coupling exists among systems, but coupling is not tightly integrated into any one system. It is difficult or impossible to have platform independence while being tightly coupled. Therefore, Web services technology follows this loosely coupled model.

Another similar technology, one that is not covered in detail in this book, is called .NET Remoting. Web services technology isn't the right technology for every application. That's where .NET Remoting comes in. This technology yields greater flexibility but is much more complicated to use. Also, it only works with objects on the .NET platform.

Here are some Web services pros:

- ✔ Crosses platforms
- ✔ Firewall friendly
- ✔ Uses a very simple model
- ✔ Language independent

And here are a few of the downsides of Web services:

- ✔ Relies on IIS
- ✔ Uses only HTTP or HTTPS protocols
- ✔ Not useful for binary data

Here are some pros of .NET Remoting:

- ✔ Very flexible
- ✔ Allows complex objects
- ✔ More control over security

And a few cons of .NET Remoting:

- ✔ Allows objects only
- ✔ Client must be aware of objects
- ✔ Requires the .NET platform, so some interoperability is lost

Figure 13-1 (earlier in this chapter) shows that Web services provide a great way to share and invoke objects across all computers in an internal network and also through a firewall to the external network. Web services do not force a network administrator to open additional ports in the firewall. Because port 80 is already open for regular Internet traffic, nothing else needs to be configured.

Interoperability

By definition, a real technological issue exists with writing new code in Visual Studio .NET and calling objects that you wrote using an earlier version of Visual Studio. Prior versions of Visual Studio enabled you to create COM objects for use in your applications or in DCOM or COM+ for distributed applications. Because .NET applications target the .NET runtime, they are said to be running *managed code*. Because the .NET Framework manages the code, it cannot manage COM objects that were not written using a technology that targets the .NET runtime. In other words, .NET assemblies cannot inherently call COM objects. To translate a call to/from .NET and COM objects, the execution environment must exchange, or *marshal,* calls between the environments. This becomes quite tricky when you are dealing with two different technologies.

.NET assemblies calling COM objects

Microsoft anticipated that many organizations would not migrate their code to .NET because they have a huge investment in COM-based code. Instead, companies will want to call COM components from their .NET projects. Microsoft provided a set of .NET assemblies for the express purpose of interacting with COM objects. All of these interoperability assemblies are located in the namespace `System.Runtime.InteropServices`. Namespaces are discussed in Chapter 3.

Fortunately, Visual Studio.NET knows that you are trying to interoperate with a COM object and automatically adds the reference to this namespace. To call a COM object from your Visual Studio.NET project, follow this procedure:

1. **To open Visual Studio .NET, choose Start⇨Programs⇨Microsoft Visual Studio .NET⇨Microsoft Visual Studio .NET.**

2. **Open your project.**

3. **Choose the Project⇨Add Reference menu to bring up the Add Reference dialog box.**

4. **Click the COM tab in the Add Reference dialog box.**

   Clicking this tab brings up the dialog box shown in Figure 13-2.

5. **Select the desired COM object.**

   For example, if you want to write a program that accesses Microsoft Application Center Test COM objects, click `Microsoft ACT Application Object Model 1.0 Type Library`.

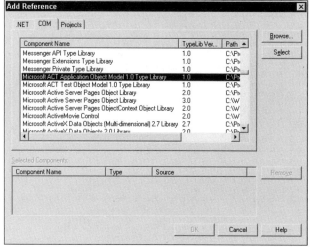

Figure 13-2:
Adding
a COM
reference
to a Visual
Studio.NET
project.

6. Click the Select button.

Clicking Select adds the current component to the list of components that are to be included in your project. You can continue to select components until you are finished.

7. When you are finished, click OK.

Clicking OK closes the dialog box and adds references to your selected components. If you added the ACT COM object that I mention in Step 5, you see a reference in the References folder in the Solution Explorer window (refer to Figure 6-2) to `ActApplicationLIB`.

8. Write your code for the COM object.

Your code can now reference the COM object just as if it were a .NET object, but you have to instruct Visual Studio.NET to use the new library (or libraries).

As an example, in Visual Basic.NET, you use the `Imports` keyword. Listing 13-1 shows how to do this.

The line numbers on the left of the code are for reference only.

Listing 13-1: Sample of using the Application Center Test COM objects

```
1: Imports ActApplicationLIB
2: Public Class WebForm1
3:     Inherits System.Web.UI.Page
4: Protected WithEvents DataGrid1 As System.Web.UI.WebControls.DataGrid
5:
6:   Private Sub Page_Load(ByVal sender As System.Object, ByVal e As
                System.EventArgs) Handles MyBase.Load
7:      'declare ACT objects
8:      Dim oProject As New ActApplicationLIB.Project()
9:      Dim oTest As ActApplicationLIB.Test
10:
11:     'declare variables
12:     Dim sProjectPath As String
13:     Dim sProjectName As String
14:
15:     'assign variable names for the ACT project path and file name
16:     sProjectPath = "\inetpub\wwwroot\interop\WSFD"
17:     sProjectName = "WSFD.act"
18:
19:     'open the ACT project
20:     oProject.Open(sProjectPath, sProjectName, False)
21:
22:     Try
23:         'declare datatable
24:         Dim myTable As DataTable = New DataTable()
25:
26:         'declare column
27:         Dim myColumn As DataColumn
28:
29:         'assign column properties
30:         myColumn = New DataColumn()
31:         myColumn.DataType = Type.GetType("System.String")
32:         myColumn.ColumnName = "Test Name"
33:         myTable.Columns.Add(myColumn)
34:
35:         'assign row properties
36:         Dim workRow As DataRow
37:         For Each oTest In oProject.Tests
38:             workRow = myTable.NewRow()
39:             workRow("Test Name") = "<a href=ACTTest.aspx?Action=View&Name="
            & oTest.Name & ">" & oTest.Name & "</a>"
40:             myTable.Rows.Add(workRow)
41:         Next
42:
43:         'bind datagrid
44:         DataGrid1.AutoGenerateColumns = True
45:         DataGrid1.DataSource = myTable
46:         DataGrid1.DataBind()
47:     Finally
48:         oProject.Close()
49:         oProject = Nothing
50:
```

```
51:     End Try
52:
53: End Sub
54:
55: End Class
```

The reason for the code shown in Listing 13-1 is to illustrate how easy it is to use a COM object within your Visual Studio .NET projects. The class definition that lies between lines 2 and 55 display a list of tests that are in an Application Center Test (also known as ACT) project and displays them in a datagrid. This is illustrated in Figure 13-3.

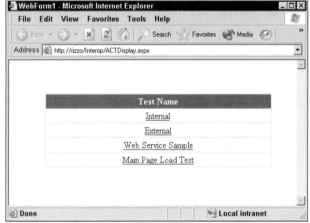

Figure 13-3: Sample datagrid that reads information from a COM object.

In Line 1, notice the reference to the new library with the `Imports` keyword. This keyword enables you to use the objects declared within this library without specifying the name of the library on each and every line of code. In other words, Line 8 can declare a new ACT project because of the reference to the COM library and the `Imports` keyword. Line 9 declares an ACT test object the same way.

Line 16 indicates where the physical path to the ACT project is located, while Line 17 indicates the name of the project (with an `ACT` file extension). Line 20 opens the ACT project.

The rest of the code simply iterates through each of the tests in the project and builds a data grid with one row for every project name. The amazing thing about this code is that the complexity of marshalling calls between .NET and COM are completely handled for you!

COM components calling .NET assemblies

Not only did Microsoft anticipate that .NET code would need to call existing COM components, but Microsoft also anticipated that in ongoing development, COM components would need to interact with newer .NET code. This .NET code could be written by another department in your company, purchased from a third party, or used with building-block services (see Chapter 10).

For your .NET components to be made available to COM, you have to perform some specific procedures. The process is not exactly straightforward.

Calling .NET assemblies from your COM components does not work directly. You have to create an additional .NET assembly that acts as an intermediary between COM and .NET. However, if you want to call a .NET object that is not a Web service from COM, you do not need an intermediary.

Interoperability assemblies for calling .NET assemblies from COM are located in the System.Runtime.InteropServices namespace.

To call a .NET Web services assembly from COM, follow these steps:

1. **Create a new Visual Studio .NET project by choosing Start⇨Programs⇨Microsoft Visual Studio .NET⇨Microsoft Visual Studio .NET.**

   Ensure that you create a new Windows Application, not a Web services application.

   You are creating an intermediary project between COM and your Web services project, not the Web services project itself. This section assumes that you've already created a Web services project that you are trying to connect to from COM.

   Also, remember that the examples are in Visual Basic .NET.

2. **To add a reference to the** InteropServices **namespace, type this line of code at the top of a code module:**

   ```
   Imports System.Runtime.InteropServices
   ```

3. **Rename your class.**

   By default, when you created your project, a class named Class1 was created for you. Change this class to a name that is more germane to the way you will use your code. For example, my Web services project saves and looks up users in a database. Therefore, this intermediate project has a class named UserServices.

4. **Add a Web Reference to your Web service.**

   To find out how to add a Web reference, see Chapter 9.

5. Add code that calls your Web service.

In your class, create code that calls your Web service code in your other project. Again, this project is only an intermediary project that bridges the gap between COM and .NET.

6. Add Interop directives.

For each class and method in your intermediary code, you need to add a directive, called `ComVisible`. It takes an argument, `True` or `False`. If `True`, this attribute indicates that the object will be made available to COM. If `False`, it will not. This way, you can pick and choose what you want to expose to COM. For our example, we want to expose everything. Use the directive, like this: `<ComVisible(True)>`.

If you want to expose a method or class, you must declare it as being `Public`.

Listing 13-2 shows how all of these bits of code come together. The server name `xyz` is the name of the Web reference.

Listing 13-2: Visual Basic .NET code that exposes a class to COM

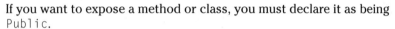

```
1: Imports System.Runtime.InteropServices
2:
3: 'expose the class to COM
4: <ComVisible(True)> _
5: Public Class UserServices
6:     Dim WSFD As New xyz.WSFD()
7:     Dim sResult As String
8:
9:     'expose the function to COM
10:    <ComVisible(True)> _
11:    Public Function Save _
12:        ( _
13:            ByVal UserID As Integer, _
14:            ByVal LastName As String, _
15:            ByVal FirstName As String, _
16:            ByVal Address1 As String, _
17:            ByVal Address2 As String, _
18:            ByVal City As String, _
19:            ByVal State As String, _
20:            ByVal Postal As String, _
21:            ByVal Country As String, _
22:            ByVal HomePhone As String, _
23:            ByVal HomeEMail As String _
24:        ) As String
25:
26:        'call the Web Service that will save the data
27:        sResult = WSFD.Save( _
28:            UserID, _
29:            LastName, _
```

(continued)

Listing 13-2: *(continued)*

```
30:              FirstName, _
31:              Address1, _
32:              Address2, _
33:              City, _
34:              State, _
35:              Postal, _
36:              Country, _
37:              HomePhone, _
38:              HomeEMail _
39:         )
40:
41:        Save = sResult
42:    End Function
43:
44:End Class
```

The code in Listing 13-2 simply does two things. First, it makes .NET calls available to COM by using the `ComVisible` directive. Second, it acts as a proxy by, in turn, making a call to a Web service.

Line 4 declares the directive (with the line continuation character "_") that the class in Line 5 will be made available to COM. Line 6 declares an object variable, `WSFD`, that references your Web service. From this point forward, simply use the `WSFD` object. Lines 27 through 39 call the `WSFD` Web service. Lines 11 through 24 act as a wrapper that exposes a method, called `Save`, but in turn calls the `WSFD` Web service method called `Save`. This method is made available to COM by using the directive `ComVisible` in Line 10 and setting its value to `True`.

7. **Compile your project.**

8. **Register your assembly.**

   Your .NET assembly must now be registered for use with COM. To do this, you use a special program called `REGASM.exe`. It is located in the folder where you installed the .NET Framework. By default, it is installed in this folder:

   ```
   C:\WINDOWS\Microsoft.NET\Framework\v1.0.3705.
   ```

   To register the assembly, you simply use this utility from a command prompt and pass it the full path and name of your new assembly created in Steps 1 through 7. For example, to register a project called DOTNET-TOCOM.exe, type this:

   ```
   REGASM DOTNETTOCOM.exe
   ```

It helps if you add the path of the .NET framework to the `path` variable within your operating system. This way, you don't have to be forced to type full path information when you use any of the .NET utilities in that path. Also if you do not change to the path where your assembly is located, you have to type the name of the full path. You can change to the *folder* (also known as a *directory*) where your assembly is located in a command prompt by using the `CD` command. For example, if your assembly is located in a folder named `c:\projects`, then type **CD\ projects** before using the `REGASM` utility.

9. **Call the .NET Object from COM.**

After you compile and register your .NET project, your COM project can now call your new .NET Windows project, which, in turn, calls your Web services project. You can set a reference from your Visual Basic 6 or earlier project or use the `CreateObject` command, like this:

```
'declare variables
Dim obj As Object
Dim sResult As String

'create the new .NET intermediary object
Set obj = CreateObject("DOTNETTOCOM.UserServices")

'call method which passes values to Web Service
sResult = obj.Save("", "Anthony", "Mann", "123 Main
    Street", "", "Portsmouth", "NH", "03801", "USA",
    "", "")
```

Notice that when you set a reference to your object or create it by using the CreateObject command, the format is

```
NET_project_name.NET_class_name.
```

WS-I

WS-I (Web Services Interoperability) is an organization to help with interoperability issues for Web services. This organization crosses all companies and industries. It is not a Microsoft initiative solely. WS-I defines a basic profile of how Web services should be constructed to interoperate with other Web services on other platforms. It also defines other ancillary functionality, including the following:

- ✔ Specifications
- ✔ Testing tools
- ✔ Benchmarks
- ✔ Scenarios
- ✔ Use cases
- ✔ Implementation guidelines

More information about each of the latest specifications can be read at www.ws-i.org.

To Migrate or Not to Migrate: That Is the Question

Throughout this book, you've seen why Web services are necessary and what they do for your applications. They're quite easy to design, implement, and deploy. However, you probably have a lot of code that was written by using a prior technology. So, do you migrate your existing code or keep it in its current format?

Because of the interoperability assemblies and the ease of using COM-based technologies with your Web services projects, it probably doesn't make sense for you to migrate your code. If your time is like most, there's too much to do already without adding the migration of your existing code to .NET to the list.

However, if your existing code needs enhancements, you may want to consider migrating the code to .NET. Migrating can enable you to take advantage of new features available in .NET. Although migrating is probably not a straightforward task, you'd be well advised to take the following into account if you do migrate.

The smaller the better

You want to migrate your code in small, logical bits. If you undertake your entire project at once, you're likely to run into problems. Taking a small project and trying to migrate the code to .NET is best. This way, you understand how to do it. Many differences exist in using Visual Studio .NET over other versions of Visual Studio. Differences include such things as

- Security
- Data access
- Namespaces
- Web development tools
- Code-behind pages
- Inheritance
- Session state

Redesign

If you are going to migrate your code to .NET, you have a unique opportunity to redesign your code to make it more efficient and provide better functionality. Perhaps you wanted to add some features to make your customers happy. Visual Studio .NET incorporates many new productivity enhancements, like handling session state and server-side controls. Your redesign can take advantage of these.

Data access

Your code performance can benefit dramatically by moving from ADO to ADO.NET. Migrating your code to Visual Studio .NET enables you to incorporate these new advanced features. New advanced and high-performance features of ADO.NET include:

- ✔ DataSets
- ✔ DataReader
- ✔ SQLClient data provider
- ✔ Connection pooling

More information about ADO.NET can be found in Chapter 2.

Part V
The Part of Tens

The 5th Wave   By Rich Tennant

*Bill Gates dreams...

*Yes, he sleeps with his glasses on.

JUSTICE DEPT.

"THAT'S RIGHT, MS. BINGAMAN, HE'S COLLECTING A ROYALTY FROM EVERYONE ON EARTH, AND THERE'S NOTHING WE CAN DO ABOUT IT."

In this part . . .

What *For Dummies* book would be complete without The Part of Tens? This one follows suit. This part gives additional resources to help guide you with respect to Web services. Chapter 14 lists ten reasons to construct Web services on the Microsoft platform. Chapter 15 lists ten additional resources for Web services.

Chapter 14

Ten Reasons to Construct Web Services with Microsoft .NET

In This Chapter

▶ Discovering benefits of the Microsoft .NET platform

▶ Revealing why Microsoft tools are superior

*W*ould you like to know why you should construct XML Web services on the Microsoft .NET platform? Check out this short chapter to find out ten reasons (in no particular order) why you should use the Microsoft .NET Platform to construct your Web services.

Huge ROI

Writing and hosting your Web services projects on the Microsoft .NET platform yields a huge return on investment (ROI). This ROI is mostly because of the other nine points listed in this chapter.

Because you're not stuck using a single development language, you don't have to retrain developers on a specific technology. Just have them do what they already know how to do. Even though there is a learning curve with understanding Web services (but a smaller learning curve after reading this book), being able to develop interoperable code without having to learn a new language is a great return on your investment. Imagine being able to write Windows code in COBOL? It's true! Even though Microsoft doesn't ship COBOL (or Visual COBOL ++) to run on the .NET Framework, some third-party vendors do just that . . . target COBOL to run on the .NET Framework.

To help you calculate the ROI by using the Visual Studio .NET development suite, Microsoft has provided a calculator. It can be found at

http://msdn.microsoft.com/vstudio/productinfo/roi/

In addition to the ROI calculator, you can find out how other companies have achieved high ROI by reading case studies on using XML Web services at

```
www.microsoft.com/net/business/casestudies.asp
```

Additionally, the cost of implementing a .NET solution is dramatically lower than Microsoft's competitor's products. In fact, as long as you have a Microsoft operating system, the .NET Framework is free.

The .NET Framework includes the compilers necessary to construct a .NET application. Theoretically, you could construct a .NET application with a text editor and use the compiler for free. However, I don't know why you would do this; I certainly don't recommend trying — unless you're a programming masochist. Microsoft has some great, highly productive development tools, like Visual Studio .NET.

Language Independence

One of the major components of the .NET Framework is the Common Language Runtime, or CLR. The CLR provides a common set of services that are used by all .NET languages. Because of the CLR, any software language that targets the CLR can be used to compile .NET applications, including Web services. The beauty of language independence means that a Web service can be written in your choice of languages. The ones that ship out of the box with the .NET Framework are the following:

- Visual Basic .NET
- Visual C++ .NET
- Visual C# .NET
- Visual J++ .NET

More information about the .NET Framework and the CLR can be found in Chapter 2. If you want to find out more information about the third-party languages that target the .NET Framework, you can find them on the Microsoft (MSDN) Web site at

```
http://msdn.microsoft.com/vstudio/partners/language/default.asp.
```

Simple Deployment

Deployment refers to transferring your Web services projects between your development, testing, and production environments. Deployment with your

Web services projects on the .NET platform couldn't be easier. You can use one of the following three deployment tools:

- **XCopy:** Enables you to copy a folder location and all subfolders to another location on your network.
- **Copy Project Wizard:** Allows you to copy an entire project from one location to another.
- **Deployment Project:** Allows you to create a project that is installed at the remote location.

In addition, you do not have to register any .NET components that you have created. In prior component models, such as COM, you had to register your objects with the system registry. There was limited support for backward compatibility of your objects, and you could not have an older version on the same computer as a newer version. COM is covered in Chapter 13. The ability to deploy your application without needing to register your components is a major advantage of .NET. Deployment is covered in Chapter 8.

No More DLL, Uh, Heck

Well, DLL rhymes with something that is a little worse than *heck,* but this is a family book, so . . . anyway, the term has been circulating around the IT industry for lots of years. In fact, ever since Windows came out approximately 15 years ago, DLLs have been a big problem.

What is it? The deal with DLLs is that they (and EXEs, for that matter) are registered in the system registry. So when these files need to be updated, so does the registry. If the registry doesn't get updated but the files do, you get unpredictable results.

And it doesn't stop there. Even if you registered everything correctly, you could find yourself in the following situation: Some users have one version of your file(s), but others have a different version. Additionally, two separate applications, by chance, may name their objects the same name. You can imagine that DLL problems made troubleshooting exceedingly difficult.

Well, the .NET platform says to heck with all that registry nonsense. Because of the self-describing nature of your Web services (through the WSDL file — see Chapter 9 to learn about WSDL files), you have no need to register your files.

You can enable your Web services projects to allow for *side-by-side deployments.* This means that you can have multiple versions of your project on a single machine at the same time without any problem. You simply run the file from a specified folder that contains the version you wish to use. It's that simple. See Chapter 12.

Managed Execution Environment

The .NET Framework is based (in part) on the concept of a *managed execution environment*. This environment is a runtime set of services that provides lots of benefits. Each software language that targets the .NET runtime, such as Visual Basic.NET and Visual C#.NET, are built to work with these services. By writing programs in these languages, you get these services automatically. Some of the services in the managed execution environment are the following:

- Automatic memory management
- Garbage collection (unused objects and variables)
- Consistent versioning paradigm
- Common types among all languages
- Interoperability of code among and between code written in different languages
- Guaranteed performance and reliability

Interoperability

Because Web services are an open standard, interoperability among your systems can be achieved with relatively few problems. XML Web services not only enable new systems and applications to be connected together, but also enable you to connect older *(legacy)* systems with your new services.

Many legacy systems are still connected by using Electronic Data Interchange, or EDI. However, with .NET applications, your systems can be connected without EDI. Although currently EDI is as essential as computers are to many businesses, over time, EDI will probably give itself up entirely to Web services. And if you're new in business and don't have EDI, you should consider all your options before you implement it — EDI can be very expensive to implement. In other words, Web services provide a low-cost alternative to system interoperability over EDI.

On the other hand, .NET applications (such as Web services projects) can be quite inexpensive to implement and maintain. This lowers a company's total cost of ownership, also known as TCO.

.NET components are not only compatible with other .NET components, but they can be compatible with other components written in prior versions of Visual Studio — even Visual Basic. Chapter 13 shows how COM (Component

Object Model) components can be used in a .NET environment, which uses Web services for component integration. The interoperability between these two technologies is known as *COM-Interop*.

Native Support

Microsoft's operating systems support .NET when you install the .NET Framework. And the upcoming .NET servers will have the framework built-in. When a software product automatically supports XML Web services, it is referred to as having *native support*. In addition, many of the server-based products and solutions have been built on the .NET Framework, so integration is a snap (relatively speaking)!

Eventually, all Microsoft operating systems, servers, and products will have native support for Web services because it is the strategic direction of Microsoft to do so.

Multi-Device Support

One of the major design goals of the .NET platform is that it runs on any device. This means that an application that is written for the .NET platform can be run with little or no additional effort on the following devices:

- ✔ Browsers (Internet Explorer and Netscape)
- ✔ Smart phones
- ✔ PDAs (personal digital assistants)
- ✔ Tablet PCs
- ✔ Any other device that comes out in the future

The .NET Framework will run on multiple devices. Obviously, a PDA or smart phone requires that less resources be used than are used by a desktop computer. To address this, Microsoft created the Compact .NET Framework. This means that your code can easily be ported to these smaller devices by using the .NET platform.

One Development Environment

With the advent of Visual Studio .NET, you now have one consistent development environment that you can use to develop any type of application. Prior to Visual Studio .NET, the development environment depended not just on the type of project but also on the languages you used. For example, compare creating a COM object with developing a Web project. A COM object might be created by using Visual Basic 6. However, you had to leave this familiar environment to create a new Web-based project within the Visual InterDev environment. *Visual InterDev* was a prior tool that Microsoft sold to create professional Web sites.

Visual Studio.NET makes little distinction between the types of projects that you create, so you (as a developer) can enjoy the relative comfort of not learning a new tool for a different type of project. You can, for example, create a Web service and also a Web site all within Visual Basic .NET.

GUI Code Separation

One major problem prior to the release of .NET was the fact that in your Web-based projects, HTML elements that were used to create a Graphical User Interface (GUI) were mixed with scripting code in the same file. This mixing of code made the following things difficult to do:

- Debug
- Change the look and feel of an application
- Programmatically access all parts of a Web form
- Have one programmer code the page and a graphic designer lay out the page
- Have multiple programmers work on separate parts of the same file

.NET addresses all these issues by separating the code that controls a Web form from the GUI elements that the user sees on the screen. The code is placed in a separate file that is linked to the HTML GUI file. The code file is called a *code-behind* file. This distinction seems simple (and in a way it is), but even the smallest changes can signify a major step forward. That's what code separation means to software development on the Microsoft platform.

Chapter 15

Ten Online Resources for Additional Web Services Information

*B*elieve it or not, this book doesn't tell you everything that you ever wanted to know about Web services. It is a good beginner's reference into the new technological world of Web services. However, if you want more info, you'll have to consult additional books or online resources. This chapter shows ten online resources that you can consult for additional information for Web services and related technologies.

Great Microsoft Resources

Not surprisingly, Microsoft has mountains of information, resources, samples, downloads, and technical support dedicated to .NET, Web services, *and* specific development applications. Check out the following sites to get just a sample of what you can find in Microsoft's cyber wonderland.

Microsoft .NET home page

```
www.microsoft.com/net
```

The Microsoft .NET home page (shown in Figure 15-1) is *the* main resource page for everything that you need to know about Microsoft .NET, including solutions, technical resources, and downloads (such as service packs). After all, .NET is at the core of Microsoft's strategy for Web services and interoperability.

Want to read some case studies about .NET? Point your browser to this Web site and choose the link for case studies. There are hundreds of case studies at this Web site, along with many other .NET-related resources.

Microsoft Web services home page

www.microsoft.com/webservices

This Microsoft site is a great resource to find out about the latest and greatest Web services resources. (See Figure 15-2.) Because Web services are made from ever-evolving technologies, you can find out about the latest specifications.

This site is also a great place to go for downloads, such as SDKs (Software Development Kits) and beta downloads. And it's an outstanding resource to read about how to fit these technologies together.

Figure 15-1:
The
Microsoft
.NET
home page.

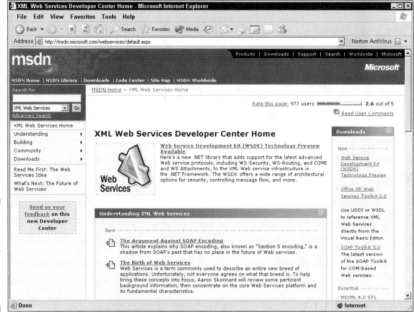

Figure 15-2:
The
Microsoft
Web
Services
home page.

Web services are a part of .NET, so this Web site differs from the .NET Web site listed previously in this chapter. For example, if you want to learn about consuming Web services within Microsoft Office, you would point your browser to this site.

Microsoft UDDI home page

```
http://uddi.microsoft.com
```

The Microsoft UDDI (also known as Universal Description, Discovery, and Integration) is covered in Chapters 8 and 9. Use this Web site, shown in Figure 15-3, to list your company and its Web services into a directory, much like the way the "yellow pages" and "white pages" work.

If you want other companies to be able to find your Web services, you must list it in a UDDI directory, such as the one Microsoft provides at this Web site. With this site, you'll be able to

- ✔ Register your company as a service provider
- ✔ List the Web services that you provide
- ✔ Enter the URL locations of where your Web services can be found

Figure 15-3:
The
Microsoft
UDDI
home page.

UDDI has a Web site in its own right. If you don't find what you want on the Microsoft UDDI page, check out UDDI.org, which I discuss later in this chapter.

Microsoft .NET architecture home page

```
http://msdn.microsoft.com/architecture
```

Design is the marriage of technology and usability. I can go on and on about the technical organization of your Web services, but *designing* your .NET applications so that they work well for users is a very important step in the process of creating fully integrated Web services.

Because you will probably be working with Web developers who can help you evaluate your Web service needs and design application architecture to meet these needs, this book doesn't cover too much in the way of design. However, I encourage you to learn more about the .NET architecture — knowing about design can help you determine whether an idea is feasible *before* you spend a lot of time, effort, and money developing a project that simply won't work.

Design is important, not only because of your Web services projects, but also because of any other projects that you create with Visual Studio .NET on the .NET platform. (Well, really, design and architecture are essential to any technological project, especially large-scale projects.) The Microsoft .NET Architecture site (see Figure 15-4) is an outstanding, timely resource that you can consult to find out about how to design your .NET projects. On the Microsoft .NET Architecture Web site, you can find useful resources about

✔ Designing your Web services for handling application state

✔ Using Web services for data center operations

✔ Attending free architecture Web casts

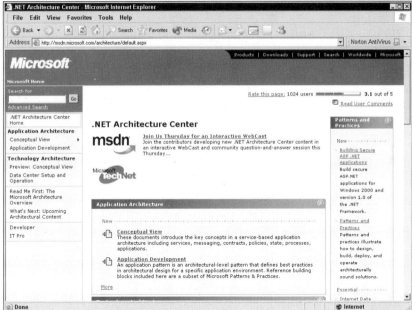

Figure 15-4:
The
Microsoft
.NET
Architecture
home page.

Microsoft Visual Studio home page

`msdn.microsoft.com/vstudio`

Microsoft Visual Studio is the premier design, development, and deployment environment for constructing any .NET project, including Web services, so it's only fitting that the Microsoft Visual Studio home page is a great resource to help you with specific tasks relating to this product. On this site, shown in Figure 15-5, you can find

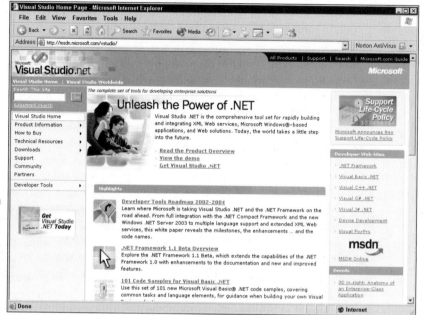

Figure 15-5:
The
Microsoft
Visual
Studio
home page.

✔ Technical resources for the specific development language that you're using, such as Visual Basic .NET, Visual C# .NET, Visual C++ .NET, and Visual J# .NET

✔ Downloads for code samples, such as basic .NET examples and more advanced samples like mobile development

✔ Downloads for service packs. Service packs are necessary to make sure that your Visual Studio .NET applications are up to date

✔ Comparison of the different Visual Studio editions (Professional, Enterprise Developer, Enterprise, and Architect)

Web Resources That Don't Fall under the Microsoft Domain

Certainly, if you're using .NET to create your Web services, using Microsoft resources is a no-brainer. But guess what, folks! There's a whole big world out there outside Microsoft land . . .even though some of the resources outside Microsoft's official domain are actually sponsored by Microsoft.

I know it's hard to believe that there's even more out there; that's why the following sections highlight the best of the Internet sites you can find. If you want to find even more resources, try doing a little search of your own. You may not see the light of day for a while, so busy will you be perusing the many sites you find.

GotDotNet home page

www.gotdotnet.com

The GotDotNet site, shown in Figure 15-6, is a community Web site for all sorts of resources and activities. Here's a smattering of the resources to give you an idea of what I mean:

- ✔ Contests to see who can build the best .NET solution, given requirements
- ✔ Message boards and chat rooms that use Microsoft Passport for validation and registration (see Chapter 10)
- ✔ Samples (and still more samples), for all kinds of applications in all .NET languages, such as those needed for ASP.NET applications, ADO.NET applications, and more

Figure 15-6:
The
GotDotNet.
com
home page.

It's a fun and informative site for everything .NET related. There's more than just Web services stuff on this site. You must visit it!

UDDI.org home page

www.uddi.org

Microsoft did not invent UDDI alone. It's a joint effort with multiple companies to create a standards-based organization, UDDI.org, which facilitates the design and development of UDDI registries, interfaces, and more. If you are interested in viewing UDDI specifications in depth, the UDDI.org site, shown in Figure 15-7, is the resource for you.

This site differs from the Microsoft UDDI site in that the Microsoft site actually allows your Web services to be registered, while the UDDI.org site simply contains specification and standards information.

You can use the UDDI.org Web site to read white papers and even read best practice information that UDDI registries, such as the Microsoft UDDI registry, must use to comply with standards.

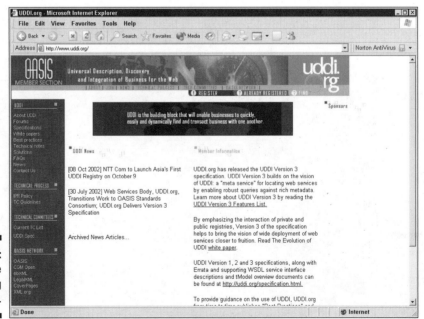

Figure 15-7: The UDDI.org home page.

W3C.org home page

www.w3c.org

Hard as it is to believe, Microsoft didn't invent XML and Web services technologies alone. In fact, in the spirit of the Internet, several companies got together and developed standards for Web services and all related technologies so that everyone would be doing roughly the same thing — and so that all users would be able to benefit from Web service technologies.

So what standards body would be involved in documenting, distributing, and otherwise tweaking the standards for these new technologies? Who else? The W3C! W3C stands for World Wide Web Consortium. The W3C has its hands in all kinds of cookie jars. It's responsible for creating open standards that are related to the Internet. In fact, the bad boys at the W3C have spent years updating all the markup languages, from SGML (the granddaddy of HTML) to XML to create sophisticated, multifaceted markup languages that make Web services work. If you want very in-depth information about any Web specification, visit this site, shown in Figure 15-8.

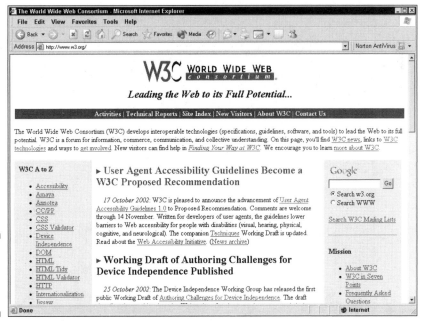

Figure 15-8: The W3C.org home page.

WebServices.org home page

www.webservices.org

WebServices.org is one of those resources that gives you a little bit of anything (and everything) you might be looking for.

The site, shown in Figure 15-9, is membership-based, meaning that you have to provide some personal information, along with a user name and password to get some of the heftier resources, but it includes downloads, standards information, and other technical information for the everyday IT geek.

This site contains information about Web services in general, not only on the Microsoft .NET platform. There are other vendors that use Web services standards (those listed on this site), such as IBM, Sun, HP, and others. In fact, on this Web site, you'll find things like

- ✔ Industry News
- ✔ Events
- ✔ White papers
- ✔ Architecture
- ✔ Standards

Figure 15-9: The Web Services.org home page.

XML.org home page

www.xml.org

Surprise. There's a whole organization (and its companion Web site, shown in Figure 15-10) devoted to that vexing markup language, XML. You only skimmed the surface of XML and SOAP in Chapters 3 and 4. This site goes into as much depth as you care to go into for XML, and it also includes information about Web services because they are so closely related.

Upon visiting this Web site, you'll probably notice that there is similar information available on some of the other Web sites mentioned in this chapter. That's because different companies and non-profit organizations have decided to create these Web sites, but many of the technologies overlap. For example, the W3C is responsible for *All Things Internet,* but XML is an Internet-related technology. Therefore, XML is covered not only on the W3C Web site, but the XML Web site as well. You'll find different information on each of the sites, so it's a good idea to visit them all!

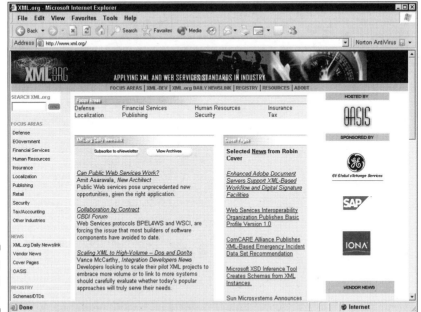

Figure 15-10:
The XML.org
home page.

Index

• E •

• *X* •

Notes

Notes

Notes

Notes

Notes

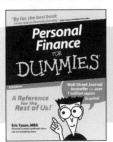

FOR DUMMIES®

A world of resources to help you grow

HOME, GARDEN & HOBBIES

Feng Shui FOR DUMMIES
A Reference for the Rest of Us!
0-7645-5295-3

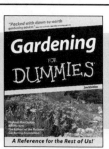

Gardening FOR DUMMIES
2nd Edition
A Reference for the Rest of Us!
0-7645-5130-2

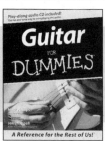

Guitar FOR DUMMIES
A Reference for the Rest of Us!
0-7645-5106-X

Also available:

Auto Repair For Dummies
(0-7645-5089-6)

Chess For Dummies
(0-7645-5003-9)

Home Maintenance For Dummies
(0-7645-5215-5)

Organizing For Dummies
(0-7645-5300-3)

Piano For Dummies
(0-7645-5105-1)

Poker For Dummies
(0-7645-5232-5)

Quilting For Dummies
(0-7645-5118-3)

Rock Guitar For Dummies
(0-7645-5356-9)

Roses For Dummies
(0-7645-5202-3)

Sewing For Dummies
(0-7645-5137-X)

FOOD & WINE

Cooking FOR DUMMIES
2nd Edition
A Reference for the Rest of Us!
0-7645-5250-3

Cookies FOR DUMMIES
A Reference for the Rest of Us!
0-7645-5390-9

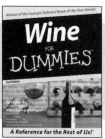

Wine FOR DUMMIES
2nd Edition
A Reference for the Rest of Us!
0-7645-5114-0

Also available:

Bartending For Dummies
(0-7645-5051-9)

Chinese Cooking For Dummies
(0-7645-5247-3)

Christmas Cooking For Dummies
(0-7645-5407-7)

Diabetes Cookbook For Dummies
(0-7645-5230-9)

Grilling For Dummies
(0-7645-5076-4)

Low-Fat Cooking For Dummies
(0-7645-5035-7)

Slow Cookers For Dummies
(0-7645-5240-6)

TRAVEL

Italy FOR DUMMIES
2nd Edition
A Travel Guide for the Rest of Us!
0-7645-5453-0

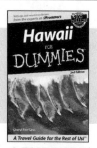

Hawaii FOR DUMMIES
2nd Edition
A Travel Guide for the Rest of Us!
0-7645-5438-7

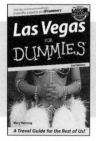

Las Vegas FOR DUMMIES
2nd Edition
A Travel Guide for the Rest of Us!
0-7645-5448-4

Also available:

America's National Parks For Dummies
(0-7645-6204-5)

Caribbean For Dummies
(0-7645-5445-X)

Cruise Vacations For Dummies 2003
(0-7645-5459-X)

Europe For Dummies
(0-7645-5456-5)

Ireland For Dummies
(0-7645-6199-5)

France For Dummies
(0-7645-6292-4)

London For Dummies
(0-7645-5416-6)

Mexico's Beach Resorts For Dummies
(0-7645-6262-2)

Paris For Dummies
(0-7645-5494-8)

RV Vacations For Dummies
(0-7645-5443-3)

Walt Disney World & Orlando For Dummies
(0-7645-5444-1)

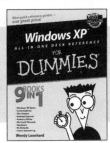
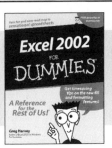

FOR DUMMIES®

Helping you expand your horizons and realize your potential

INTERNET

0-7645-0894-6

0-7645-1659-0

0-7645-1642-6

Also available:

America Online 7.0 For Dummies
(0-7645-1624-8)

Genealogy Online For Dummies
(0-7645-0807-5)

The Internet All-in-One Desk Reference For Dummies
(0-7645-1659-0)

Internet Explorer 6 For Dummies
(0-7645-1344-3)

The Internet For Dummies Quick Reference
(0-7645-1645-0)

Internet Privacy For Dummies
(0-7645-0846-6)

Researching Online For Dummies
(0-7645-0546-7)

Starting an Online Business For Dummies
(0-7645-1655-8)

DIGITAL MEDIA

0-7645-1664-7

0-7645-1675-2

0-7645-0806-7

Also available:

CD and DVD Recording For Dummies
(0-7645-1627-2)

Digital Photography All-in-One Desk Reference For Dummies
(0-7645-1800-3)

Digital Photography For Dummies Quick Reference
(0-7645-0750-8)

Home Recording for Musicians For Dummies
(0-7645-1634-5)

MP3 For Dummies
(0-7645-0858-X)

Paint Shop Pro "X" For Dummies
(0-7645-2440-2)

Photo Retouching & Restoration For Dummies
(0-7645-1662-0)

Scanners For Dummies
(0-7645-0783-4)

GRAPHICS

0-7645-0817-2

0-7645-1651-5

0-7645-0895-4

Also available:

Adobe Acrobat 5 PDF For Dummies
(0-7645-1652-3)

Fireworks 4 For Dummies
(0-7645-0804-0)

Illustrator 10 For Dummies
(0-7645-3636-2)

QuarkXPress 5 For Dummies
(0-7645-0643-9)

Visio 2000 For Dummies
(0-7645-0635-8)

FOR DUMMIES®

The advice and explanations you need to succeed

SELF-HELP, SPIRITUALITY & RELIGION

0-7645-5302-X

0-7645-5418-2

0-7645-5264-3

Also available:

The Bible For Dummies
(0-7645-5296-1)

Buddhism For Dummies
(0-7645-5359-3)

Christian Prayer For Dummies
(0-7645-5500-6)

Dating For Dummies
(0-7645-5072-1)

Judaism For Dummies
(0-7645-5299-6)

Potty Training For Dummies
(0-7645-5417-4)

Pregnancy For Dummies
(0-7645-5074-8)

Rekindling Romance For Dummies
(0-7645-5303-8)

Spirituality For Dummies
(0-7645-5298-8)

Weddings For Dummies
(0-7645-5055-1)

PETS

0-7645-5255-4

0-7645-5286-4

0-7645-5275-9

Also available:

Labrador Retrievers For Dummies
(0-7645-5281-3)

Aquariums For Dummies
(0-7645-5156-6)

Birds For Dummies
(0-7645-5139-6)

Dogs For Dummies
(0-7645-5274-0)

Ferrets For Dummies
(0-7645-5259-7)

German Shepherds For Dummies
(0-7645-5280-5)

Golden Retrievers For Dummies
(0-7645-5267-8)

Horses For Dummies
(0-7645-5138-8)

Jack Russell Terriers For Dummies
(0-7645-5268-6)

Puppies Raising & Training Diary For Dummies
(0-7645-0876-8)

EDUCATION & TEST PREPARATION

0-7645-5194-9

0-7645-5325-9

0-7645-5210-4

Also available:

Chemistry For Dummies
(0-7645-5430-1)

English Grammar For Dummies
(0-7645-5322-4)

French For Dummies
(0-7645-5193-0)

The GMAT For Dummies
(0-7645-5251-1)

Inglés Para Dummies
(0-7645-5427-1)

Italian For Dummies
(0-7645-5196-5)

Research Papers For Dummies
(0-7645-5426-3)

The SAT I For Dummies
(0-7645-5472-7)

U.S. History For Dummies
(0-7645-5249-X)

World History For Dummies
(0-7645-5242-2)

Available wherever books are sold. Go to www.dummies.com or call 1-877-762-2974 to order direct.

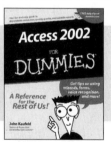

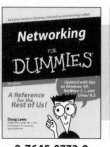